Presented to E. & H. College
by L. S. Campbell, July 1930.

Volume 2
P9-DNQ-912

SELECTED LITERARY
AND POLITICAL PAPERS
AND ADDRESSES OF
WOODROW WILSON

VOLUME TWO

Woodrow Wilson

SELECTED
LITERARY AND
POLITICAL PAPERS
AND ADDRESSES
OF
WOODROW WILSON

IN THREE VOLUMES
VOLUME II

PUBLISHED BY ARRANGEMENT
WITH HARPER & BROTHERS

GROSSET & DUNLAP
PUBLISHERS   NEW YORK

CONTENTS

PAGE

FIRST INAUGURAL ADDRESS AS PRESIDENT OF THE
UNITED STATES 1
Delivered March 4, 1913. From official publi-
cation in Mr. Wilson's files.

FREEMEN NEED NO GUARDIANS 8
From the *Fortnightly Review,* February, 1913,
Vol. 99, pp. 209–218.

THE TARIFF 25
First special address to Congress asking immediate revision of the Payne Aldrich Tariff
April 8, 1913. From the *Congressional Record,*
63d Congress, 1st Session, Vol. 50, p. 130.

THE DEDICATION OF CONGRESS HALL 30
Address delivered at Philadelphia, October 25,
1913. From the *Congressional Record,* 63d
Congress, 1st Session, Vol. 50, pp. 5809–5810.

A NEW LATIN-AMERICAN POLICY 37
Address delivered before the Southern Commercial Congress at Mobile, Ala., October 27,
1913. From official publication in Mr.
Wilson's files.

PANAMA CANAL TOLLS 44
Address to Congress on the Panama Canal tolls
problem, March 5, 1914. From the *Congressional Record,* 63d Congress, 2d Session, Vol.
51, p. 4313.

A PRESIDENT'S DIFFICULTIES 46
Speech to the members of the National Press
Club, Washington, March 20, 1914. From the
New York *Times,* March 21, 1914.

  PAGE

"The Idea of America Is to Serve Humanity" .   52
        Address to the graduating class of the United
        States Naval Academy, Annapolis, June 5,
        1914. From the White House files.

Be Worthy of the Men of 1776   58
        Address at Independence Hall, Philadelphia,
        July 4, 1914. From original copy in the White
        House files.

American Neutrality—An Appeal by the Presi-
        dent   70
        Presented in the Senate, August 19, 1914.
        From original copy in Mr. Wilson's files.

Militant Christianity   73
        Address at Y. M. C. A. celebration, Pittsburgh,
        October 24, 1914. From the White House files.

The Federal Reserve System   86
        Letter to William Gibbs McAdoo, Secretary of
        the Treasury, November 17, 1914. From the
        Commercial and Financial Chronicle, November
        21, 1914. Vol. 99, pp. 1496–1497.

Work of the Federal Trade Board   92
        Address before the American Electric Railway
        Association, Washington, January 29, 1915.
        From the Commercial and Financial Chronicle,
        February 6, 1915, Vol. 100, pp. 436–438.

Co-operation in the Business of Government . 107
        Address delivered before the United States
        Chamber of Commerce, Washington, February
        3, 1915. From official publication in Mr.
        Wilson's files.

Meaning of the Civil War 123
        Address delivered at Arlington, May 31, 1915.
        From the White House files.

Democracy No Longer an Experiment   126

Address to the Grand Army of the Republic,
Washington, September 28, 1915. From the
New York *Times,* September 29, 1915.

Be Not Afraid of Our Foreign-Born Citizens . . 130

Address to the Daughters of the American
Revolution, Washington, October 11, 1915.
From the White House files.

A New Kind of Church Life   139

Address before the Federal Council of Churches,
Columbus, Ohio, December 10, 1915. From the
Congressional Record, 64th Congress, 1st Ses-
sion, Vol. 53, pp. 15751–15753.

"You Cannot Fool All the People All the Time"   152

Address at the First Annual Banquet of the
Motion Picture Board of Trade, Hotel Bilt-
more, New York, January 27, 1916. From the
White House files.

Public Officials Swell Up   158

Address to the National Press Club, May 15,
1916. From the White House files.

First Commitment to the Idea of a League of
Nations   169

Address before the League to Enforce Peace,
Washington, May 27, 1916. From official publication in Mr. Wilson's files.

I Am All Sorts of a Democrat   175

Address before the Associated Advertising
Clubs, Philadelphia, June 29, 1916. From the
White House files.

We Are Servants of the Rank and File of the
People   182

Address before the Press Club, New York, June
30, 1916. From the *Congressional Record,* 64th
Congress, 1st Session, Vol. 53, pp. 11925–11926.

PAGE

LOYALTY MEANS SELF-SACRIFICE 188
    Address on Citizenship delivered at Washington
    before the Conference on Americanization, July
    13, 1916. From the White House files.

ABRAHAM LINCOLN 194
    Acceptance of the Lincoln Memorial, Hodgen-
    ville, Kentucky, September 4, 1916. From the
    Congressional Record, 64th Congress, 1st Ses-
    sion, Vol. 53, Appendix, p. 2160.

LABOR AND CAPITAL 200
    Address delivered at Shadow Lawn, September
    23, 1916. From the New York *Times*, Septem-
    ber 24, 1916.

THE MEXICAN PROBLEM AGAIN: AN INTERVIEW . . 212
    From the *Ladies' Home Journal*, October, 1916.

ESSENTIAL TERMS OF PEACE IN EUROPE 218
    Address to the United States Senate, January
    22, 1917. From Senate Document 685, 64th
    Congress, 2d Session.

SUBMARINE WARFARE AND THE BREAK WITH GERMANY 228
    Address to Congress February 3, 1917. From
    the *Congressional Record*, 64th Congress, 2d
    Session, Vol. 54, pp. 2578-2579.

FOR DECLARATION OF WAR AGAINST GERMANY . . . 234
    Address delivered at a joint session of the two
    houses of Congress, April 2, 1917. From the
    65th Congress, 1st Session, Senate Document
    No. 5.

"AMERICA WAS BORN TO SERVE MANKIND" 248
    Memorial Day Address at Arlington National
    Cemetery, May 30, 1917. From Official Bulletin
    No. 18.

CONTENTS

IX:

PAGE

THE BIBLE 251
Letter from the soldiers and sailors of the
United States, August, 1917. From the *Con-
gressional Record,* Vol. 55, p. 6041.

FOURTH LIBERTY LOAN 262
Address opening the campaign for the Fourth
Liberty Loan delivered in New York City, September 27, 1918. From official government
publication in Mr. Wilson's files.

ARMISTICE TERMS 273
Message to the German Government through
Secretary Lansing and Mr. Frederick Oederlin,
Charge d'Affaires of Switzerland, October 23,
1918. From official U. S. Bulletin, No. 445.

ANNUAL MESSAGE 279
Address delivered at a joint session of the two
houses of Congress, December 2, 1918. From
official government publication in Mr. Wilson's
files.

CHRISTMAS GREETINGS TO THE SOLDIERS OF THE
UNITED STATES 299
Address to American troops at Humes, France,
December 25 1918. From official government
publication in Mr. Wilson's files.

AT THE GUILDHALL, LONDON 303
Response to an address of welcome by the Lord
Mayor at the Guildhall, London, December 28,
1918. From official government publication in
Mr. Wilson's files.

AT HIS GRANDFATHER'S CHURCH AT CARLISLE . . . 308
Address at the Lowther Street Congregational
Church, Carlisle, England, December 29, 1918.
From original copy in Mr. Wilson's files.

IN FREE TRADE HALL, MANCHESTER 310
Address given at a luncheon, December 30,

PAGE

1918. From official government publication in
in Mr. Wilson's files.

OPENING THE PEACE CONFERENCE 316
Address at the First Plenary Session, Paris,
January 18, 1919. From official government
publication in Mr. Wilson's files.

"MAKE THIS LEAGUE OF NATIONS A VITAL THING" . 318
Address before the Second Plenary Session of
the Peace Conference; Paris, January 25, 1919.
From official government publication in Mr.
Wilson's files.

BEFORE THE INTERNATIONAL LAW SOCIETY 325
Address at Paris, May 9, 1919. From the New
York *Times*, May 11, 1919.

"THAT QUICK COMRADESHIP OF LETTERS" 330
Address at the Institute of France, Paris,
May 10, 1919. From original in Mr. Wilson's
files.

SURESNES CEMETERY SPEECH 334
Memorial Day Address at Suresnes Cemetery,
near Paris, May 30, 1919. From original in
Mr. Wilson's files.

EXPOSITION OF THE LEAGUE TO THE FOREIGN RELA-
TIONS COMMITTEE 341
Statement to the members of the Senate Com-
mittee on Foreign Relations, August 19, 1919.
From 66th Congress, 1st Session. Senate
Document No. 76.

ADDRESS 350
Delivered at Columbus, Ohio, September 4, 1919.

ADDRESS 369
Delivered at Pueblo, Colo., September 25, 1919.

PAGE

NATIONAL REFERENDUM OF THE LEAGUE OF NATIONS .   392
An appeal to the country to make the Presidential Election an expression of the nation's opinion on the League of Nations, October 3, 1920. From the New York *Times,* October 4, 1920.

THE ROAD AWAY FROM REVOLUTION 395
From the *Atlantic Monthly,* August, 1923.

"HIGH SIGNIFICANCE OF ARMISTICE DAY" 399
Last Public Address delivered over the Radio, November 10, 1923.

FIRST INAUGURAL ADDRESS AS PRESIDENT OF THE UNITED STATES

DELIVERED MARCH 4, 1913. FROM OFFICIAL PUBLICATION IN MR. WILSON'S FILES.

MY FELLOW CITIZENS:

There has been a change of government. It began two years ago, when the House of Representatives became Democratic by a decisive majority. It has now been completed. The Senate about to assemble will also be Democratic. The offices of President and Vice-President have been put into the hands of Democrats. What does the change mean? That is the question that is uppermost in our minds to-day. That is the question I am going to try to answer, in order, if I may, to interpret the occasion.

It means much more than the mere success of a party. The success of a party means little except when the Nation is using that party for a large and definite purpose. No one can mistake the purpose for which the Nation now seeks to use the Democratic Party. It seeks to use it to interpret a change in its own plans and point of view. Some old things with which we had grown familiar, and which had begun to creep into the very habit of our thought and of our lives, have altered their aspect as we have latterly looked critically upon them, with fresh, awakened eyes; have dropped their disguises and shown themselves alien and sinister. Some new things, as we look frankly upon them, willing to comprehend their real character, have come to assume the aspect of things long believed in and familiar, stuff of our own convictions. We have been refreshed by a new insight into our own life.

We see that in many things that life is very great. It is incomparably great in its material aspects, in its body of wealth, in the diversity and sweep of its energy, in the industries which have been conceived and built up by the genius of individual men and the limitless enterprise of groups of men. It is great, also, very great, in its moral force.

Nowhere else in the world have noble men and women exhibited in more striking forms the beauty and the energy of sympathy and helpfulness and counsel in their efforts to rectify wrong, alleviate suffering, and set the weak in the way of strength and hope. We have built up, moreover, a great system of government, which has stood through a long age as in many respects a model for those who seek to set liberty upon foundations that will endure against fortuitous change, against storm and accident. Our life contains every great thing, and contains it in rich abundance.

But the evil has come with the good, and much fine gold has been corroded. With riches has come inexcusable waste. We have squandered a great part of what we might have used, and have not stopped to conserve the exceeding bounty of nature, without which our genius for enterprise would have been worthless and impotent, scorning to be careful, shamefully prodigal as well as admirably efficient. We have been proud of our industrial achievements, but we have not hitherto stopped thoughtfully enough to count the human cost, the cost of lives snuffed out, of energies overtaxed and broken, the fearful physical and spiritual cost to the men and women and children upon whom the dead weight and burden of it all has fallen pitilessly the years through. The groans and agony of it all had not yet reached our ears, the solemn, moving undertone of our life, coming up out of the mines and factories and out of every home where the struggle had its intimate and familiar seat. With the great Government went many deep secret things which we too long delayed to look into and scrutinize with candid, fearless eyes. The great Government we loved has too often been made use of for private and selfish purposes, and those who used it had forgotten the people.

At last a vision has been vouchsafed us of our life as a whole. We see the bad with the good, the debased and decadent with the sound and vital. With this vision we approach new affairs. Our duty is to cleanse, to reconsider, to restore, to correct the evil without imparing the good, to purify and humanize every process of our common life without weakening or sentimentalizing it. There has been something crude and heartless and unfeeling in our haste to succeed and be great. Our thought has been "Let every man look out for himself, let every generation look out for itself," while we reared giant machinery which made it impossible that any but those who stood at the levers of control should have a chance to look out for themselves. We had not forgotten our morals. We remembered well enough that we had set up a policy which was meant to serve the humblest as well as the most powerful, with an eye single to the standards of justice and fair play, and remembered it with pride. But we were very heedless and in a hurry to be great.

We have come now to the sober second thought. The scales of heedlessness have fallen from our eyes. We have made up our minds to square every process of our national life again with the standards we so proudly set up at the beginning and have always carried at our hearts. Our work is a work of restoration.

We have itemized with some degree of particularity the things that ought to be altered and here are some of the chief items: A tariff which cuts us off from our proper part in the commerce of the world, violates the just principles of taxation, and makes the Government a facile instrument in the hands of private interests; a banking and currency system based upon the necessity of the Government to sell its bonds fifty years ago and perfectly adapted to concentrating cash and restricting credits; an industrial system which, take it on all its sides, financial as well as administrative, holds capital in leading strings, restricts the liberties and limits the opportunities of labor, and exploits without renewing or conserving the natural resources of the country; a body of agricultural activities never yet given the efficiency of great business undertakings or served as it should be through the instrumentality of science taken directly to the farm, or afforded the facilities of credit best suited to its practical needs; watercourses undeveloped, waste places unreclaimed, forests untended, fast disappearing without plan or prospect of renewal, unregarded waste heaps at every mine. We have studied as perhaps no other nation has the most effective means of production, but we have not studied cost or economy as we should either as organizers of industry, as statesmen, or as individuals.

Nor have we studied and perfected the means by which government may be put at the service of humanity, in safeguarding the health of the Nation, the health of its men and its women and its children, as well as their rights in the struggle for existence. This is no sentimental duty. The firm basis of government is justice, not pity. These are matters of justice. There can be no equality or opportunity, the first essential of justice in the body politic, if men and women and children be not shielded in their lives, their very vitality, from the consequences of great industrial and social processes which they can not alter, control, or singly cope with. Society must see to it that it does not itself crush or weaken or damage its own constituent parts. The first duty of law is to keep sound the society it serves. Sanitary laws, pure food laws, and laws determining conditions of labor which individuals are powerless to determine for themselves are intimate parts of the very business of justice and legal efficiency.

These are some of the things we ought to do, and

not leave the others undone, the old-fashioned, nev-
er-to-be-neglected, fundamental safeguarding of
property and of individual right. This is the high
enterprise of the new day: To lift everything that
concerns our life as a Nation to the light that shines
from the hearthfire of every man's conscience and
vision of the right. It is inconceivable that we
should do this as partisans; it is inconceivable we
should do it in ignorance of the facts as they are
or in blind haste. We shall restore, not destroy.
We shall deal with our economic system as it is
and as it may be modified, not as it might be if we
had a clean sheet of paper to write upon; and step
by step we shall make it what it should be, in the
spirit of those who question their own wisdom and
seek counsel and knowledge, not shallow self-satis-
faction or the excitement of excursions whither they
can not tell. Justice, and only justice, shall alway
be our motto.

And yet it will be no cool process of mere science.
The Nation has been deeply stirred, stirred by a solemn passion, stirred by the knowledge of wrong, of
ideals lost, of government too often debauched and
made an instrument of evil. The feelings with
which we face this new age of right and opportunity sweep across our heartstrings like some air out
of God's own presence, where justice and mercy
are reconciled and the judge and the brother are
one. We know our task to be no mere task of politics but a task which shall search us through and
through, whether we be able to understand our time
and the need of our people, whether we be indeed

their spokesmen and interpreters, whether we have
the pure heart to comprehend and the rectified will
to choose our high course of action.

This is not a day of triumph; it is a day of dedication. Here muster, not the forces of party, but the
forces of humanity. Men's hearts wait upon us;
men's lives hang in the balance; men's hopes call
upon us to say what we will do. Who shall live up
to the great trust? Who dares fail to try? I summon all honest men, all patriotic, all forward-look-
ing men, to my side. God helping me, I will not
fail them, if they will but counsel and sustain me!

WASHINGTON, MARCH 4, 1913.

FREEMEN NEED NO GUARDIANS![1]

FROM THE "FORTNIGHTLY REVIEW," FEBRUARY, 1913,
VOL. 99, PP. 209-218.

THERE are two theories of government that have been contending with each other ever since government began. One of them is the theory which in America is associated with the name of a very great man, Alexander Hamilton. A great man, but in my judgment, not a great American. He did not think in terms of American life. Hamilton believed that the only people who could understand government, and therefore the only people who were qualified to conduct it, were the men who had the biggest financial stake in the commercial and industrial enterprises of the country.

That theory, though few have now the hardihood to profess it openly, has been the working theory upon which our government has lately been conducted. It is astonishing how persistent it is. It is amazing how quickly the political party which had Lincoln for its first leader—Lincoln, who not only denied, but in his own person so completely disproved, the aristocratic theory—it is amazing how quickly that party founded on faith in the people forgot the precepts of Lincoln and fell under the

---

[1] This interview was published so near in point of time to the first inaugural that it seems to be an appendix and hence is published as the second article of this volume.—THE EDITORS.

delusion that the "masses" needed the guardianship of "men of affairs."

For indeed, if you stop to think about it, nothing could be a further departure from original Americanism, from faith in the ability of a confident, resourceful, and independent people than the discouraging doctrine that somebody has got to provide prosperity for the rest of us. And yet that is exactly the doctrine on which the government of the United States has been conducted lately. Who have been consulted when important measures of government, like tariff acts, and currency acts, and railroad acts were under consideration? The people whom the tariff chiefly affects, the people for whom the currency is supposed to exist, the people who pay the duties and ride on the railroads? Oh! no. What do they know about such matters! The gentlemen whose ideas have been sought are the big manufacturers, the bankers, and the heads of the great railroad combinations. The masters of the government of the United States are the combined capitalists and manufacturers of the United States. It is written over every intimate page of the records of Congress; it is written all through the history of conferences at the White House, that the suggestions of economic policy in this country have come from one source, not from many sources; the benevolent guardians, the kind-hearted trustees who have taken the troubles of government off our hands have become so conspicuous that almost anybody can write out a list of them. They have become so conspicuous that their names are mentioned upon almost ev-

ery political platform. The men who have undertaken the interesting job of taking care of us do not
force us to requite them with anonymously directed
gratitude. We know them by name.

Suppose you go to Washington and try to get at
your government. You will always find that while
you are politely listened to, the men really consulted
are the men who have the biggest stake—the big
bankers, the big manufacturers, the big masters of
commerce, the heads of railroad corporations and of
steamship corporations. I have no objection to these
men being consulted, because they also, though they
do not themselves seem to admit it, are part of the
people of the United States. But I do very seriously
object to these gentlemen being chiefly consulted, and
particularly to their being exclusively consulted, and
if the government of the United States is to do the
right thing by the people of the United States it has
got to do it directly and not through the intermedi-
ation of these gentlemen. Every time it has come to
a critical question, these gentlemen have been yielded
to, and their demands have been treated as the demands that should be followed as a matter of course.

The government of the United States at present
is a foster-child of the special interests. It is not
allowed to have a will of its own. It is told at every
move, "Don't do that; you will interfere with our
prosperity." And when we ask, "Where is our
prosperity lodged?" a certain group of gentlemen
say, "With us." The government of the United
States in recent years has not been administered
by the common people of the United States. You

know just as well as I do—it is not an indictment
against anybody, it is a mere statement of the facts—
that the people have stood outside and looked on at
their own government and that all they have had to
determine in past years has been which crowd they
would look on at; whether they would look on at this
little group or that little group who had managed
to get the control of affairs in its hands. Have you
ever heard, for example, of any hearing before any
great committee of the Congress in which the people
of the country as a whole were represented, except
it may be by the Congressmen themselves? The men
who appear at those meetings in order to argue for
this schedule in the tariff, for this measure or against
that measure, are men who represent special interests. They may represent them very honestly; they
may intend no wrong to their fellow citizens, but
they are speaking from the point of view always of
a small portion of the population. I have sometimes
wondered why men, particularly men of means, men
who didn't have to work for their living shouldn't
constitute themselves attorneys for the people, and
every time a hearing is held before a committee of
Congress should not go and ask, "Gentlemen, in
considering these things suppose you consider the
whole country? Suppose you consider the citizens
of the United States?"

Now I don't want a smug lot of experts to sit
down behind closed doors in Washington and play
Providence to me. There is a Providence to which
I am perfectly willing to submit. But as for other
men setting up as Providence over myself, I seri-

ously object. I have never met a political saviour
in the flesh, and I never expect to meet one. I am
reminded of Gelett Burgess' verses:—

> "I never saw a purple cow,
> I never hope to see one,
> But this I'll tell you anyhow,
> I'd rather see than be one."

That is the way I feel about this saving of my
fellow-countrymen. I'd rather see a saviour of the
United States than set up to be one, because I have
found out, I have actually found out, that men I
consult with know more than I do—especially if I
consult with enough of them. I never came out of
a committee meeting or a conference without seeing
more of the question that was under discussion than
I had seen when I went in. And that to my mind is
an image of government. I am not willing to be
under the patronage of the trusts, no matter how
providential a government presides over the process
of their control of my life.

I am one of those who absolutely reject the trustee theory, the guardianship theory. I have never
found a man who knew how to take care of me, and,
reasoning from that point out, I conjecture that
there isn't any man who knows how to take care of
the people of the United States. I suspect that the
people of the United States understand their own
interests better than any group of men in the confines of the country understand them. The men who
are sweating blood to get their foothold in the world
of endeavour understand the conditions of business

in the United States very much better than the men
who have arrived and are at the top. They know
what the thing is that they are struggling against.
They know how difficult it is to start a new enterprise. They know how far they have to search for
credit that will put them upon an even footing with
the men who have already built up industry in this
country. They know that somewhere by somebody
the development of industry in this country is being
controlled.

I do not say this with the slightest desire to create
any prejudice against wealth; on the contrary, I
should be ashamed of myself if I excited class feeling of any kind. But I do mean to suggest this:
that the wealth of the country has, in recent years,
come from particular sources; it has come from
those sources which have built up monopoly. Its
point of view is a special point of view. It is the point
of view of those men who do not wish that the people should determine their own affairs, because they
do not believe that the people's judgment is sound.
They want to be commissioned to take care of the
United States and of the people of the United States,
because they believe that they, better than anybody
else, understand the interests of the United States.
I do not challenge their character; I challenge their
point of view. We cannot afford to be governed as
we have been governed in the last generation, by
men who occupy so narrow, so prejudiced, so limited
a point of view.

The government of our country cannot be lodged
in any special class. The policy of a great nation

cannot be tied up with any particular set of interests. I want to say, again and again, that my arguments do not touch the character of the men to whom I am opposed. I believe that the very wealthy men who have got their money by certain kinds of corporate enterprises have closed in their horizon, and that they do not see and do not understand the rank and file of the people. It is for that reason that I want to break up the little coterie that has determined what the government of the nation should do. The list of the men who used to determine what New Jersey should and should not do did not exceed half a dozen, and they were always the same men. These very men now are, some of them, frank enough to admit that New Jersey has finer energy in her because more men are consulted and the whole field of action is widened and liberalised.

We have got to relieve our government from the domination of special classes, not because these special classes are bad, necessarily, but because no special class can understand the interests of a great community.

I believe, as I believe in nothing else, in the average integrity and the average intelligence of the American people, and I do not believe that the intelligence of America can be put into commission anywhere. I do not believe that there is any group of men of any kind to whom we can afford to give that kind of trusteeship.

I will not live under trustees if I can help it. No group of men less than the majority has a right to tell me how I have got to live in America. I will

submit to the majority, because I have been trained
to do it—though I may sometimes have my private
opinion even of the majority. I do not care how
wise, how patriotic, the trustees may be, I have never
heard of any group of men in whose hands I am
willing to lodge the liberties of America in trust.

If any part of our people want to be wards, if
they want to have guardians put over them, if they
want to be taken care of, if they want to be children,
patronised by the government, why, I am sorry, because it will sap the manhood of America. But I
don't believe they do. I believe they want to stand
on the firm foundation of law and right and take
care of themselves. I, for my part, don't want to
belong to a nation, I believe that I do not belong to
a nation, that needs to be taken care of by guardians.
I want to belong to a nation, and I am proud that
I do belong to a nation, that knows how to take care
of itself. If I thought that the American people
were reckless, were ignorant, were vindictive, I
might shrink from putting the government into
their hands. But the beauty of democracy is that
when you are reckless you destroy your own established conditions of life; when you are vindictive,
you wreak vengeance upon yourself; the whole stability of democratic polity rests upon the fact that
every interest is every man's interest.

The theory that the men of biggest affairs, whose
field of operation is the widest, are the proper men
to advise the government is, I am willing to admit,
rather a plausible theory. If my business covers the
United States not only, but covers the world, it is

to be presumed that I have a pretty wide scope in
my vision of business. But the flaw is that it is my
own business that I have a vision of, and not the
business of the men who lie outside of the scope of
the plans I have made for a profit out of the particular transactions I am connected with. And you
can't, by putting together a large number of men
who understand their own business, no matter how
large it is, make up a body of men who will understand the business of the nation as contrasted with
their own business interest.

In a former generation, half a century ago, there
were a great many men associated with the government whose patriotism we are not privileged to deny
nor to question, who intended to serve the people,
but had become so saturated with the point of view
of a governing class, that it was impossible for them
to see America as the people of America themselves
saw it. Then there arose that interesting figure, the
immortal figure of the great Lincoln, who stood up
declaring that the politicians, the men who had governed this country, did not see from the point of
view of the people. When I think of that tall,
gaunt figure rising in Illinois, I have a picture of
a man free, unentangled, unassociated with the governing influences of the country, ready to see things
with an open eye, to see them steadily, to see them
whole, to see them as the men he rubbed shoulders
with and associated with saw them. What the
country needed in 1860 was a leader who understood and represented the thought of the whole people, as contrasted with that of a special class which

imagined itself the guardian of the country's welfare.

Now, likewise, the trouble with our present political condition is that we need some man who has not been associated with the governing classes and the governing influences of this country to stand up and speak for us; we need to hear a voice from the outside calling upon the American people to assert again their rights and prerogatives in the possession of their own government.

My thought about both Mr. Taft and Mr. Roosevelt is that of entire respect, but these gentlemen have been so intimately associated with the powers that have been determining the policy of this government for almost a generation, that they cannot look at the affairs of the country with a view of a new age and of a changed set of circumstances. They sympathise with the people; their hearts no doubt go out to the great masses of unknown men in this country; but their thought is in close habitual association with those who have framed the policies of the country during all our lifetime. Those men have framed the protective tariff, have developed the trusts, have coördinated and ordered all the great economic forces of this country in such fashion that nothing but an outside force breaking in can disturb their domination and control. It is with this in mind, I believe, that the country can say to these gentlemen: "We do not deny your integrity; we do not deny your purity of purpose; but the thought of the people of the United States has not yet penetrated to your consciousness. You are

willing to act for the people, but you are not willing
to act through the people. Now we propose to act
for ourselves.''

I sometimes think that the men who are now governing us are unconscious of the chains in which
they are held. I do not believe that men such as
we know, among our public men at least—most of
them—have deliberately put us into leading strings
to the special interests. The special interests have
grown up. They have grown up by processes which
at last, happily, we are beginning to understand.
And, having grown up, having occupied the seats
of greatest advantage nearest the ear of those who
are conducting government, having contributed the
money which was necessary to the elections, and
therefore having been kindly thought of after elections, there has closed around the government of the
United States a very interesting, a very able, a very
aggressive coterie of gentlemen who are most definite and explicit in their ideas as to what they want.

They don't have to consult us as to what they
want. They don't have to resort to anybody. They
know their plans, and therefore they know what will
be convenient for them. It may be that they have
really thought what they have said they thought; it
may be that they know so little of the history of
economic development and of the interests of the
United States as to believe that their leadership is
indispensable for our prosperity and development.
I don't have to prove that they believe that, because they themselves admit it. I have heard them
admit it on many occasions.

I want to say to you very frankly that I do not feel vindictive about it. Some of the men who have exercised this control are excellent fellows; they really believe that the prosperity of the country depends upon them. They really believe that if the leadership of economic development in this country dropped from their hands, the rest of us are too muddle-headed to undertake the task. They not only comprehend the power of the United States within their grasp, but they comprehend it within their imagination. They are honest men, they have just as much right to express their views as I have to express mine or you to express yours, but it is just about time that we examined their views and determined their validity.

As a matter of fact, their thought does not cover the process of their own undertaking. As a university president, I learned that the men who dominate our manufacturing processes could not conduct their business for twenty-four hours without the assistance of the experts with whom the universities were supplying them. Modern industry depends upon technical knowledge; and all that these gentlemen did was to manage the external features of great combinations and their financial operation, which had very little to do with the intimate skill with which the enterprises were conducted. I know men not catalogued in the public prints, men not spoken of in public discussion, who are the very bone and sinew of the industry of the United States.

Do our masters of industry speak in the spirits and interest even of those whom they employ? When men ask me what I think about the labour question and labouring men, I feel that I am being asked what I know about the vast majority of the people, and I feel as if I were being asked to separate myself, as belonging to a particular class, from that great body of my fellow-citizens who sustain and conduct the enterprises of the country. Until we get away from that point of view it will be impossible to have a free government.

I have listened to some very honest and eloquent orators whose sentiments were noteworthy for this: that when they spoke of the people, they were not thinking of themselves; they were thinking of somebody whom they were commissioned to take care of. They were always planning to do things for the American people, and I have seen them visibly shiver when it was suggested that they arranged to have something done by the people for themselves. They said, "What do they know about it?" I always feel like replying, "What do *you* know about it? You know your own interests, but who has told you our interests and what do you know about them?" For the business of every leader of government is to hear what the nation is saying and to know what the nation is enduring. It is not his business to judge *for* the nation, but to judge *through* the nation as its spokesman and voice. I do not believe that this country could have safely allowed a continuation of the policy of the men who have viewed affairs in any other light.

The hypothesis under which we have been ruled is that of government through a board of trustees, through a selected number of the big business men of the country who know a lot that the rest of us do not know, and who take it for granted that our ignorance would wreck the prosperity of the country. The idea of the Presidents we have recently had has been that they were Presidents of a National Board of Trustees. That is not my idea. I have been president of one board of trustees, and I do not care to have another on my hands. I want to be President of the people of the United States. There was many a time when I was president of the board of trustees of a university when the undergraduates knew more than the trustees did; and it has been in my thought ever since that if I could have dealt directly with the people who constituted Princeton University I could have carried it forward much faster than I could dealing with a board of trustees.

Mark you, I am not saying that these leaders knew that they were doing us an evil, or that they intended to do us an evil. For my part I am very much more afraid of the man who does a bad thing and does not know it is bad than of the man who does a bad thing and knows it is bad; because I think that in public affairs stupidity is more dangerous than knavery, because harder to fight and dislodge. If a man does not know enough to know what the consequences are going to be to the country, then he cannot govern the country in a way that is for its benefit. These gentlemen, whatever may have been their intentions, linked the government up with the men who control the finances. They may have done it innocently, or they may have done it corruptly, without affecting my argument at all. And they themselves cannot escape from that alliance.

Here is the old question of campaign funds: if I take a hundred thousand dollars from a group of men representing a particular interest that has a big stake in a certain schedule of the tariff, I take it with the knowledge that those gentlemen will expect me not to forget their interest in that schedule, and that they will take it as an implicit honor that I should see to it that they are not damaged by too great a change in that schedule. Therefore, if I take their money, I am bound to them by a tacit implication of honor. Perhaps there is no ground for objection to this situation so long as the function of government is conceived to be to look after the trustees of prosperity, who in turn will look after the people; but on any other theory than that of trusteeship no interested campaign contributions can be tolerated for a moment—save those of the millions of citizens who thus support the doctrines they believe and the men whom they recognized as their spokesmen.

I tell you the men I am interested in are the men who, under the conditions we have had, never had their voices heard, who never got a line in the newspapers, who never got a moment on the platform, who never had access to the ears of Governors or Presidents or of anybody who was responsible for the conduct of public affairs, but who went silently and patiently to their work every day carrying the burden of the world. How are they to be understood by the masters of finance, if only the masters of finance are consulted?

That is what I mean when I say, "Bring the government back to the people." I do not mean anything demagogic; I do not mean to talk as if we wanted a great mass of men to rush in and destroy something. That is not the idea. I want the people to come and take possession of their own premises; for I hold that the government belongs to the people, and that they have a right to that intimate access to it which will determine every turn of its policy.

America is never going to submit to guardianship. America is never going to choose thraldom instead of freedom. Look what there is to decide! There is the tariff question. Can the tariff question be decided in favour of the people so long as the monopolies are the chief counsellors at Washington? There is the currency question. Are we going to settle the currency question so long as the government listens only to the counsel of those who command the banking situation?

Then there is the question of conservation. What is our fear about conservation? The hands that are being stretched out to monopolise our forests, to prevent the use of our great power-producing streams, the hands that are being stretched into the bowels of the earth to take possession of the great riches that lie hidden in Alaska and elsewhere in the incomparable domain of the United States, are the hands of monopoly. Are these men to continue to stand at the elbow of government and tell us how we are to save ourselves—from themselves? You cannot settle the question of conservation while monopoly

is close to the ears of those who govern. And the
question of conservation is a great deal bigger than
the question of saving our forests and our mineral
resources and our waters; it is as big as the life and
happiness and strength and elasticity and hope of
our people.

There are tasks awaiting the government of the
United States which it cannot perform until every
pulse of that government beats in unison with the
needs and the desires of the whole body of the
American people. Shall we not give the people
access of sympathy, access of authority, to the instrumentalities which are to be indispensable to their
lives?

THE TARIFF

FIRST SPECIAL ADDRESS TO CONGRESS ASKING IMMEDIATE
REVISION OF THE PAYNE-ALDRICH TARIFF, APRIL 8,
1913. FROM THE "CONGRESSONAL RECORD," 63D CON-
GRESS, 1ST SESSION, VOL. 50, P. 130.

GENTLEMEN OF THE CONGRESS:
I am very glad indeed to have this opportunity to address the two Houses directly and to
verify for myself the impression that the President
of the United States is a person, not a mere department of the Government hailing Congress from some
isolated island of jealous power, sending messages,
not speaking naturally and with his own voice—that
he is a human being trying to coöperate with other
human beings in a common service. After this pleasant experience I shall feel quite normal in all our
dealings with one another.

I have called the Congress together in extraordinary session because a duty was laid upon the party
now in power at the recent elections which it ought
to perform promptly, in order that the burden carried by the people under existing law may be light-
ened as soon as possible, and in order, also, that the
business interests of the country may not be kept
too long in suspense as to what the fiscal changes are
to be to which they will be required to adjust themselves. It is clear to the whole country that the tariff

duties must be altered. They must be changed to
meet the radical alteration in the conditions of our
economic life which the country has witnessed within
the last generation. While the whole face and method
of our industrial and commercial life were being
changed beyond recognition the tariff schedules have
remained what they were before the change began,
or have moved in the direction they were given when
no large circumstance of our industrial development
was what it is to-day. Our task is to square them
with the actual facts. The sooner that is done the
sooner we shall escape from suffering from the facts
and the sooner our men of business will be free to
thrive by the law of nature—the nature of free business—instead of by the law of legislation and
artificial arrangement.

We have seen tariff legislation wander very far
afield in our day—very far indeed from the field in
which our prosperity might have had a normal growth
and stimulation. No one who looks the facts squarely
in the face or knows anything that lies beneath the
surface of action can fail to perceive the principles
upon which recent tariff legislation has been based.
We long ago passed beyond the modest notion of
"protecting" the industries of the country and moved
boldly forward to the idea that they were entitled
to the direct patronage of the Government. For a
long time—a time so long that the men now active
in public policy hardly remember the conditions that
preceded it—we have sought in our tariff schedules
to give each group of manufacturers or producers
what they themselves thought that they needed in

order to maintain a practically exclusive market as against the rest of the world. Consciously or unconsciously, we have built up a set of privileges and exemptions from competition behind which it was easy by any, even the crudest, forms of combination to organize monopoly; until at last nothing is normal, nothing is obliged to stand the tests of efficiency and economy, in our world of big business, but everything thrives by concerted arrangement. Only new principles of action will save us from a final hard crystallization of monopoly and a complete loss of the influences that quicken enterprise and keep independent energy alive.

It is plain what those principles must be. We must abolish everything that bears even the semblance of privilege or of any kind of artificial advantage, and put our business men and producers under the stimulation of a constant necessity to be efficient, economical, and enterprising, masters of competitive supremacy, better workers and merchants than any in the world. Aside from the duties laid upon articles which we do not, and probably can not, produce, therefore, and the duties laid upon luxuries and merely for the sake of the revenues they yield, the object of the tariff duties henceforth laid must be effective competition, the whetting of American wits by contest with the wits of the rest of the world.

It would be unwise to move toward this end headlong, with reckless haste, or with strokes that cut at the very roots of what has grown up amongst us by long process and at our own invitation. It does not alter a thing to upset it and break it and deprive

it of a chance to change. It destroys it. We must
make changes in our fiscal laws, in our fiscal system,
whose object is development, a more free and wholesome development, not revolution or upset or confusion. We must build up trade, especially foreign
trade. We need the outlet and the enlarged field of
energy more than we ever did before. We must build
up industry as well, and must adopt freedom in the
place of artificial stimulation only so far as it will
build, not pull down. In dealing with the tariff the
method by which this may be done will be a matter
of judgment exercised item by item. To some not
accustomed to the excitements and responsibilities
of greater freedom our methods may in some respects
and at some points seem heroic but remedies may be
heroic and yet be remedies. It is our business to
make sure that they are genuine remedies. Our object is clear. If our motive is above just challenge
and only an occasional error of judgment is charge-
able against us, we shall be fortunate.

We are called upon to render the country a great
service in more matters than one. Our responsibility
should be met and our methods should be thorough,
as thorough as moderate and well considered, based
upon the facts as they are, and not worked out as
if we were beginners. We are to deal with the facts
of our own day, with the facts of no other and to
make laws which square with those facts. It is best,
indeed it is necessary, to begin with the tariff. I
will urge nothing upon you now at the opening of
your session which can obscure that first object or
divert our energies from that clearly defined duty.

At a later time I may take the liberty of calling your attention to reforms which should press close upon the heels of the tariff changes, if not accompany them, of which the chief is the reform of our banking and currency laws; but just now I refrain. For the present, I put these matters on one side and think only of this one thing—of the changes in our fiscal system which may best serve to open once more the free channels of prosperity to a great people whom we would serve to the utmost and throughout both rank and file.

I sincerely thank you for your courtesy.

THE DEDICATION OF CONGRESS HALL

ADDRESS DELIVERED AT PHILADELPHIA OCTOBER 25, 1913. FROM THE "CONGRESSIONAL RECORD," 63D CONGRESS, 1ST SESSION, VOL. 50, PP. 5809-5810.

NO American could stand in this place to-day and think of the circumstances which we are come together to celebrate without being most profoundly stirred. There has come over me since I sat down here a sense of deep solemnity, because it has seemed to me that I saw ghosts crowding—a great assemblage of spirits no longer visible, but whose influence we still feel as we feel the molding power of history itself. The men who sat in this hall, to whom we now look back with a touch of deep sentiment, were men of flesh and blood, face to face with extremely difficult problems. The population of the United States then was hardly three times the present population of the city of Philadelphia, and yet that was a Nation as this is a Nation, and the men who spoke for it were setting their hands to work which was to last, not only that their people might be happy, but that an example might be lifted up for the instruction of the rest of the world.

I like to read the quaint old accounts such as Mr. Day has read to us this afternoon. Strangers came to America to see what the young people that had sprung up here were like, and they found men in

counsel who knew how to construct governments.
They found men deliberating here who had none of
the appearance of novices, none of the hesitation of
men who did not know whether the work they were
doing was going to last or not; men who addressed
themselves to a problem of construction as familiarly
as we attempt to carry out the traditions of a Government established these 137 years.

I feel to-day the compulsion of these men, the compulsion of examples which were set up in this place.
And of what do their examples remind us? They
remind us not merely of public service but of public
service shot through with principle and honor. . . .

They were not historic men. They did not say:

Look upon us as those who shall hereafter be illustrious.

They said:

Look upon us who are doing the first free work of
constitutional liberty in the world, and who must do
it in soberness and truth, or it will not last.

Politics, ladies and gentlemen, is made up in just
about equal parts of compensation and sympathy.
No man ought to go into politics who does not comprehend the task that he is going to attack. He may
comprehend it so completely that it daunts him, that
he doubts whether his own spirit is stout enough and
his own mind able enough to attempt its great undertakings, but unless he comprehend it he ought
not to enter it. After he has comprehended it, there
should come into his mind those profound impulses
of sympathy which connect him with the rest of mankind, for politics is a business of interpretation, and

no men are fit for it who do not see and seek more
than their own advantage and interest.

We have stumbled upon many unhappy circumstances in the hundred years that have gone by since
the event that we are celebrating. Almost all of
them have come from self-centered men, men who
saw in their own interest the interest of the country,
and who did not have vision enough to read it in
wider terms, in the universal terms of equity and
justice and the rights of mankind. I hear a great
many people at Fourth of July celebrations laud the
Declaration of Independence who in between Julys
shiver at the plain language of our bills of rights.
The Declaration of Independence was, indeed, the
first audible breath of liberty, but the substance of
liberty is written in such documents as the declaration of rights attached, for example, to the first constitution of Virginia which was a model for the
similar documents read elsewhere into our great fundamental charters. That document speaks in very
plain terms. The men of that generation did not
hesitate to say that every people has a right to choose
its own forms of government—not once, but as often
as it pleases—and to accommodate those forms of government to its existing interests and circumstances.
Not only to establish but to alter is the fundamental
principle of self-government.

We are just as much under compulsion to study
the particular circumstances of our own day as the
gentlemen were who sat in this hall and set us
precedents, not of what to do but how to do it. Liberty inheres in the circumstances of the day. Human

happiness consists in the life which human beings are leading at the time that they live. I can feed my memory as happily upon the circumstances of the revolutionary and constitutional period as you can, but I can not feed all my purposes with them in Washington now. Every day problems arise which wear some new phase and aspect, and I must fall back, if I would serve my conscience, upon those things which are fundamental rather than upon those things which are superficial, and ask myself this question, How are you going to assist in some small part to give the American people and, by example, the peoples of the world more liberty, more happiness, more substantial prosperity; and how are you going to make that prosperity a common heritage instead of a selfish possession? . . .

I come here to-day partly in order to feed my own spirit. I did not come in compliment. When I was asked to come, I knew immediately upon the utterance of the invitation that I had to come, that to be absent would be as if I refused to drink once more at the original fountains of inspiration for our own government.

The men of the day which we now celebrate had a very great advantage over us, ladies and gentlemen, in this one particular : Life was simple in America then. All men shared the same circumstances in almost equal degree. We think of Washington, for example, as an aristocrat, as a man separated by training, separated by family and neighborhood tradition, from the ordinary people of the rank and file of the country. Have you forgotten the personal

history of George Washington? Do you not know
that he struggled as poor boys now struggle for a
meager and imperfect education; that he worked at
his surveyor's tasks in the lonely forests; that he
knew all the roughness, all the hardships, all the
adventure, all the variety of the common life of that
day; and that if he stood a little stiffly in this place,
if he looked a little aloof, it was because life had
dealt hardly with him? All his sinews had been
stiffened by the rough work of making America. He
was a man of the people, whose touch had been with
them since the day he saw the light first in the old
Dominion of Virginia. And the men who came after
him, men, some of whom had drunk deep at the
sources of philosophy and of study, were, nevertheless, also men who on this side of the water knew no
complicated life but the simple life of primitive
neighborhoods. Our task is very much more difficult. That sympathy which alone interprets public
duty is more difficult for a public man to acquire now
than it was then, because we live in the midst of circumstances and conditions infinitely complex.

No man can boast that he understands America.
No man can boast that he has lived the life of America, as almost every man who sat in this hall in those
days could boast. No man can pretend that except
by common counsel he can gather into his consciousness what the varied life of this people is. The duty
that we have to keep open eyes and open hearts and
accessible understandings is a very much more difficult duty to perform than it was in their day. Yet
how much more important that it should be per-

formed, for fear we make infinite and irreparable
blunders. The city of Washington is in some respects
self-contained, and it is easy there to forget what
the rest of the United States is thinking about. I
count it a fortunate circumstance that almost all the
windows of the White House and its offices open upon
unoccupied spaces that stretch to the banks of the
Potomac and then out into Virginia and on to the
heavens themselves, and that as I sit there I can
constantly forget Washington and remember the
United States. Not that I would intimate that all
of the United States lies south of Washington, but
there is a serious thing back of my thought. If you
think too much about being re-elected, it is very difficult to be worth re-electing. You are so apt to forget that the comparatively small number of persons,
numerous as they seem to be when they swarm, who
come to Washington to ask for things, do not constitute an important proportion of the population of
the country, that it is constantly necessary to come
away from Washington and renew one's contact with
the people who do not swarm there, who do not ask for
anything, but who do trust you without their personal counsel to do your duty. Unless a man gets these
contacts he grows weaker and weaker. He needs
them as Hercules needed the touch of mother earth.
If you lift him up too high or he lifts himself too high,
he loses the contact and therefore loses the inspiration.

I love to think of those plain men, however far
from plain their dress sometimes was, who assembled
in this hall. One is startled to think of the variety
of costume and color which would now occur if we

were let loose upon the fashions of that age. Men's lack of taste is largely concealed now by the limitations of fashion. Yet these men, who sometimes dressed like the peacock, were, nevertheless, of the ordinary flight of their time. They were birds of a feather; they were birds come from a very simple breeding; they were much in the open heaven. They were beginning, when there was so little to distract their attention, to show that they could live upon fundamental principles of government. We talk those principles, but we have not time to absorb them. We have not time to let them into our blood, and thence have them translated into the plain mandates of action.

The very smallness of this room, the very simplicity of it all, all the suggestions which come from its restoration, are reassuring things—things which it becomes a man to realize. Therefore my theme here to-day, my only thought, is a very simple one. Do not let us go back to the annals of those sessions of Congress to find out what to do, because we live in another age and the circumstances are absolutely different; but let us be men of that kind; let us feel at every turn the compulsions of principle and of honor which they left; let us free our vision from temporary circumstances and look abroad at the horizon and take into our lungs the great air of freedom which has blown through this country and stolen across the seas and blessed people everywhere; and, looking east and west and north and south, let us remind ourselves that we are the custodians, in some degree, of the principles which have made men free and governments just.

A NEW LATIN-AMERICAN POLICY

ADDRESS DELIVERED BEFORE THE SOUTHERN COMMER-
CIAL CONGRESS AT MOBILE, ALA., OCTOBER 27, 1913.
FROM OFFICIAL PUBLICATION IN MR. WILSON'S FILES.

I T is with unaffected pleasure that I find myself
here to-day. I once before had the pleasure, in
another southern city, of addressing the Southern
Commercial Congress. I then spoke of what the
future seemed to hold in store for this region, which
so many of us love and toward the future of which
we all look forward with so much confidence and
hope. But another theme directed me here this time.
I do not need to speak of the South. She has, perhaps, acquired the gift of speaking for herself. I
come because I want to speak of our present and
prospective relations with our neighbors to the south.
I deemed it a public duty, as well as a personal pleasure, to be here to express for myself and for the Government I represent the welcome we all feel to those
who represent the Latin-American States.

The future, ladies and gentlemen, is going to be
very different for this hemisphere from the past.
These States lying to the south of us, which have
always been our neighbors, will now be drawn closer
to us by innumerable ties, and, I hope, chief of all,
by the tie of a common understanding of each other.
Interest does not tie nations together; it sometimes

separates them. But sympathy and understanding does unite them, and I believe that by the new route that is just about to be opened, while we physically cut two continents asunder, we spiritually unite them. It is a spiritual union which we seek.

I wonder if you realize, I wonder if your imaginations have been filled with the significance of the tides of commerce. Your governor alluded in very fit and striking terms to the voyage of Columbus, but Columbus took his voyage under compulsion of circumstances. Constantinople had been captured by the Turks and all the routes of trade with the East had been suddenly closed. If there was not a way across the Atlantic to open those routes again, they were closed forever, and Columbus set out not to discover America, for he did not know that it existed, but to discover the eastern shores of Asia. He set sail for Cathay and stumbled upon America. With that change in the outlook of the world, what happened? England, that had been at the back of Europe with an unknown sea behind her, found that all things had turned as if upon a pivot and she was at the front of Europe; and since then all the tides of energy and enterprise that have issued out of Europe have seemed to be turned westward across the Atlantic. But you will notice that they have turned westward chiefly north of the Equator and that it is the northern half of the globe that has seemed to be filled with the media of intercourse and of sympathy and of common understanding.

Do you not see now what is about to happen? These great tides which have been running along

parallels of latitude will now swing southward
athwart parallels of latitude, and that opening gate
at the Isthmus of Panama will open the world to a
commerce that she has not known before, a commerce
of intelligence, of thought and sympathy between
North and South. The Latin American States, which,
to their disadvantage, have been off the main lines,
will now be on the main lines. I feel that these gentlemen honoring us with their presence to-day will
presently find that some part, at any rate, of the
center of gravity of the world has shifted. Do you
realize that New York, for example, will be nearer
the western coast of South American than she is now
to the eastern coast of South America? Do you
realize that a line drawn northward parallel with the
greater part of the western coast of South America
will run only about 150 miles west of New York?
The great bulk of South America, if you will look
at your globes (not at your Mercator's projection),
lies eastward of the continent of North America. You
will realize that when you realize that the canal will
run southeast, not southwest, and that when you get
into the Pacific you will be farther east than you
were when you left the Gulf of Mexico. These things
are significant, therefore, of this, that we are closing
one chapter in the history of the world and are
opening another, of great, unimaginable significance.

There is one peculiarity about the history of the
Latin American States which I am sure they are
keenly aware of. You hear of ''concessions'' to foreign capitalists in Latin America. You do not hear
of concessions to foreign capitalists in the United

States. They are not granted concessions. They are
invited to make investments. The work is ours,
though they are welcome to invest in it. We do not
ask them to supply the capital and do the work. It
is an invitation, not a privilege; and States that are
obliged, because their territory does not lie within
the main field of modern enterprise and action, to
grant concessions are in this condition, that foreign
interests are apt to dominate their domestic affairs,
a condition of affairs always dangerous and apt to
become intolerable. What these States are going
to see, therefore, is an emancipation from the subor-
dination, which has been inevitable, to foreign enterprise and an assertion of the splendid character
which, in spite of these difficulties, they have again
and again been able to demonstrate. The dignity,
the courage, the self-possession, the self-respect of
the Latin American States, their achievements in the
face of all these adverse circumstances, deserve nothing but the admiration and applause of the world.
They have had harder bargains driven with them in
the matter of loans than any other peoples in the
world. Interest has been exacted of them that was
not exacted of anybody else, because the risk was
said to be greater; and then securities were taken
that destroyed the risk—an admirable arrangement
for those who were forcing the terms! I rejoice in
nothing so much as in the prospect that they will
now be emancipated from these conditions, and we
ought to be the first to take part in assisting in that
emancipation. I think some of these gentlemen have
already had occasion to bear witness that the De-

partment of State in recent months has tried to serve them in that wise. In the future they will draw closer and closer to us because of circumstances of which I wish to speak with moderation and, I hope, without indiscretion.

We must prove ourselves their friends, and champions upon terms of equality and honor. You cannot be friends upon any other terms than upon the terms of equality. You cannot be friends at all except upon the terms of honor. We must show ourselves friends by comprehending their interest whether it squares with our own interest or not. It is a very perilous thing to determine the foreign policy of a nation in the terms of material interest. It not only is unfair to those with whom you are dealing, but it is degrading as regards your own actions.

Comprehension must be the soil in which shall grow all the fruits of friendship, and there is a reason and a compulsion lying behind all this which is dearer than anything else to the thoughtful men of America. I mean the development of constitutional liberty in the world. Human rights, national integrity, and opportunity as against material interests—that, ladies and gentlemen, is the issue which we now have to face. I want to take this occasion to say that the United States will never again seek one additional foot of territory by conquest. She will devote herself to showing that she knows how to make honorable and fruitful use of the territory she has, and she must regard it as one of the duties of friendship to see that from no quarter are material interests made superior to human liberty and national opportunity.

I say this, not with a single thought that anyone will gainsay it, but merely to fix in our consciousness what our real relationship with the rest of America is. It is the relationship of a family of mankind devoted to the development of true constitutional liberty. We know that that is the soil out of which the best enterprise springs. We know that this is a cause which we are making in common with our neighbors, because we have had to make it for ourselves.

Reference has been made here to-day to some of the national problems which confront us as a Nation. What is at the heart of all our national problems? It is that we have seen the hand of material interest sometimes about to close upon our dearest rights and possessions. We have seen material interests threaten constitutional freedom in the United States. Therefore we will now know how to sympathize with those in the rest of America who have to contend with such powers, not only within their borders but from outside their borders also.

I know what the response of the thought and heart of America will be to the program I have outlined, because America was created to realize a program like that. This is not America because it is rich. This is not America because it has set up for a great population great opportunities of material prosperity. America is a name which sounds in the ears of men everywhere as a synonym with individual opportunity because a synonym of individual liberty. I would rather belong to a poor nation that was free than to a rich nation that had ceased to be in love with liberty. But we shall not be poor if we love liberty, because the nation that loves liberty truly sets every man free to do his best and be his best, and that means the release of all the splendid energies of a great people who think for themselves. A nation of employees cannot be free any more than a nation of employers can be.

In emphasizing the points which must unite us in sympathy and in spiritual interest with the Latin American peoples we are only emphasizing the points of our own life, and we should prove ourselves untrue to our own traditions if we proved ourselves untrue friends to them.

Do not think, therefore, gentlemen, that the questions of the day are mere questions of policy and diplomacy. They are shot through with the principles of life. We dare not turn from the principle that morality and not expediency is the thing that must guide us and that we will never condone iniquity because it is most convenient to do so. It seems to me that this is a day of infinite hope, of confidence in a future greater than the past has been, for I am fain to believe that in spite of all the things that we wish to correct the nineteenth century that now lies behind us has brought us a long stage toward the time when, slowly ascending the tedious climb that leads to the final uplands, we shall get our ultimate view of the duties of mankind. We have breasted a considerable part of that climb and shall presently—it may be in a generation or two—come out upon those great heights where there shines unobstructed the light of the justice of God.

PANAMA CANAL TOLLS

ADDRESS TO CONGRESS ON THE PANAMA CANAL TOLLS
PROBLEM, MARCH 5, 1914. FROM THE "CONGRESSIONAL
RECORD," 63D CONGRESS, 2D SESSION, VOL. 51, P. 4313.

GENTLEMEN OF THE CONGRESS:
I have come to you upon an errand which
can be very briefly performed, but I beg that you will
not measure its importance by the number of sentences in which I state it. No communication I have
addressed to the Congress carried with it graver or
more far-reaching implications as to the interest of
the country, and I come now to speak upon a matter with regard to which I am charged in a peculiar
degree, by the Constitution itself, with personal responsibility.

I have come to ask you for the repeal of that provision of the Panama Canal Act of August 24, 1912,
which exempts vessels engaged in the coastwise trade
of the United States from payment of tolls, and to
urge upon you the justice, the wisdom, and the
large policy of such a repeal with the utmost earnest-
ness of which I am capable.

In my own judgment, very fully considered and
maturely formed, that exemption constitutes a mistaken economic policy from every point of view, and
is, moreover, in plain contravention of the treaty
with Great Britain concerning the canal concluded

on November 18, 1901. But I have not come to urge
upon you my personal views. I have come to state
to you a fact and a situation. Whatever may be our
own differences of opinion concerning this much debated measure, its meaning is not debated outside the
United States. Everywhere else the language of the
treaty is given but one interpretation, and that interpretation precludes the exemption I am asking you
to repeal. We consented to the treaty; its language
we accepted, if we did not originate it; and we are
too big, too powerful, too self-respecting a nation to
interpret with a too strained or refined reading the
words of our own promises just because we have
power enough to give us leave to read them as we
please. The large thing to do is the only thing we
can afford to do, a voluntary withdrawal from a position everywhere questioned and misunderstood. We
ought to reverse our action without raising the question whether we were right or wrong, and so once
more deserve our reputation for generosity and for
the redemption of every obligation without quibble
or hesitation.

I ask this of you in support of the foreign policy
of the administration. I shall not know how to deal
with other matters of even greater delicacy and
nearer consequence if you do not grant it to me in
ungrudging measure.

A PRESIDENT'S DIFFICULTIES[1]

SPEECH TO THE MEMBERS OF THE NATIONAL PRESS CLUB, WASHINGTON, MARCH 20, 1914. FROM THE NEW YORK "TIMES," MARCH 21, 1914.

I WAS just thinking of my sense of confusion of identity, sometimes, when I read the articles about myself. I have never read an article about myself in which I have recognized myself, and I have come to have the impression that I must be some kind of a fraud, because I think a great many of these articles are written in absolute good faith. I tremble to think of the variety and falseness in the impressions I make—and it is being borne in on me so that it may change my very disposition—that I am a cold and removed person who has a thinking machine inside which he adjusts to the circumstances, which he does not allow to be moved by any winds of affection or emotion of any kind, that turns like a cold searchlight on anything that is presented to his attention and makes it work.

I am not aware of having any detachable apparatus inside of me. On the contrary, if I were to interpret myself, I would say that my constant embarrassment

---

[1] Mr. Wilson had been elected a member of the National Press Club as an author long before he became President. The occasion of this speech was a "housewarming" at the club's new headquarters. The President's talk was an impromptu one, delivered informally, and was not intended for publication. According to the New York *Times*, Mr. Wilson "was in a happy mood, and his remarks were constantly punctuated with laughter and applause."

is to restrain the emotions that are inside of me. You
may not believe it, but I sometimes feel like a fire
from a far from extinct volcano, and if the lava does
not seem to spill over it is because you are not high
enough to see the caldron boil. Because, truly, gentlemen, in the position which I now occupy there is
a sort of, I do not know how else to express it than
to say, passionate sense of being connected with my
fellow men in a peculiar relationship of responsibility,
not merely the responsibility of office, but God knows
there are enough things in this world that need to
be corrected.

I have mixed, first and last, with all sorts and conditions of men—there are mighty few kinds of men
that have to be described to me, and there are mighty
few kinds of experiences that have to be described
to me—and when I think of the number of men who
are looking to me as the representative of a party,
with the hope for all varieties of salvage from the
things they are struggling in the midst of, it makes
me tremble. It makes me tremble not only with a
sense of my own inadequacy and weakness, but as
if I were shaken by the very things that are shaking
them and, if I seem circumspect, it is because I am
so diligently trying not to make any colossal blunders. If you just calculate the number of blunders a
fellow can make in twenty-four hours if he is not
careful and if he does not listen more than he talks,
you would see something of the feeling that I have.

I was amused the other day at a remark that Senator Newlands made. I had read him the trust message that I was to deliver to Congress some ten days

before I delivered it, and I never stop "doctoring" things of that kind until the day I have to deliver them. When he heard it read to Congress he said: "I think it was better than it was when you read it to me." I said: "Senator, there is one thing which I do not think you understand. I not only use all the brains I have, but all I can borrow, and I have borrowed a lot since I read it to you first."

That, I dare say, is what gives the impression of circumspectness. I am listening; I am diligently trying to collect all the brains that are borrowable in order that I will not make more blunders than it is inevitable that a man should make who has great limitations of knowledge and capacity. And the emotion of the thing is so great that I suppose I must be some kind of a mask to conceal it. I really feel sometimes as if I were masquerading when I catch a picture of myself in some printed description. In between things that I have to do as a public officer I never think of myself as the President of the United States, because I never have had any sense of being identified with that office.

I feel like a person appointed for a certain length of time to administer that office, and I feel just as much outside of it at this moment as I did before I was elected to it. I feel just as much outside of it as I still feel outside of the Government of the United States. No man could imagine himself the Government of the United States; but he could understand that some part of his fellow-citizens had told him to go and run a certain part of it the best he knew how. That would not make him the Government itself or the thing itself. It would just make him responsible for running it the best he knew how. The machine is so much greater than himself, the office is so much greater than he can ever be, and the most he can do is to look grave enough and self-possessed enough to seem to fill it.

I can hardly refrain every now and again from tipping the public a wink, as much as to say, "It is only 'me' that is inside this thing. I know perfectly well that I will have to get out presently. I know that then I will look just my own proper size, and that for the time being the proportions are somewhat refracted and misrepresented to the eye by the large thing I am inside of, from which I am tipping you this wink."

For example, take matters of this sort. I will not say whether it is wise or unwise, simple or grave, but certain precedents have been established that in certain companies the President must leave the room first, and people must give way to him. They must not sit down if he is standing up. It is a very uncomfortable thing to have to think of all the other people every time I get up and sit down, and all that sort of thing. So that when I get guests in my own house and the public is shut out I adjourn being President and take leave to be a gentleman. If they draw back and insist upon my doing something first, I firmly decline.

There are blessed intervals when I forget by one means or another that I am President of the United States. One means by which I forget is to get a rattling good detective story, get after some imag-

inary offender, and chase him all over—preferably
any continent but this, because the various parts of
this continent are becoming painfully suggestive to
me. The Post Offices, and many other things which
stir reminiscence have "sicklied them o'er with a
pale cast of thought." There are Post Offices to
which I wouldn't think of mailing a letter, which
I can't think of without trembling with the knowledge of all the heart-burnings of the struggle there
was in getting somebody installed as Postmaster.

Now, if I were free I would come not infrequently
up to these rooms. You know I never was in Washington but for a very few times, and for a very few
hours, until I came last year, and I never expect to
see the inside of the public buildings in Washington until my term is over. The minute I turn up
anywhere I am personally conducted to beat the
band. The Curator and the Assistant Curator and
every other blooming official turns up, and they show
me so much attention that I don't see the building.
I would have to say "Stand aside and let me see
what you are showing me."

Some day after I am through with this office I
am going to come back to Washington and see it.
In the meantime I am in the same category as the
National Museum, the Monument, the Smithsonian
Institution, or the Congressional Library, and everything that comes down here has to be shown the
President. If I only knew the appearance to assume—apparently I can assume other appearances
that do not show what is going on inside—I would
like to have it pointed out, so that I could practice

it before the looking glass and see if I could not
look like the Monument. Being regarded as a national exhibit, it will be much simpler than being
shaken hands with by the whole United States.

And yet, even that is interesting to me, simply because I like human beings. It is a pretty poor
crowd that does not interest you. I think they would
have to be all members of that class that devotes itself to "expense regardless of pleasure" in order to
be entirely uninteresting. These look so much alike
—spend their time trying to look so much alike—
and so relieve themselves of all responsibility of
thought—that they are very monotonous, indeed, to
look at; whereas, a crowd picked up off the street
is just a jolly lot—a job lot of real human beings,
is just a jolly lot—a job lot of real human beings pul-
sating with life, with all kinds of passions and desires.

It would be a great pleasure if, unobserved and
unattended, I could be knocked around as I have
been accustomed to being knocked around all my
life; if I could resort to any delightful quarter, to
any place in Washington that I chose. I have sometimes thought of going to some costumer's—some
theatrical costumer's—and buying an assortment of
beards, rouge and coloring and all the known means
of disguising myself, if it were not against the law.

You see I have a scruple as President against
breaking the law and disguising one's self is against
the law, but if I could disguise myself and not get
caught I would go out, be a free American citizen
once more and have a jolly time. I might then meet
some of you gentlemen and actually tell you what I
really thought.

"THE IDEA OF AMERICA IS TO SERVE HUMANITY"

ADDRESS TO THE GRADUATING CLASS OF THE UNITED STATES NAVAL ACADEMY, ANNAPOLIS, JUNE 5, 1914. FROM THE WHITE HOUSE FILES.

DURING the greater part of my life I have been associated with young men, and on occasions it seems to me without number have faced bodies of youngsters going out to take part in the activities of the world, but I have a consciousness of a different significance on this occasion from that which I have felt on other similar occasions. When I have faced the graduating classes at universities I have felt that I was facing a great conjecture. They were going out into all sorts of pursuits and with every degree of preparation for the particular thing they were expecting to do; some without any preparation at all, for they did not know what they expected to do. But in facing you I am facing men who are trained for a special thing. You know what you are going to do, and you are under the eye of the whole Nation in doing it. For you, gentlemen, are to be part of the power of the Government of the United States. There is a very deep and solemn significance in that fact, and I am sure that every one of you feels it. The moral is perfectly obvious. Be ready and fit for anything that you have to do. And keep ready and fit. Do not grow slack. Do not suppose that your education is over because you have received your diplomas from the academy. Your education has just begun. Moreover, you are to have a very peculiar privilege which not many of your predecessors have had. You are yourselves going to become teachers. You are going to teach those 50,000 fellow countrymen of yours who are the enlisted men of the Navy. You are going to make them fitter to obey your orders and to serve the country. You are going to make them fitter to see what the orders mean in their outlook upon life and upon the service; and that is a great privilege, for out of you is going the energy and intelligence which are going to quicken the whole body of the United States Navy.

I congratulate you upon that prospect, but I want to ask you not to get the professional point of view. I would ask it of you if you were lawyers; I would ask it of you if you were merchants; I would ask it of you whatever you expected to be. Do not get the professional point of view. There is nothing narrower or more unserviceable than the professional point of view, to have the attitude toward life that it centers in your profession. It does not. Your profession is only one of the many activities which are meant to keep the world straight, and to keep the energy in its blood and in its muscle. We are all of us in this world, as I understand it, to set forward the affairs of the whole world, though we play a special part in that great function. The Navy goes all over the world, and I think it is to be congratulated upon having that sort of illustration of what the

world is and what it contains; and inasmuch as you
are going all over the world you ought to be the better able to see the relation that your country bears
to the rest of the world.

It ought to be one of your thoughts all the time
that you are sample Americans—not merely sample
Navy men, not merely sample soldiers, but sample
Americans—and that you have the point of view of
America with regard to her Navy and her Army;
that she is using them as the instruments of civilization, not as the instruments of aggression. The
idea of America is to serve humanity, and every time
you let the Stars and Stripes free to the wind you
ought to realize that that is in itself a message that
you are on an errand which other navies have sometimes forgotten; not an errand of conquest, but an
errand of service. I always have the same thought
when I look at the flag of the United States, for I
know something of the history of the struggle of
mankind for liberty. When I look at that flag it
seems to me as if the white stripes were strips of
parchment upon which are written the rights of man,
and the red stripes the streams of blood by which
those rights have been made good. Then in the little
blue firmament in the corner have swung out the
stars of the States of the American Union. So, it
is, as it were, a sort of floating charter that has come
down to us from Runnymede, when men said, ''We
will not have masters; we will be a people, and we
will seek our own liberty.''

You are not serving a government, gentlemen; you
are serving a people. For we who for the time be-

ing constitute the Government are merely instruments for a little while in the hands of a great Nation which chooses whom it will to carry out its decrees and who invariably rejects the man who forgets the ideals which it intended him to serve. So that I hope that wherever you go you will have a generous, comprehending love of the people you come into contact with, and will come back and tell us, if you can, what service the United States can render to the remotest parts of the world; tell us where you see men suffering; tell us where you think advice will lift them up; tell us where you think that the counsel of statesmen may better the fortunes of unfortunate men; always having it in mind that you are champions of what is right and fair all 'round for the public welfare, no matter where you are, and that it is that you are ready to fight for and not merely on the drop of a hat or upon some slight punctilio, but that you are champions of your fellow men, particularly of that great body one hundred million strong whom you represent in the United States.

What do you think is the most lasting impression that those boys down at Vera Cruz are going to leave? They have had to use some force—I pray God it may not be necessary for them to use any more—but do you think that the way they fought is going to be the most lasting impression? Have men not fought ever since the world began? Is there anything new in using force? The new things in the world are the things that are divorced from force. The things that show the moral compulsions of the human conscience, those are the things by

which we have been building up civilization, not by
force. And the lasting impression that those boys
are going to leave is this, that they exercise self-
control; that they are ready and diligent to make the
place where they went fitter to live in than they
found it; that they regarded other people's rights;
that they did not strut and bluster, but went quietly,
like self-respecting gentlemen, about their legitimate
work. And the people of Vera Cruz, who feared the
Americans and despised the Americans, are going to
get a very different taste in their mouths about
the whole thing when the boys of the Navy and the
Army come away. Is that not something to be proud
of, that you know how to use force like men of conscience and like gentlemen, serving your fellow men
and not trying to overcome them? Like that gallant
gentleman who has so long borne the heats and perplexities and distresses of the situation in Vera Cruz
—Admiral Fletcher. I mention him, because his
service there has been longer and so much of the
early perplexities fell upon him. I have been in almost daily communication with Admiral Fletcher, and
I have tested his temper. I have tested his discre-
tion. I know that he is a man with a touch of states-
manship about him, and he has grown bigger in my
eye each day as I have read his dispatches, for he has
sought always to serve the thing he was trying to do
in the temper that we all recognize and love to believe is typically American.

I challenge you youngsters to go out with these
conceptions, knowing that you are part of the Government and force of the United States and that men

will judge us by you. I am not afraid of the verdict.
I can not look in your faces and doubt what it will
be, but I want you to take these great engines of
force out onto the seas like adventurers enlisted for
the elevation of the spirit of the human race. For
that is the only distinction that America has. Other
nations have been strong, other nations have piled
wealth as high as the sky, but they have come into
disgrace because they used their force and their
wealth for the oppression of mankind and their own
aggrandizement; and America will not bring glory
to herself, but disgrace, by following the beaten
paths of history. We must strike out upon new
paths, and we must count upon you gentlemen to be
the explorers who will carry this spirit and spread
this message all over the seas and in every port of
the civilized world.

You see, therefore, why I said that when I faced
you I felt there was a special significance. I am
not present on an occasion when you are about to
scatter on various errands. You are all going on the
same errand, and I like to feel bound with you in
one common organization for the glory of America.
And her glory goes deeper than all the tinsel, goes
deeper than the sound of guns and the clash of
sabers; it goes down to the very foundation of those
things that have made the spirit of men free and
happy and content.

BE WORTHY OF THE MEN OF 1776

ADDRESS AT INDEPENDENCE HALL, PHILADELPHIA, JULY 4, 1914. FROM ORIGINAL COPY IN THE WHITE HOUSE FILES.

WE are assembled to celebrate the 138th anniversary of the birth of the United States. I suppose that we can more vividly realize the circumstances of that birth standing on this historic spot than it would be possible to realize than anywhere else. The Declaration of Independence was written in Philadelphia; it was adopted in this historic building by which we stand. I have just had the privilege of sitting in the chair of the great man who presided over the deliberations of those who gave the Declaration to the world. My hand rests at this moment upon the table upon which the Declaration was signed. We can feel that we are almost in the visible and tangible presence of a great historic transaction.

Have you ever read the Declaration of Independence, or attended with close comprehension to the real character of it when you have heard it read? If you have, you will know that it is not a Fourth of July oration. The Declaration of Independence was a document preliminary to war. It was a vital piece of practical business, not a piece of rhetoric; and if you will pass beyond those preliminary passages

which we are accustomed to quote about the rights
of men and read into the heart of the document you
will see that it is very express and detailed, that it
consists of a series of definite specifications concerning actual public business of the day. Not the business of our day, for the matter with which it deals is
past, but the business of that first revolution by
which the Nation was set up, the business of 1776.
Its general statements, its general declarations cannot mean anything to us unless we append to it a
similiar specific body of particulars as to what we
consider the essential business of our own day.

Liberty does not consist, my fellow-citizens, in mere
general declarations of the rights of men. It consists
in the translation of those declarations into definite
action. Therefore, standing here where the Declaration was adopted, reading its business-like sentences,
we ought to ask ourselves what there is in it for us.
There is nothing in it for us unless we can translate
it into the terms of our own conditions and of our
own lives. We must reduce it to what the lawyers
call a bill of particulars. It contains a bill of particulars, but the bill of particulars of 1776. If we
would keep it alive, we must fill it with a bill of particulars of the year 1914.

The task to which we have constantly to re-address
ourselves is the task of proving that we are worthy
of the men who drew this great Declaration and know
what they would have done in our circumstances.
Patriotism consists in some very practical things,—
practical in that they belong to the life of every day,
that they wear no extraordinary distinction about

them, that they are connected with commonplace
duty. The way to be patriotic in America is not only
to love America, but to love the duty that lies nearest to our hand and know that in performing it we
are serving our country. There are some gentlemen
in Washington, for example, at this very moment,
who are showing themselves very patriotic in a way
which does not attract wide attention but seems to
belong to mere everyday obligations. Those members of the House and Senate who stay in hot Washington to maintain a quorum of the Houses and
transact the all-important business of the Nation are
doing an act of patriotism. I honor them for it, and
I am glad to stay there and stick by them until the
work is done.

It is patriotic, also, to learn what the facts of our
national life are and to face them with candor. I
have heard a great many facts stated about the present business condition of this country, for example,
—a great many allegations of fact, at any rate, but
the allegations do not tally with one another. And
yet I know that truth always matches with truth;
and when I find some insisting that everything is
going wrong and others insisting that everything is
going right, and when I know from a wide observation of the general circumstances of the country
taken as a whole that things are going extremely
well, I wonder what those who are crying out that
things are wrong are trying to do. Are they trying
to serve the country? or are they trying to serve
something smaller than the country? Are they trying to put hope into the hearts of the men who work

and toil every day, or are they trying to plant discouragement and despair in those hearts? And why do they cry that everything is wrong and yet do nothing to set it right? If they love America and anything is wrong amongst us, it is their business to put their hand with ours to the task of setting it right. When the facts are known and acknowledged, the duty of all patriotic men is to accept them in candor and to address themselves hopefully and confidently to the common counsel which is necessary to act upon them wisely and in universal concert.

I have had some experiences in the last fourteen months which have not been entirely reassuring. It was universally admitted, for example, my fellow-citizens, that the banking system of this country needed reorganization. We set the best minds that we could find to the task of discovering the best method of reorganization. But we met with hardly anything but criticism from the bankers of the country; we met with hardly anything but resistance from the majority of those at least who spoke at all concerning the matter. And yet so soon as that Act was passed there was a universal chorus of applause, and the very men who had opposed the measure joined in that applause. If it was wrong the day before it was passed, why was it right the day after it was passed? Where had been the candor of criticism not only, but the concert of counsel which makes legislative action vigorous and safe and successful?

It is not patriotic to concert measures against one another; it is patriotic to concert measures for one another.

In one sense the Declaration of Independence has
lost its significance. It has lost its significance as a
declaration of national independence. Nobody outside America believed when it was uttered that we
could make good our independence; now nobody anywhere would dare to doubt that we are independent
and can maintain our independence. As a declaration of independence, therefore, it is a mere historic
document. Our independence is a fact so stupendous
that it can be measured only by the size and energy
and variety and wealth and power of one of the
greatest nations in the world. But it is one thing to
be independent and it is another thing to know what
to do with your independence. It is one thing to
come to your majority and another thing to know
what you are going to do with your life and your
energies; and one of the most serious questions for
sober-minded men to address themselves to in the
United States is this, What are we going to do with
the influence and power of this great nation? Are
we going to play the old rôle of using that power for
our aggrandizement and material benefit only? You
know what that may mean. It may upon occasion
mean that we shall use it to make the peoples of
other nations suffer in the way in which we said it
was intolerable to suffer when we uttered our Declaration of Independence.

The Department of State at Washington is constantly called upon to back up the commercial enterprises and the industrial enterprises of the United
States in foreign countries, and it at one time went
so far in that direction that all its diplomacy came

to be designation as "dollar diplomacy." It was
called upon to support every man who wanted to earn
anything anywhere if he was an American. But
there ought to be a limit to that. There is no man
who is more interested than I am in carrying the
enterprise of American business men to every quarter of the globe. I was interested in it long before
I was suspected of being a politician. I have been
preaching it year after year as the great thing that
lay in the future for the United States, to show her
wit and skill and enterprise and influence in every
country in the world. But observe the limit to all
that which is laid upon us perhaps more than upon
any other nation in the world. We set this nation up,
at any rate we professed to set it up, to vindicate the
rights of men. We did not name any differences
between one race and another. We did not set up
any barriers against any particular people. We
opened our gates to all the world and said: "Let all
men who wish to be free come to us and they will be
welcome." We said, "This independence of ours is
not a selfish thing for our own exclusive private use.
It is for everybody to whom we can find the means of
extending it." We cannot with that oath taken in
our youth, we cannot with that great ideal set before
us when we were a young people and numbered
only a scant three millions, take upon ourselves
now that we are a hundred million strong any other
conception of duty than we then entertained. If
American enterprise in foreign countries, particularly in those foreign countries which are not strong
enough to resist us, takes the shape of imposing upon

and exploiting the mass of the people of that country it ought to be checked and not encouraged. I am willing to get anything for an American that money and enterprise can obtain except the suppression of the rights of other men. I will not help any man buy a power which he ought not to exercise over his fellow-beings.

You know, my fellow-countrymen, what a big question there is in Mexico. Eighty-five per cent. of the Mexican people have never been allowed to have any genuine participation in their own government or to exercise any substantial rights with regard to the very land they live upon. All the rights that men most desire have been exercised by the other fifteen per cent. Do you suppose that that circumstance is not sometimes in my thought? I know that the American people have a heart that will beat just as strong for those millions in Mexico as it will beat or has beaten for any other millions elsewhere in the world, and that when once they conceive what is at stake in Mexico they will know what ought to be done in Mexico. I hear a great deal said about the loss of property in Mexico and the loss of the lives of foreigners and I deplore these things with all my heart. Undoubtedly upon the conclusion of the present disturbed conditions in Mexico those who have been unjustly deprived of their property or in any wise unjustly put upon ought to be compensated. Men's individual rights have no doubt been invaded, and the invasion of those rights has been attended by many deplorable circumstances which ought sometime in the proper way to be accounted for. But back of it all is the struggle of a people to come into its own, and while we look upon the incidents in the foreground let us not forget the great tragic reality in the background which towers above the whole picture.

A patriotic American is a man who is not niggardly and selfish in the things that he enjoys that make for human liberty and the rights of man. He wants to share them with the whole world, and he is never so proud of the great flag under which he lives as when it comes to mean to other people as well as to himself a symbol of hope and liberty. I would be ashamed of this flag if it ever did anything outside America that we would not permit it to do inside of America.

The world is becoming more complicated every day, my fellow-citizens. No man ought to be foolish enough to think that he understands it all. And, therefore, I am glad that there are some simple things in the world. One of the simple things is principle. Honesty is a perfectly simple thing. It is hard for me to believe that in most circumstances when a man has a choice of ways he does not know which is the right way and which is the wrong way. No man who has chosen the wrong way ought even to come into Independence Square; it is holy ground which he ought not to tread upon. He ought not to come where immortal voices have uttered the great sentences of such a document as this Declaration of Independence upon which rests the liberty of a whole nation.

And so I say that it is patriotic sometimes to prefer

the honor of the country to its material interest. Would you rather be deemed by all the nations of the world incapable of keeping your treaty obligations in order that you might have free tolls for American ships? The treaty under which we gave up that right may have been a mistaken treaty, but there was no mistake about its meaning.

When I have made a promise as a man I try to keep it, and I know of no other rule permissible to a nation. The most distinguished nation in the world is the nation that can and will keep its promises even to its own hurt. And I want to say parenthetically that I do not think anybody was hurt. I cannot be enthusiastic for subsidies to a monopoly, but let those who are enthusiastic for subsidies ask themselves whether they prefer subsidies to unsullied honor.

The most patriotic man, ladies and gentlemen, is sometimes the man who goes in the direction that he thinks right even when he sees half the world against him. It is the dictate of patriotism to sacrifice yourself if you think that that is the path of honor and of duty. Do not blame others if they do not agree with you. Do not die with bitterness in your heart because you did not convince the rest of the world, but die happy because you believe that you tried to serve your country by not selling your soul. Those were grim days, the days of 1776. Those gentlemen did not attach their names to the Declaration of Independence on this table expecting a holiday on the next day, and that 4th of July was not itself a holiday. They attached their signatures to that significant document knowing that if they failed it was certain that every one of them would hang for the failure. They were committing treason in the interest of the liberty of three million people in America. All the rest of the world was against them and smiled with cynical incredulity at the audacious undertaking. Do you think that if they could see this great Nation now they would regret anything that they then did to draw the gaze of a hostile world upon them? Every idea must be started by somebody, and it is a lonely thing to start anything. Yet if it is in you, you must start it if you have a ened people that wishes and intends to govern and you profess to be working for.

I am sometimes very much interested when I see gentlemen supposing that popularity is the way to success in America. The way to success in this great country with its fair judgments is to show that you are not afraid of anybody except God and his final verdict. If I did not believe that, I would not believe in democracy. If I did not believe that, I would not believe that people can govern themselves. If I did not believe that the moral judgment would be the last judgment, the final judgment, in the minds of men as well as at the tribunal of God, I could not believe in popular government. But I do believe these things, and, therefore, I earnestly believe in the democracy not only of America but of every awakened people that wishes and intends to govern and control its own affairs.

It is very inspiring, my friends, to come to this that may be called the original fountain of independence and liberty in America and here drink

draughts of patriotic feeling which seem to renew
the very blood in one's veins. Down in Washington
sometimes when the days are hot and the business
presses intolerably and there are so many things
to do that it does not seem possible to do anything
in the way it ought to be done, it is always possible
to lift one's thought above the task of the moment
and, as it were, to realize that great thing of which
we are all parts, the great body of American feeling and American principle. No man could do the
work that has to be done in Washington if he allowed himself to be separated from that body of
principle. He must make himself feel that he is a
part of the people of the United States, that he is
trying to think not only for them, but with them, and
then he cannot feel lonely. He not only cannot feel
lonely but he cannot feel afraid of anything.

My dream is that as the years go on and the world
knows more and more of America it will also drink
at these fountains of youth and renewal; that it also
will turn to America for those moral inspirations
which lie at the basis of all freedom; that the world
will never fear America unless it feels that it is engaged in some enterprise which is inconsistent with
the rights of humanity; and that America will come
into the full light of the day when all shall know
that she puts human rights above all other rights
and that her flag is the flag not only of America but
of humanity.

What other great people has devoted itself to this
exalted ideal? To what other nation in the world
can all eyes look for an instant sympathy that thrills

the whole body politic when men anywhere are fighting for their rights? I do not know that there will ever be a declaration of independence and of grievances for mankind, but I believe that if any such document is ever drawn it will be drawn in the spirit of the American Declaration of Independence, and that America has lifted high the light which will shine unto all generations and guide the feet of mankind to the goal of justice and liberty and peace.

AMERICAN NEUTRALITY—AN APPEAL
BY THE PRESIDENT

PRESENTED IN THE SENATE, AUGUST 19, 1914. FROM ORIG-
INAL COPY IN MR. WILSON'S FILES.

MY FELLOW COUNTRYMEN: I suppose that every thoughtful man in America has asked himself, during these last troubled weeks, what influence the European war may exert upon the United States, and I take the liberty of addressing a few words to you in order to point out that it is entirely within our own choice what its effects upon us will be and to urge very earnestly upon you the sort of speech and conduct which will best safeguard the Nation against distress and disaster.

The effect of the war upon the United States will depend upon what American citizens say and do. Every man who really loves America will act and speak in the true spirit of neutrality, which is the spirit of impartiality and fairness and friendliness to all concerned. The spirit of the Nation in this critical matter will be determined largely by what individuals and society and those gathered in public meetings do and say, upon what newspapers and magazines contain, upon what ministers utter in their pulpits, and men proclaim as their opinions on the street.

The people of the United States are drawn from

many nations, and chiefly from the nations now at war. It is natural and inevitable that there should be the utmost variety of sympathy and desire among them with regard to the issues and circumstances of the conflict. Some will wish one nation, others another, to succeed in the momentous struggle. It will be easy to excite passion and difficult to allay it. Those responsible for exciting it will assume a heavy responsibility, responsibility for no less a thing than that the people of the United States, whose love of their country and whose loyalty to its Government should unite them as Americans all, bound in honor and affection to think first of her and her interests, may be divided in camps of hostile opinion, hot against each other, involved in the war itself in impulse and opinion if not in action.

Such divisions amongst us would be fatal to our peace of mind and might seriously stand in the way of the proper performance of our duty as the one great nation at peace, the one people holding itself ready to play a part of impartial mediation and speak the counsels of peace and accommodation, not as a partisan, but as a friend.

I venture, therefore, my fellow countrymen, to speak a solemn word of warning to you against that deepest, most subtle, most essential breach of neutrality which may spring out of partisanship, out of passionately taking sides. The United States must be neutral in fact as well as in name during these days that are to try men's souls. We must be impartial in thought as well as in action, must put a curb upon our sentiments as well as upon every transaction that might be construed as a preference of one party to the struggle before another.

My thought is of America. I am speaking, I feel sure, the earnest wish and purpose of every thoughtful American that this great country of ours, which is, of course, the first in our thoughts and in our hearts, should show herself in this time of peculiar trial a Nation fit beyond others to exhibit the fine poise of undisturbed judgment, the dignity of self-control, the efficiency of dispassionate action; a Nation that neither sits in judgment upon others nor is disturbed in her own counsels and which keeps herself fit and free to do what is honest and disinterested and truly serviceable for the peace of the world.

Shall we not resolve to put upon ourselves the restraints which will bring to our people the happiness and the great and lasting influence for peace we covet for them?

MILITANT CHRISTIANITY

ADDRESS AT Y. M. C. A. CELEBRATION, PITTSBURGH, OCTOBER 24, 1914. FROM THE WHITE HOUSE FILES.

I FEEL almost as if I were a truant, being away from Washington to-day, but I thought that perhaps if I were absent the Congress would have the more leisure to adjourn. I do not ordinarily open my office at Washington on Saturday. Being a schoolmaster, I am accustomed to a Saturday holiday, and I thought I could not better spend a holiday than by showing at least something of the true direction of my affections; for by long association with the men who have worked for this organization I can say that it has enlisted my deep affection.

I am interested in it for various reasons. First of all, because it is an association of young men. I have had a good deal to do with young men in my time, and I have formed an impression of them which I believe to be contrary to the general impression. They are generally thought to be arch radicals. As a matter of fact, they are the most conservative people I have ever dealt with. Go to a college community and try to change the least custom of that little world and find out the conservatives will rush at you. Moreover, young men are embarrassed by having inherited their fathers' opinions. I have often said that the use of a university is to make young gentlemen as unlike their fathers as possible. I do not say that with the least disrespect for the fathers; but every man who is old enough to have a son in college is old enough to have become very seriously immersed in some particular business and is almost certain to have caught the point of view of that particular business. And it is very useful to his son to be taken out of that narrow circle, conducted to some high place where he may see the general map of the world and of the interests of mankind, and there be shown how big the world is and how much of it his father may happen to have forgotten. It would be worth while for men, middle-aged and old, to detach themselves more frequently from the things that command their daily attention and to think of the sweeping tides of humanity.

Therefore I am interested in this association, because it is intended to bring young men together before any crust has formed over them, before they have been hardened to any particular occupation, before they have caught an inveterate point of view; while they still have a searchlight that they can swing and see what it reveals of all the circumstances of the hidden world.

I am the more interested in it because it is an association of young men who are Christians. I wonder if we attach sufficient importance to Christianity as a mere instrumentality in the life of mankind. For one, I am not fond of thinking of Christianity as the means of saving *individual* souls. I have always been very impatient of processes and institutions which said that their purpose was to put every man

in the way of developing his character. My advice
is: Do not think about your character. If you will
think about what you ought to do for other people,
your character will take care of itself. Character is
a by-product, and any man who devotes himself to
its cultivation in his own case will become a selfish
prig. The only way your powers can become great
is by exerting them outside the circle of your own
narrow, special, selfish interests. And that is the reason of Christianity. Christ came into the world to
save others, not to save himself; and no man is a true
Christian who does not think constantly of how he
can lift his brother, how he can assist his friend, how
he can enlighten mankind, how he can make virtue
the rule of conduct in the circle in which he lives.
An association merely of young men might be an
association that had its energies put forth in every
direction, but an association of Christian young men
is an association meant to put its shoulders under
the world and lift it, so that other men may feel that
they have companions in bearing the weight and
heat of the day; that other men may know that there
are those who care for them, who would go into places
of difficulty and danger to rescue them, who regard
themselves as their brother's keeper.

And, then, I am glad that it is an association.
Every word of its title means an element of strength.
Young men are strong. Christian young men are the
strongest kind of young men, and when they associate themselves together they have the incomparable
strength of organization. The Young Men's Christian Association once excited, perhaps it is not too

much to say, the hostility of the organized churches of the Christian world, because the movement looked as if it were so nonsectarian, as if it were so outside the ecclesiastical field, that perhaps it was an effort to draw young men away from the churches and to substitute this organization for the great bodies of Christian people who joined themselves in the Christian denominations. But after a while it appeared that it was a great instrumentality that belonged to all the churches; that it was a common instrument for sending the light of Christianity out into the world in its most practical form, drawing young men who were strangers into places where they could have companionship that stimulated them and suggestions that kept them straight and occupations that amused them without vicious practice; and then, by surrounding themselves with an atmosphere of purity and of simplicity of life, catch something of a glimpse of the great ideal which Christ lifted when He was elevated upon the cross.

I remember hearing a very wise man say once, a man grown old in the service of a great church, that he had never taught his son religion dogmatically at any time; that he and the boy's mother had agreed that if the atmosphere of that home did not make a Christian of the boy, nothing that they could say would make a Christian of him. They knew that Christianity was catching, and if they did not have it, it would not be communicated. If they did have it, it would penetrate while the boy slept, almost; while he was unconscious of the sweet influences that were about him, while he reckoned nothing of instruction, but merely breathed into his lungs the wholesome air of a Christian home. That is the principle of the Young Men's Christian Association—to make a place where the atmosphere makes great ideals contagious. That is the reason that I said, though I had forgotten that I said it, what is quoted on the outer page of the program—that you can test a modern community by the degree of its interest in its Young Men's Christian Association. You can test whether it knows what roads it wants to travel or not. You can test whether it is deeply interested in the spiritual and essential prosperity of its rising generation. I know of no test that can be more conclusively put to a community than that.

I want to suggest to the young men of this association that it is the duty of young men not only to combine for the things that are good, but to combine in a militant spirit. There is a fine passage in one of Milton's prose writings which I am sorry to say I can not quote, but the meaning of which I can give you, and it is worth hearing. He says that he has no patience with a cloistered virtue that does not go out and seek its adversary. Ah, how tired I am of the men who are merely on the defensive, who hedge themselves in, who perhaps enlarge the hedge enough to include their little family circle and ward off all the evil influences of the world from that loved and hallowed group. How tired I am of the men whose virtue is selfish because it is merely self-protective! And how much I wish that men by the hundred thousand might volunteer to go out and seek an adversary and subdue him!

I have had the fortune to take part in affairs of a considerable variety of sorts, and I have tried to hate as few persons as possible, but there is an exquisite combination of contempt and hate that I have for a particular kind of person, and that is the moral coward. I wish we could give all our cowards a perpetual vacation. Let them go off and sit on the side lines and see us play the game; and put them off the field if they interfere with the game. They do nothing but harm, and they do it by that most subtle and fatal thing of all, that of taking the momentum and the spirit and the forward dash out of things. A man who is virtuous and a coward has no marketable virtue about him. The virtue, I repeat, which is merely self-defensive is not serviceable even, I suspect, to himself. For how a man can swallow and not taste bad when he is a coward and thinking only of himself I can not imagine.

Be militant! Be an organization that is going to do things! If you can find older men who will give you countenance and acceptable leadership, follow them; but if you can not, organize separately and dispense with them. There are only two sorts of men worth associating with when something is to be done. Those are young men and men who never grow old. Now, if you find men who have grown old, about whom the crust has hardened, whose hinges are stiff, whose minds always have their eye over the shoulder thinking of things as they *were* done, do not have anything to do with them. It would not be Christian to exclude them from your organization, but merely use them to pad the roll. If you can find older men who will lead you acceptably and keep you in countenance, I am bound as an older man to advise you to follow them. But suit yourselves. Do not follow people that stand still. Just remind them that this is not a statical proposition; it is a movement, and if they can not get a move on them they are not serviceable.

Life, gentlemen—the life of society, the life of the world—has constantly to be fed from the bottom. It has to be fed by those great sources of strength which are constantly rising in new generations. Red blood has to be pumped into it. New fiber has to be supplied. That is the reason I have always said that I believe in popular institutions. If you can guess beforehand whom your rulers are going to be, you can guess with a very great certainty that most of them will not be fit to rule. The beauty of popular institutions is that you do not know where the man is going to come from, and you do not care so he is the right man. You do not know whether he will come from the avenue or from the alley. You do not know whether he will come from the city or the farm. You do not know whether you will ever have heard that name before or not. Therefore you do not limit at any point your supply of new strength. You do not say it has got to come through the blood of a particular family or through the processes of a particular training, or by any thing except the native impulse and genius of the man himself. The humblest hovel, therefore, may produce you your greatest man. A very humble hovel did produce you one of your greatest men. That is

the process of life, this constant surging up of the
new strength of unnamed, unrecognized, uncata-
logued men who are just getting into the running,
who are just coming up from the masses of the unrecognized multitude. You do not know when you
will see above the level masses of the crowd some
great stature lifted head and shoulders above the
rest, shouldering its way, not violently but gently,
to the front, and saying, "Here am I; follow me."
And his voice will be your voice, his thought will be
your thought, and you will follow him as if you were
following the best things in yourselves.

When I think of an association of Christian young
men I wonder that it has not already turned the
world upside down. I wonder, not that it has done
so much, for it has done a great deal, but that it has
done so little; and I can only conjecture that it does
not realize its own strength. I can only imagine that
it has not yet got its pace. I wish I could believe,
and I do believe, that at 70 it is just reaching its
majority, and that from this time on a dream greater
even than George Williams ever dreamed will be
realized in the great accumulating momentum of
Christian men throughout the world. For, gentlemen, this is an age in which the principles of men
who utter public opinion dominate the world. It
makes no difference what is done for the time being.
After the struggle is over the jury will sit, and nobody can corrupt that jury.

At one time I tried to write history. I did not
know enough to write it, but I knew from experience how hard it was to find an historian out, and I

trusted I would not be found out. I used to have this comfortable thought as I saw men struggling in the public arena. I used to think to myself, "This is all very well and very interesting. You probably assess yourself in such and such a way. Those who are your partisans assess you thus and so. Those who are your opponents urge a different verdict. But it does not make very much difference, because after you are dead and gone some quiet historian will sit in a secluded room and tell mankind for the rest of time just what to think about you, and his verdict, not the verdict of your partisans and not the verdict of your opponents, will be the verdict of posterity." I say that I used to say that to myself. It very largely was not so. And yet it was true in this sense: If the historian really speaks the judgment of the succeeding generation, then he really speaks the judgment also of the generations that succeed it, and his assessment, made without the passion of the time, made without partisan feeling in the matter—in other circumstances, when the air is cool—is the judgment of mankind upon your actions.

Now, is it not very important that we who shall constitute a portion of the jury should get our best judgments to work and base them upon Christian forbearance and Christian principles, upon the idea that it is impossible by sophistication to establish that a thing that is wrong is right? And yet, while we are going to judge with the absolute standard of righteousness, we are going to judge with Christian feeling, being men of a like sort ourselves, suffering the same temptations, having the same weaknesses, knowing the same passions; and while we do not condemn, we are going to seek to say and to live the truth. What I am hoping for is that these 70 years have just been a running start, and that now there will be a great rush of Christian principle upon the strongholds of evil and of wrong in the world. Those strongholds are not as strong as they look. Almost every vicious man is afraid of society, and if you once open the door where he is, he will run. All you have to do is to fight, not with cannon but with light.

May I illustrate it in this way? The Government of the United States has just succeeded in concluding a large number of treaties with the leading nations of the world, the sum and substance of which is this, that whenever any trouble arises the light shall shine on it for a year before anything is done; and my prediction is that after the light has shone on it for a year it will not be necessary to do anything; that after we know what happened, then we will know who was right and who was wrong. I believe that light is the greatest sanitary influence in the world. That, I suppose, is scientific commonplace, because if you want to make a place wholesome the best instrument you can use is the sun; to let his rays in, let him search out all the miasma that may lurk there. So with moral light: It is the most wholesome and rectifying, as well as the most revealing thing in the world, provided it be genuine moral light; not the light of inquisitiveness, not the light of the man who likes to turn up ugly things, not the light of the man who disturbs what is corrupt for the mere sake of the sensation that he creates by disturbing it, but the moral light, the light of the man who discloses it in order that all the sweet influences of the world may go in and make it better.

That, in my judgment, is what the Young Men's Christian Association can do. It can point out to its members the things that are wrong. It can guide the feet of those who are going astray; and when its members have realized the power of the Christian principle, then they will not be men if they do not unite to see that the rest of the world experiences the same emancipation and reaches the same happiness of release.

I believe in the Young Men's Christian Association because I believe in the progress of moral ideas in the world; and I do not know that I am sure of anything else. When you are after something and have formulated it and have done the very best thing you know how to do you have got to be sure for the time being that that is the thing to do. But you are a fool if in the back of your head you do not know it is possible that you are mistaken. All that you can claim is that that is the thing as you see it now and that you can not stand still; that you must push forward the things that are right. It may turn out that you made mistakes, but what you do know is your way. I was once a college reformer, until discouraged, and I remember a classmate of mine saying, "Why, man, can't you let anything alone?" I said, "I let everything alone that you can show me is not itself moving in the wrong direction, but I am not going to let those things alone that I see are going down-hill''; and I borrowed this illustration from an ingenious writer. He says, "If you have a post that is painted white and want to keep it white, you can not let it alone; and if anybody says to you, 'Why don't you let that post alone?' you will say, 'Because I want it to stay white, and therefore I have got to paint it at least every second year.' " There isn't anything in this world that will not change if you absolutely let it alone, and therefore you have constantly to be attending to it to see that it is being taken care of in the right way and that, if it is part of the motive force of the world, it is moving in the right direction.

That means that eternal vigilance is the price, not only of liberty, but of a great many other things. It is the price of everything that is good. It is the price of one's own soul. It is the price of the souls of the people you love; and when it comes down to the final reckoning you have a standard that is immutable. What shall a man give in exchange for his own soul? Will he sell that? Will he consent to see another man sell his soul? Will he consent to see the conditions of his community such that men's souls are debauched and trodden underfoot in the mire? What shall he give in exchange for his own soul, or any other man's soul? And since the world, the world of affairs, the world of society, is nothing less and nothing more than all of us put together, it is a great enterprise for the salvation of the soul in this world as well as in the next. There is a text in Scripture that has always interested me profoundly. It says godliness is profitable in this life as well as

in the life that is to come; and if you do not start it
in this life, it will not reach the life that is to come.
Your measurements, your directions, your whole momentum, have to be established before you reach the
next world. This world is intended as the place in
which we shall show that we know how to grow in
the stature of manliness and of righteousness.

I have come here to bid Godspeed to the great work
of the Young Men's Christian Associaiton. I love
to think of the gathering force of such things as this
in the generations to come. If a man had to measure
the accomplishments of society, the progress of reform, the speed of the world's betterment, by the few
little things that happened in his own life, by the
trifling things that he can contribute to accomplish,
he would indeed feel that the cost was much greater
than the result. But no man can look at the past of
the history of this world without seeing a vision of
the future of the history of this world; and when
you think of the accumulated moral forces that have
made one age better than another age in the progress of mankind, then you can open your eyes to the
vision. You can see that age by age, though with a
blind struggle in the dust of the road, though often
mistaking the path and losing its way in the mire,
mankind is yet—sometimes with bloody hands and
battered knees—nevertheless struggling step after
step up the slow stages to the day when he shall
live in the full light which shines upon the uplands,
where all the light that illumines mankind shines
direct from the face of God.

THE FEDERAL RESERVE SYSTEM

LETTER TO WILLIAM GIBBS MCADOO, SECRETARY OF THE TREASURY, NOVEMBER 17, 1914. FROM THE "COMMER-CIAL AND FINANCIAL CHRONICLE," NOVEMBER 21, 1914, VOL. 99, PP. 1496-1497.

WASHINGTON, *November 17, 1914.*

MY DEAR MR. SECRETARY:

I warmly appreciate your letter of yester-day, for I share your feelings entirely about the significance of the opening of the Federal Reserve banks for business.

I do not know that any special credit belongs to me for the part I was privileged to play in the estab-lishment of this new system of which we confidently hope so much; in it the labor and knowledge and forethought and practical experience and sagacity of many men are embodied, who have coöperated with unusual wisdom and admirable public spirit. None of them, I am sure, will be jealous of the distribu-tion of the praise for the great piece of legislation upon which the new system rests; they will only re-joice unselfishly to see the thing accomplished upon which they had set their hearts.

It has been accomplished, and its accomplishment is of the deepest significance, both because of the things it has done away with and because of the things it has supplied that the country lacked, and had long needed. It has done away with agitation and suspicion, because it has done away with certain fundamental wrongs. It has supplied means of accommodation in the business world and an instrumentality by which the interests of all, without regard to class, may readily be served.

We have only to look back ten years or so to realize the deep perplexities and dangerous ill humors out of which we have now at last issued as if from a bewildering fog, a noxious miasma. Ten or twelve years ago the country was torn and excited by an agitation which shook the very foundations of her political life, brought her business ideals into question, condemned her social standards, denied the honesty of her men of affairs, the integrity of her economic processes, the morality and good faith of many of the things which her law sustained.

Those who had power, whether in business or in politics, were almost universally looked upon with suspicion, and little attempt was made to distinguish the just from the unjust. They in their turn seemed to distrust the people and to wish to limit their control. There was ominous antagonism between classes. Capital and labor were in sharp conflict without prospect of accommodation between them. Interests harshly clashed which should have coöperated.

This was not merely the work of irresponsible agitators. There were real wrongs which cried out to be righted and fearless men had called attention to them, demanding that they be dealt with by law. We were living under a tariff which had been purposely contrived to confer private favors upon those who were coöperating to keep the party that originated it in power and in all that too fertile soil all the bad, interlaced growth and jungle of monopoly had sprung up. Credit, the very life of trade, the very air men must breathe if they would meet their opportunities, was too largely in control of the same small groups who had planted and cultivated monopoly. The control of all big business, and, by consequence, of all little business, too, was for the most part potentially, if not actually, in their hands. And the thing stood so until the Democrats came into power last year. The legislation of the past year and a half has in very large measure done away with these things. With a correction, suspicion and ill-will will pass away. For not only have these things been righted, but new things have been put into action which are sure to prove the instruments of a new life, in which the mists and distempers which have so embarrassed us will be cleared away; the wrongs and misunderstandings corrected which have brought distrust upon so many honest men unjustly. That is the main ground of my own satisfaction.

The tariff has been recast with a view to supporting the Government rather than supporting the favored beneficiaries of the Government. A system of banking and currency issues has been created which puts credit within the reach of every man who can show a going business, and the supervision and control of the system is in the hands of a responsible agency of the Government itself. A trade tribunal has been created by which those who attempt unjust and oppressive practices in business can be brought to book. Labor has been made something else in the view of the law than a mercantile commodity—something human and linked with the privileges of life itself. The soil has everywhere been laid bare out of which monopoly is slowly to be eradicated. And undoubtedly the means by which credit has been set free is at the heart of all these things—is the key piece of the whole structure.

This is the more significant because of its opportuneness. It is brought to its final accomplishment just as it is most imperatively needed. The war, which has involved the whole of the heart of Europe, has made it necessary that the United States should mobilize its resources in the most effective way possible and make her credit and her usefulness good for the service of the whole world. It has created, too, special difficulties, peculiar situations to be dealt with, like the great embarrassment in selling our immense cotton crop, which all the world needs, but against which, for the time being, the markets of the world are in danger of being artificially shut. The situation the bankers of the country are meeting as far as possible in a businesslike fashion and in the spirit of the new time which is opening before us.

The railroads of the country are almost as much affected, not so much because their business is curtailed as because their credit is called in question by doubt as to their earning capacity. There is no other interest so central to the business welfare of the country as this. No doubt, in the light of the new day, with its new understandings, the problems of the railroads will also be met and dealt with in a spirit of candor and justice.

For the future is clear and bright with promise of the best things. While there was agitation and suspicion and distrust and bitter complaint of wrong, groups and classes were at war with one another, did not see that their interests were common, and suffered only when separated and brought into conflict. Fundamental wrongs once righted, as they may now easily and quickly be, all differences will clear away.

We are all in the same boat, though apparently we have forgotten it. We now know the port for which we are bound. We have and shall have, more and more as our new understandings ripen, a common discipline of patriotic purpose. We shall advance, and advance together, with a new spirit, a new enthusiasm, a new cordiality of spirit and co-operation. It is an inspiring prospect. Our task is henceforth to work, not for any single interest, but for all the interests of the country as a united whole.

The future will be very different from the past, which we shall presently look back upon, I venture to say, as if upon a bad dream. The future will be different in action and different in spirit, a time of healing because a time of just dealing and co-operation between men made equal before the law in fact as well as in name. I am speaking of this because the new banking system seems to me to symbolize all of it. The opening of the Federal Reserve banks seems to me to be the principal agency we have created for the emancipation we seek. The 16th of November,

1914, will be notable as marking the time when we were best able to realize just what had happened.

In the anxious times through which we have been passing, you have, my dear Mr. Secretary, been able to do many noteworthy things to strengthen and facilitate the business operations of the country. Henceforth, you have a new instrument at hand which will render many parts of your task easy. I heartily congratulate you upon the part you yourself have played in its conception and creation and upon the successful completion of the difficult work of organization.

A new day has dawned for the beloved country whose lasting prosperity and happiness we so earnestly desire.

Sincerely yours,
WOODROW WILSON.

WORK OF THE FEDERAL TRADE BOARD

ADDRESS BEFORE THE AMERICAN ELECTRIC RAILWAY
   ASSOCIATION, WASHINGTON, JANUARY 29, 1915. FROM
   THE "COMMERCIAL AND FINANCIAL CHRONICLE," FEB-
   RUARY 6, 1915, VOL. 100, PP. 436-438.

IT is a real pleasure to me to be here and to look
this company in the face. I know how important the interests that you represent are. I know
that they represent some of the chief channels
through which the vigor and activity of the nation
flow. I am also very glad, indeed, to have you come
and look at some portion, at any rate, of the Government of the United States. Many things are reported and supposed about that Government and it
is thoroughly worth your while to come out and see
for yourselves.

I have always maintained that the only way in
which men could understand one another was by
meeting one another. If I believed all that I read
in the newspapers I would not understand anybody.
I have met many men whose horns dropped away
the moment I was permitted to examine their character. For, after all, in a vast country like this the
most difficult thing is a common understanding. We
are constantly forming get-together conventions,
and I sometimes think that we make the mistake of
confining these associations in their membership to
those who are interested only in some particular

group of the various industries of the country. The important thing is for the different enterprises of the country to understand one another; and the most important thing of all is for us to comprehend our life as a nation and understand each other as fellow-citizens.

It seems to me that I can say with a good deal of confidence that we are upon the eve of a new era of enterprise and of prosperity. Enterprise has been checked in this country for almost twenty years, because men were moving amongst a maze of interrogation points. They did not know what was going to happen to them. All sorts of regulation were proposed, and it was a matter of uncertainty what sort of regulation was going to be adopted. All sorts of charges were made against business, as if business were at default, when most men knew that the great majority of business men were honest, were public-spirited, were intending the right thing, and the many were made afraid because the few did not do what was right.

The most necessary thing, therefore, was for us to agree, as we did by slow stages agree, upon the main particulars of what ought not to be done and then to put our laws in such shape as to correspond with that general judgment. That, I say, was a necessary preliminary not only to a common understanding, but also to a universal co-operation. The great forces of a country like this can not pull separately; they have got to pull together. And except upon a basis of common understanding as to the law and as to the proprieties of conduct, it is impossible to pull

together. I, for one, have never doubted that all
America was of one principle. I have never doubted
that all America believed in doing what was fair
and honorable and of good report. But the method,
the method of control by law against the small
minority that was recalcitrant against these principles, was a thing that it was difficult to determine
upon; and it was a very great burden, let me say,
to fall upon a particular administration of this Government to have to undertake practically the whole
business of final definition. That is what has been
attempted by the Congress now about to come to a
close. It has attempted the definitions for which
the country had been getting ready, or trying to get
ready, for half a generation. It will require a period
of test to determine whether they have successfully
defined them or not; but no one needs to have it
proved to him that it was necessary to define them
and remove the uncertainties, and that, the uncertainties being removed, common understandings are
possible and a universal co-operation.

You, gentlemen, representing these arteries of
which I have spoken, that serve to release the forces
of communities and serve, also, to bind community
with community, are surely in a better position than
the men perhaps of any other profession to understand how communities constitute units—how even
a nation constitutes a unit; and that what is detrimental and hurtful to a part you, above all men,
ought to know is detrimental to all. You can not
demoralize some of the forces of a community without being in danger of demoralizing all the forces

of a community. Your interest is not in the congestion of life, but in the release of life. Your interest is not in isolation, but in union, the union of parts of this great country, so that every energy in those parts will flow freely and with full force from county to county throughout the whole nation.

What I have come to speak of this afternoon is this unity of our interest, and I want to make some—I will not say "predictions," but to use a less dangerous though bigger word—prognostications. I understand that there is among the medical profession diagnosis and prognosis. I dare say the prognosis is more difficult than the diagnosis, since it has to come first; and not being a physician, I have all the greater courage in the prognosis. I have noticed all my life that I could speak with the greatest freedom about those things that I did not understand; but there are some things that a man is bound to try to think out whether he fully comprehends them or not. The thought of no single man can comprehend the life of a great Nation like this, and yet men in public life upon whom the burden of guidance is laid must attempt to comprehend as much of it as they can. Their strength will lie in common counsel; their strength will lie in taking counsel of as many informed persons as possible in each department with which they have to deal; but some time or other the point will come when they have to make a decision based upon a prognosis. We have had to do that in attempting the definitions of law which have been attempted by this Congress, and now it is necessary for us, in order to go forward with the con-

fident spirit with which I believe we can go forward,
to look ahead and see the things that are likely to
happen.

In the first place, I feel that the mists and miasmic
airs of suspicion that have filled the business world
have now been blown away. I believe that we have
passed the era of suspicion and have come into the
era of confidence. Knowing the elements we have to
deal with, we can deal with them; and with that
confidence of knowledge we can have confidence of
enterprise. That enterprise is going to mean this:
Nobody is henceforth going to be afraid of or suspicious of any business merely because it is big. If
my judgment is correct, nobody has been suspicious
of any business merely because it was big; but they
have been suspicious whenever they thought that
the bigness was being used to take an unfair advantage. We all have to admit that it is easier for a
big fellow to take advantage of you than for a little
fellow to take advantage of you; therefore, we in-
stinctively watch the big fellow with a little closer
scrutiny than we watch the little fellow. But, bond
having been given for the big fellow, we can sleep o'
nights. Bond having been given that he will keep
the peace, we do not have to spend our time and
waste our energy watching him. The conditions of
confidence being established, nobody need think that
if he is taller than the rest anybody is going to throw
a stone at him simply because he is a favorable tar-
get—always provided there is fair dealing and real
service.

Because the characteristic of modern business,

gentlemen, is this: The number of cases in which men do business on their own individual, private capital is relatively small in our day. Almost all the greater enterprises are done on what is, so far as the managers of that business are concerned, other people's money. That is what a joint-stock company means. It means, "Won't you lend us your resources to conduct this business and trust us, a little group of managers, to see that you get honest and proper returns for your money?" and no man who manages a joint-stock company can know for many days together, without fresh inquiry, who his partners are, because the stock is constantly changing hands, and the partners are seldom the same people for long periods together. Which amounts to saying that, inasmuch as you are using the money of everybody who chooses to come in, your responsibility is to everybody who has come in or who may come in. That is simply another way of saying that your business is, so far forth, a public business, and you owe it to the public to take them into your confidence in regard to the way in which it is conducted.

The era of private business in the sense of business conducted with the money of the partners—I mean of the managing partners—is practically passed, not only in this country, but almost everywhere. Therefore, almost all business has this direct responsibility to the public in general: We owe a constant report to the public, whose money we are constantly asking for in order to conduct the business itself. Therefore, we have got to trade not only on our efficiency, not only on the service that we render, but on the confidence that we cultivate. There is a new atmosphere for business. The oxygen that the lungs of modern business takes in is the oxygen of the public confidence, and if you have not got that, your business is essentially paralyzed and asphyxiated.

I take it that we are in a position now to come to a common understanding, knowing that only a common understanding will be the stable basis of business, and that what we want for business hereafter is the same kind of liberty that we want for the individual. The liberty of the individual is limited with the greatest sharpness where his actions come into collision with the interests of the community he lives in. My liberty consists in a sort of parole. Society says to me, "You may do what you please until you do something that is in violation of the common understanding, of the public interest; then your parole is forfeited. We will take you into custody. We will limit your activities. We will penalize you if you use this thing that you call your liberty against our interest." Business does not want, and ought not to ask for, more liberty than the individual has; and I have always in my own thought summed up individual liberty, and business liberty, and every other kind of liberty, in the phrase that is common in the sporting world, "A free field and no favor."

There have been times—I will not specify them, but there have been times—when the field looked free, but when there were favors received from the managers of the course; when there were advantages given; inside tracks accorded; practices which would block the other runners; rules which would exclude the amateur who wanted to get in. That may be a free field, but there is favor, there is partiality, there is preference, there is covert advantage taken of somebody, and while it looks very well from the grandstand, there are men whom you can find who were not allowed to get in to the track and test their powers against the other men who were racing for the honors of the day.

I think it is a serviceable figure. It means this: That you are not going to be barred from the contest because you are big and strong, and you are not going to be penalized because you are big and strong, but you are going to be made to observe the rules of the track and not get in anybody's way except as you can keep ahead of him by having more vigor and skill than he has. When we get that understanding, that we are all sports, and that we are not going to ask for, not only, but we are not going to condescend to take, advantage of anything that does not belong to us, then the atmosphere will clear so that it will seem as if the sun had never shone as it does that day. It is the spirit of true sportsmanship that ought to get into everything, and men who, when they get beaten that way, squeal, do not deserve our pity.

Some men are going to get beaten because they have not the brains, they have not the initiative, they have not the skill, they have not the knowledge, they have not the same capacity that other men have. They will have to be employees, they will have to be used where they can be used. We do not need

to conceal from ourselves that there are varieties
of capacities in the world. Some men have heads,
but they are not particularly furnished. I overheard
two men one day talking about a third man, and
one of them referred to his head. "Head," the other
said, "head, that isn't a head, that's just a knot.
The Almighty put there there to keep him from
raveling out." And we have to admit that there
are such persons.

Now, liberty does not consist in framing laws to
put such men at the front and say they have got to
be allowed to keep pace with the rest, because that
would hold the whole process of civilization back.
But it does consist in saying no matter how feather-
weight the other man is you must not arbitrarily
interfere with him; that there must be an absolutely
free field and no favor to anybody. There are,
therefore, I suppose, certain rules of the game. I
will mention what seems to me some of them. I have
already mentioned one of them by way of illustration. First of all, is the rule of publicity, not doing
anything under cover, letting the public know what
you are doing and judge of it according as it is.
There are a great many businesses in this country
that have fallen under suspicion because they were
so secretive when there was nothing to secrete that
was dishonorable. The minute I keep everything in
my pocket and will not show anybody what is there,
they conjecture what may be in my pocket; whereas
if I turn my pockets inside out, the conjecture is, at
any rate, dissipated.

There is no use inviting suspicion by secretiveness. If a business is being honorably done and successfully done, you ought to be pleased to turn it inside out and let the people whom you are inviting to invest in it see exactly how it is done and with what results. Publicity, which is required in sports, is required in business. Let's see how you are running the game.

Then, in the second place, there is a full equivalent for the money you receive, the full equivalent in service; not trying to skimp in the service in order to increase profits above a reasonable return, but trying to make the profits proportioned to the satisfaction of the people that you serve. There isn't any more solid foundation for business than that. If you thoroughly satisfy the people you are serving, you are welcome to their money. They are not going to grudge it, because they will feel that they are getting a quid pro quo—they are getting something such as was promised them when their money was asked of them.

Then, in the third place, this game requires something more than ordinary sports. It requires a certain kind of conscience in business, a certain feeling that we are, after all, in this world because we are expected to make good according to the standards of the people we live with. That, after all, is the chief compulsion that is laid on all of us. I am not aware of being afraid of jail; I do not feel uneasy when I pass a penitentiary, but I would feel extremely uneasy if I knew I had done something which some fine, honorable friend of mine would condemn if I passed before him. I would look carefully at his eyes to see if he suspected anything, and I would feel unhappy until I had made a clean breast of it with him. That is what we are afraid of, and that is what we ought to be afraid of.

We are sustained by the moral judgment of honorable men, and there isn't anything else in this world that I know of that is worth while. How honors must hurt a man if he feels that they have been achieved dishonorably. They are an arrow in his heart, not a quickening or tonic to his spirit in any respect.

If he feels that he has cheated the people that trusted him, then, no matter what fortune he piles up, they never can contribute to his peace of mind for a moment. So I say that the conscience in business is the motive spring of the whole thing; the pride of doing the thing as it ought to be done.

I ask every man in this room who employs other men if he would not pay the best salary he has if he could be assured that the man he employed was of that quality. You know that is the sort of men that you want, the men who will take a pride in doing the thing right and have a clean conscience towards you who employ them. Now, all of us are employees of the public; it doesn't make any difference what our business is or how small it is, we are, so far as we get money for it, employees of the public and our clear, clean consciences toward our employers are the basis of our success and, it goes without saying, the basis of our happiness.

Then, the fourth rule, as it seems to me, is the rule of having the spirit of service. I know a lot of

cant is talked about that, and I get very sick of the
cant, as I dare say you do, but when I talk about
the spirit of service I am not meaning a sentiment;
I am not meaning a state of mind; I am meaning
something very concrete, that you want to see to it
that the thing that you do for the public and get
money for is the best thing of that kind that can
be done. This is what I mean by the spirit of service.

I have known many a man who gave up profit for
mental satisfaction. I know men in this city—there
are men in the Scientific Bureau of this government
whom I could cite—who could make very big sal-
aries, but who prefer the satisfaction of doing things
that will serve the whole community, and doing them
just as well as they possibly can be done.

I for one am proud of the scientific bureaus of this
Government. There are men in it of the most self-
sacrificing spirit and of the highest scientific efficiency, who do things on a petty salary which some
other man would not do at all, because if you have
to pay a man a salary to produce the best product
of his brain, then he scales the product down to the
salary.

Here are men who scale the product up to the
highest standards of scientific ideals. They have
hitched their wagons to a star, and the star is apt
to lift their names above the names of the rest of
us. So I say that if your earning capacity is the
capacity to earn the public confidence you can go
about your business like free men. Nobody is going
to molest you, and everybody is going to say, "If
you earn big profits; if you have treated the people

from whom you are making your profits as they
ought to be treated; if you treat the employees whom
you use in earning these profits as they ought to be
treated; if your methods of competition are clear
and above reproach, why, then, you can pile those
profits as high as the Rockies and nobody will be
jealous of it.'' Because you will have earned them
in a sense that is the handsomest sense of all.

It is in this spirit that we all ought to regard the
laws, that we all ought to criticize the laws, and
that we all ought to co-operate in the enforcement of
the laws. Government is merely an attempt to express the conscience of everybody, the average conscience of the nation, in the rules that everybody is
commanded to obey. That is all it is. If the Government is going faster than the public conscience, it
will presently have to pull up; if it is not going as
fast as the public conscience, it will presently have
to be whipped up. Because the public conscience is
going to say, ''We want our laws to express our
character,'' and our character must have this kind of
solidity underneath it, the moral judgment of right
and wrong.

The only reason we quarrel with reformers sometimes is because they are, or suppose that they are,
a little more enlightened than the rest of us and
they want us all of a sudden to be just as enlightened as they are, and we cannot stand the pace.
That is all that makes us uneasy about reformers.
If we could get our second wind, if we could keep
the pace as long as they do we might be able to run
as fast as they do, but we are more heavily weighted

with clay than they are. We cannot go as fast. And we like companionship. We want to wait for the rest of them. We do not want to be in a lonely advance climbing some heights of perfection where there is no good inn to stop at over-night.

That is the homely, and, I dare say, obvious lesson, which I have meant to give utterance to this afternoon. I think that I understand what you are after. I hope that you understand what we are after. All I ask is that if anything is being done that ought not to be done, the fault in it be conclusively pointed out and the way to correct the mistake be explicitly shown. There is an old rule that ought to obtain in politics as in everything else, and it is expressed in a very homely way. It is the rule of "Put up or shut up." Someone said, "If you wish me to consider you witty I must really trouble you to make a joke." If you wish me to consider you wise, I must really trouble you to show the goods; to show how the thing can be done; to show how it can be better done. Because nobody is fool enough to suppose that the way he has determined that the thing ought to be done, is necessarily the best way to do it, but it is the best way to do it until you show a better way. That is a perfectly obvious rule.

So again I say it is the rule of "Put up or shut up." And I do not mean that in any sort of disrespect. The market for ideas is a highly competitive market, and the rules of competition are necessarily fair. There is only one test for an idea and that is "Is it good?" You may for the time being dress it with such rhetoric that it will look good, and the best thing that is characteristic of countries like our own is that every man who has an idea is constantly invited to the platform. And there is nothing better for an idea by way of test than exposure to the atmosphere. If you let enough people hear it stated often enough, it will certainly seek its proper level.

That is the reason I believe in free speech. I have been subjected to free speech myself, and it is hard to endure sometimes, because the office of the President seems to be a clearing-house for original ideas. I am brought more original ideas per diem, I dare say, than any other person in the country, and therefore, pay the penalty of freedom of speech. Perhaps my mind does not register original ideas readily enough, because some of them do not register at all. I am perfectly willing to admit that that is the fault of the register and not the fault of the idea. All I have to say is that if you have ideas the register is entirely at your service.

CO-OPERATION IN THE BUSINESS OF GOVERNMENT

ADDRESS DELIVERED BEFORE THE UNITED STATES CHAM-
BER OF COMMERCE, WASHINGTON, FEBRUARY 3, 1915.
FROM OFFICIAL PUBLICATION IN MR. WILSON'S FILES.

I FEEL that it is hardly fair to you for me to come in in this casual fashion among a body of men who have been seriously discussing great questions, and it is hardly fair to me, because I come in cold, not having had the advantage of sharing the atmosphere of your deliberations and catching the feeling of your conference. Moreover, I hardly know just how to express my interest in the things you are undertaking. When a man stands outside an organization and speaks to it he is too apt to have the tone of outside commendation, as who should say, "I would desire to pat you on the back and say 'Good boys; you are doing well!'" I would a great deal rather have you receive me as if for the time being I were one of your own number.

Because the longer I occupy the office that I now occupy the more I regret any lines of separation; the more I deplore any feeling that one set of men has one set of interests and another set of men another set of interests; the more I feel the solidarity of the Nation—the impossibility of separating one interest from another without misconceiving it; the necessity that we should all understand one another, in order that we may understand ourselves.

There is an illustration which I have used a great many times. I will use it again, because it is most serviceable to my own mind. We often speak of a man who cannot find his way in some jungle or some desert as having "lost himself." Did you never reflect that that is the only thing he has not lost? *He* is *there*. He has lost the rest of the world. He has no fixed point by which to steer. He does not know which is north, which is south, which is east, which is west; and if he did know, he is so confused that he would not know in which of those directions his goal lay. Therefore, following his heart, he walks in a great circle from right to left and comes back to where he started—to himself again. To my mind that is a picture of the world. If you have lost sight of other interests and do not know the relation of your own interests to those other interests, then you do not understand your own interests, and have lost yourself. What you want is orientation, relationship to the points of the compass; relationship to the other people in the world; vital connections which you have for the time being severed.

I am particularly glad to express my admiration for the kind of organization which you have drawn together. I have attended banquets of chambers of commerce in various parts of the country and have got the impression at each of those banquets that there was only one city in the country. It has seemed to me that those associations were meant in order to destroy men's perspective, in order to de-

stroy their sense of relative proportions. Worst of
all, if I may be permitted to say so, they were intended to boost something in particular. Boosting
is a very unhandsome thing. Advancing enterprise
is a very handsome thing, but to exaggerate local
merits in order to create disproportion in the general development is not a particularly handsome
thing or a particularly intelligent thing. A city cannot grow on the face of a great state like a mushroom
on that one spot. Its roots are throughout the state,
and unless the state it is in, or the region it draws
from, can itself thrive and pulse with life as a whole,
the city can have no healthy growth. You forget
the wide rootages of everything when you boost some
particular region. There are dangers which probably you all understand in the mere practice of
advertisement. When a man begins to advertise
himself there are certain points that are somewhat
exaggerated, and I have noticed that men who exaggerate most, most quickly lose any proper conception
of what their own proportions are. Therefore, these
local centers of enthusiasm may be local centers of
mistake if they are not very wisely guided and if
they do not themselves realize their relations to the
other centers of enthusiasm and of advancement.

The advantage about a Chamber of Commerce of
the United States is that there is only one way to
boost the United States, and that is by seeing to it
that the conditions under which business is done
throughout the whole country are the best possible
conditions. There cannot be any disproportion about
that. If you draw your sap and your vitality from

all quarters, then the more sap and vitality there is in you the more there is in the commonwealth as a whole, and every time you lift at all you lift the whole level of manufacturing and mercantile enterprise. Moreover, the advantage of it is that you cannot boost the United States in that way without understanding the United States. You learn a great deal. I agreed with a colleague of mine in the Cabinet the other day that we had never attended in our lives before a school to compare with that we were now attending for the purpose of gaining a liberal education.

Of course, I learn a great many things that are not so, but the interesting thing about that is this: Things that are not so do not match. If you hear enough of them, you see there is no pattern whatever; it is a crazy quilt. Whereas, the truth always matches, piece by piece, with other parts of the truth. No man can lie consistently, and he cannot lie about everything if he talks to you long. I would guarantee that if enough liars talked to you, you would get the truth; because the parts that they did not invent would match one another, and the parts that they did invent would *not* match one another. Talk long enough, therefore, and see the connections clearly enough, and you can patch together the case as a whole. I had somewhat that experience about Mexico, and that was about the only way in which I learned anything that was true about it. For there had been vivid imaginations and many special interests which depicted things as they wished me to believe them to be.

Seriously, the task of this body is to match all the facts of business throughout the country and to see the vast and consistent pattern of it. That is the reason I think you are to be congratulated upon the fact that you cannot do this thing without common counsel. There isn't any man who knows enough to comprehend the United States. It is a co-operative effort, necessarily. You cannot perform the functions of this Chamber of Commerce without drawing in not only a vast number of men, but men, and a number of men, from every region and section of the country. The minute this association falls into the hands, if it ever should, of men from a single section or men with a single set of interests most at heart, it will go to seed and die. Its strength must come from the uttermost parts of the land and must be compounded of brains and comprehensions of every sort. It is a very noble and handsome picture for the imagination, and I have asked myself before I came here to-day, what relation you could bear to the Government of the United States and what relation the Government could bear to you?

There are two aspects and activities of the Government with which you will naturally come into most direct contact. The first is the Government's power of inquiry, systematic and disinterested inquiry, and its power of scientific assistance. You get an illustration of the latter, for example, in the Department of Agriculture. Has it occurred to you, I wonder, that we are just upon the eve of a time when our Department of Agriculture will be of infinite importance to the whole world? There is a shortage of food in the world now. That shortage will be much more serious in a few months from now than it is now. It is necessary that we should plant a great deal more; it is necessary that our lands should yield more per acre than they do now; it is necessary that there should not be a plow or a spade idle in this country if the world is to be fed. And the methods of our farmers must feed upon the scientific information to be derived from the State departments of agriculture, and from that taproot of all, the United States Department of Agriculture. The object and use of that department is to inform men of the latest developments and disclosures of science with regard to all the processes by which soils can be put to their proper use and their fertility made the greatest possible. Similarly with the Bureau of Standards. It is ready to supply those things by which you can set norms, you can set bases, for all the scientific processes of business.

I have a great admiration for the scientific parts of the Government of the United States, and it has amazed me that so few men have discovered them. Here in these departments are quiet men, trained to the highest degree of skill, serving for a petty re-muneration along lines that are infinitely useful to mankind; and yet in some cases they waited to be discovered until this Chamber of Commerce of the United States was established. Coming to this city, officers of that association found that there were things that were infinitely useful to them and with which the whole United States ought to be put into communication.

The Government of the United States is very properly a great instrumentality of inquiry and information. One thing we are just beginning to do that
we ought to have done long ago: We ought long
ago to have had our Bureau of Foreign and Domestic
Commerce. We ought long ago to have sent the best
eyes of the Government out into the world to see
where the opportunities and openings of American
commerce and American genius were to be found—
men who were not sent out as the commercial agents
of any particular set of business men in the United
States, but who were eyes for the whole business
community. I have been reading consular reports
for twenty years. In what I came to regard as an
evil day the Congressman from my district began to
send me the consular reports, and they ate up more
and more of my time. They are very interesting,
but they are a good deal like what the old lady said
of the dictionary, that it was very interesting but a
little disconnected. You get a picture of the world
as if a spotlight were being dotted about over the
surface of it. Here you see a glimpse of this, and
here you see a glimpse of that, and through the
medium of some consuls you do not see anything at
all. Because the consul has to have eyes and the
consul has to know what he is looking for. A lit-
erary friend of mine said that he used to believe in
the maxim that "everything comes to the man who
waits," but he discovered after awhile by practical
experience that it needed an additional clause, "provided he knows what he is waiting for." Unless
you know what you are looking for and have trained

eyes to see it when it comes your way, it may pass
unnoticed. We are just beginning to do, systemati-
cally and scientifically, what we ought long ago to
have done, to employ the Government of the United
States to survey the world in order that American
commerce might be guided.

But there are other ways of using the Government
of the United States, ways that have long been tried,
though not always with conspicuous success or fortunate results. You can use the Government of the
United States by influencing its legislation. That
has been a very active industry, but it has not always
been managed in the interest of the whole people.
It is very instructive and useful for the Government
of the United States to have such means as you are
ready to supply for getting a sort of consensus of
opinion which proceeds from no particular quarter
and originates with no particular interest. Information is the very foundation of all right action in
legislation.

I remember once, a good many years ago, I was attending one of the local chambers of commerce of
the United States at a time when everybody was
complaining that Congress was interfering with business. If you have heard that complaint recently and
supposed that it was original with the men who
made it, you have not lived as long as I have. It
has been going on ever since I can remember. The
complaint came most vigorously from men who were
interested in large corporate development. I took
the liberty to say to that body of men, whom I did
not know, that I took it for granted that there were

a great many lawyers among them, and that it was
likely that the more prominent of those lawyers were
the intimate advisors of the corporations of that
region. I said that I had met a great many lawyers
from whom the complaint had come most vigorously,
not only that there was too much legislation with
regard to corporations, but that it was ignorant legislation. I said, "Now, the responsibility is with you.
If the legislation is mistaken, you are on the inside
and know where the mistakes are being made. You
know not only the innocent and right things that
your corporations are doing, but you know the other
things, too. Knowing how they are done, you can
be expert advisors as to how the wrong things can
be prevented. If, therefore, this thing is handled
ignorantly, there is nobody to blame but yourselves."
If we on the outside cannot understand the thing
and cannot get advice from the inside, then we will
have to do it with the flat hand and not with the
touch of skill and discrimination. Isn't that true?
Men on the inside of business know how business is
conducted and they cannot complain if men on the
outside make mistakes about business if they do not
come from the inside and give the kind of advice
which is necessary.

The trouble has been that when they came in the
past—for I think the thing is changing very rapidly—they came with all their bristles out; they
came on the defensive; they came to see, not what
they could accomplish, but what they could prevent.
They did not come to guide; they came to block.
That is of no use whatever to the general body politic.

What has got to pervade us like a great motive
power is that we cannot, and must not, separate our
interests from one another, but must pool our interests. A man who is trying to fight for his single
hand is fighting against the community and not fighting with it. There are a great many dreadful things
about war, as nobody needs to be told in this day
of distress and of terror, but there is one thing about
war which has a very splendid side, and that is the
consciousness that a whole nation gets that they must
all act as a unit for a common end. And when peace
is as handsome as war there will be no war. When
men, I mean, engage in the pursuits of peace in the
same spirit of self-sacrifice and of conscious service
of the community with which, at any rate, the common soldier engages in war, then shall there be wars
no more. You have moved the vanguard for the
United States in the purposes of this association just
a little nearer that ideal. That is the reason I am
here, because I believe it.

There is a specific matter about which I, for one,
want your advice. Let me say, if I may say it without disrespect, that I do not think you are prepared
to give it right away. You will have to make some
rather extended inquiries before you are ready to
give it. What I am thinking of is competition in
foreign markets as between the merchants of different
nations.

I speak of the subject with a certain degree of
hesitation, because the thing farthest from my
thought is taking advantage of nations now disabled
from playing their full part in that competition, and

seeking a sudden selfish advantage because they are for the time being disabled. Pray believe me that we ought to eliminate all that thought from our minds and consider this matter as if we and the other nations now at war were in the normal circumstances of commerce.

There is a normal circumstance of commerce in which we are apparently at a disadvantage. Our anti-trust laws are thought by some to make it illegal for merchants in the United States to form combinations for the purpose of strengthening themselves in taking advantage of the opportunities of foreign trade. That is a very serious matter for this reason: There are some corporations, and some firms for all I know, whose business is great enough and whose resources are abundant enough to enable them to establish selling agencies in foreign countries; to enable them to extend the long credits which in some cases are necessary in order to keep the trade they desire; to enable them, in other words, to orangize their business in foreign territory in a way which the smaller man cannot afford to do. His business has not grown big enough to permit him to establish selling agencies. The export commission merchant, perhaps, taxes him a little too highly to make that an available competitive means of conducting and extending his business.

The question arises, therefore, how are the smaller merchants, how are the younger and weaker corporations going to get a foothold as against the combinations which are permitted and even encouraged

by foreign governments in this field of competition?
There are governments which, as you know, distinctly encourage the formation of great combinations in each particular field of commerce in order
to maintain selling agencies and to extend long
credits, and to use and maintain the machinery which
is necessary for the extension of business; and
American merchants feel that they are at a very considerable disadvantage in contending against that.
The matter has been many times brought to my attention, and I have each time suspended judgment.
I want to be shown this: I want to be shown how
such a combination can be made and conducted in
a way which will not close it against the use of
everybody who wants to use it. A combination has
a tendency to exclude new members. When a group
of men get control of a good thing, they do not see
any particular point in letting other people into the
good thing. What I would like very much to be
shown, therefore, is a method of co-operation which
is not a method of combination. Not that the two
words are mutually exclusive, but we have come to
have a special meaning attached to the word "combination." Most of our combinations have a safety
lock, and you have to know the combination to get
in. I want to know how these co-operative methods
can be adopted for the benefit of everybody who
wants to use them, and I say frankly if I can be
shown that, I am for them. If I cannot be shown
that, I am against them. I hasten to add that I
hopefully expect I *can* be shown that.

You, as I have just now intimated, probably can-

not show it to me offhand, but by the methods which
you have the means of using you certainly ought
to be able to throw a vast deal of light on the subject. Because the minute you ask the small merchant, the small banker, the country man, how he
looks upon these things and how he thinks they ought
to be arranged in order that he can use them, if he
is like some of the men in country districts whom
I know, he will turn out to have had a good deal of
thought upon that subject and to be able to make
some very interesting suggestions whose intelligence
and comprehensiveness will surprise some city gentlemen who think that only the cities understand the
business of the country. As a matter of fact, you do
not have time to think in a city. It takes time to
think. You can get what you call opinions by con-
tagion in a city and get them very quickly, but you
do not always know where the germ came from. And
you have no scientific laboratory method by which
to determine whether it is a good germ or a bad germ.

There are thinking spaces in this country, and
some of the thinking done is very solid thinking indeed, the thinking of the sort of men that we all
love best, who think for themselves, who do not see
things as they are told to see them, but look at them
and see them independently; who, if they are told
they are white when they are black, plainly say that
they are black—men with eyes and with a courage
back of those eyes to tell what they see. The country is full of those men. They have been singularly
reticent sometimes, singularly silent, but the country
is full of them. And what I rejoice in is that you

have called them into the ranks. For your methods are bound to be democratic in spite of you. I do not mean democratic with a big "D," though I have a private conviction that you cannot be democratic with a small "d" long without becoming democratic with a big "D." Still that is just between ourselves. The point is that when we have a *consensus* of opinion, when we have this common counsel, then the legislative processes of this Government will be infinitely illuminated.

I used to wonder when I was Governor of one of the States of this great country where all the bills came from. Some of them had a very private complexion. I found upon inquiry—it was easy to find—that practically nine-tenths of the bills that were introduced had been handed to the members who introduced them by some constituent of theirs, had been drawn up by some lawyer whom they might or might not know, and were intended to do something that would be beneficial to a particular set of persons. I do not mean, necessarily, beneficial in a way that would be hurtful to the rest; they may have been perfectly honest, but they came out of cubbyholes all over the State. They did not come out of public places where men had got together and compared views. They were not the products of common counsel, but the products of private counsel, a very necessary process if there is no other, but a process which it would be a very happy thing to dispense with if we could get another. And the only other process is the process of common counsel.

Some of the happiest experiences of my life have

been like this. We had once when I was president
of a university to revise the whole course of study.
Courses of study are chronically in need of revision.
A committee of, I believe, fourteen men was directed
by the faculty of the university to report a revised
curriculum. Naturally, the men who had the most
ideas on the subject were picked out and, naturally,
each man came with a very definite notion of the
kind of revision he wanted, and one of the first discoveries we made was that no two of us wanted
exactly the same revision. I went in there with all
my war paint on to get the revision I wanted, and
I dare say, though it was perhaps more skillfully
concealed, the other men had their war paint on, too.
We discussed the matter for six months. The result
was a report which no one of us had conceived or
foreseen, but with which we were all absolutely satisfied. There was not a man who had not learned in
that committee more than he had ever known before
about the subject, and who had not willingly revised
his prepossessions; who was not proud to be a par-
ticipant in a genuine piece of common counsel. I
have had several experiences of that sort, and it has
led me, whenever I confer, to hold my particular
opinion provisionally, as my contribution to go into
the final result but not to dominate the final result.

That is the ideal of a government like ours, and
an interesting thing is that if you only talk about
an idea that will not work long enough, everybody
will see perfectly plainly that it will not work;
whereas, if you do not talk about it, and do not have
a great many people talk about it, you are in danger

of having the people who handle it think that it will
work.   Many minds are necessary to compound a
workable method of life in a various and populous
country; and as I think about the whole thing and
picture the purposes, the infinitely difficult and complex purposes which we must conceive and carry out,
not only does it minister to my own modesty, I hope,
of opinion, but it also fills me with a very great
enthusiasm.   It is a splendid thing to be part of a
great wide-awake Nation.   It is a splendid thing to
know that your own strength is infinitely multiplied
by the strength of other men who love the country as
you do.   It is a splendid thing to feel that the wholesome blood of a great country can be united in
common purposes, and that by frankly looking one
another in the face and taking counsel with one
another, prejudices will drop away, handsome understandings will arise, a universal spirit of service will
be engendered, and that with this increased sense of
community of purpose will come a vastly enhanced individual power of achievement; for we will be lifted
by the whole mass of which we constitute a part.

Have you never heard a great chorus of trained
voices lift the voice of the prima donna as if it soared
with easy grace above the whole melodious sound?
It does not seem to come from the single throat that
produces it.   It seems as if it were the perfect accent and crown of the great chorus.   So it ought to
be with the statesman.   So it ought to be with every
man who tries to guide the counsels of a great nation.
He should feel that his voice is lifted upon the chorus
and that it is only the crown of the common theme.

MEANING OF THE CIVIL WAR

ADDRESS DELIVERED AT ARLINGTON, MAY 31, 1915. FROM
THE WHITE HOUSE FILES.

I HAVE not come here to-day to deliver an address, but merely reverently to take part in expressing the sentiment of this impressive day. It
is necessarily a day of reminiscences. Reminiscence
is not always a profitable exercise. It generally belongs to those, appropriately to those only, who have
left the active stage of life and have nothing to think
about except the things that are gone and dead. It
does not behoove a nation to walk with its eyes over
its shoulder. Its business is constantly in the years
that lie ahead of it and in the present that challenges
it to the display of its power. But there are reminiscences which are stimulating and wholesome, and
among those reminiscences are chiefly to be ranked
the recollections of days of heroism, days when great
nations found it possible to express the best that was
in them by the ardent exercise of every power that
was in them.

That is what gives dignity to a day like this. It is
not a day of regret. It is not a day of weakening
memory. It is a day of stimulation. But, my
friends, these stimulating memories we are sometimes apt to minimize because we do not see the full
significance of them. We are constantly speaking

of the great war of which we think to-day as a war
which saved the Union, and it did indeed save the
Union, but it was a war that did a great deal more
than that. It created in this country what had never
existed before,—a national consciousness. It was not
the salvation of the Union; it was the rebirth of
the Union. It was the time when America for the
first time realized its unity and saw the vision of its
united destiny.

The solemn lesson of these memories for us is not
that we must be ready to save the Union again, for
there is none among us who threaten its life, but
that we must see to it that the unity then realized,
the vision then seen, is exemplified in us and in the
things that we do. There is no stimulation in any
lesson unless it be the stimulation to duty. There
is no stimulation in any occasion if it be merely the
pleasure of recollection; it must also be the ardor
and courage of hope. Greater days lie before this
nation than it has ever seen yet; and the solemn
consciousness of those who bear office in this time is
that they must make their best endeavor to embody
in what they do and say and are, the best things in
the United States.

It does not do to talk too much about one's self,
and I do not think that it is wholesome for the
United States to talk too much about itself. I do not
want to know what you are to-day so much as I want
to know what you are going to do to-morrow. The
only test I know of that is competent to determine
what you are is the test of what you do. Iet us not
think of our characters; let us think of our duties

and of the actions that lie before us. I have always
maintained that the man who lives to cultivate his
own character will result only in cultivating an intolerable prig, because his object will be himself.
Character, my friends, is a by-product; it is produced in the great manufacture of daily duty. Duty
is not easy to determine. Duty for a nation is made
up of so many complicated elements that no man can
determine it. No group of men without wide common counsel can possibly determine what the duty of
the day is. That is the strength of a democracy,
because there daily rises in the great body of a
democracy the expression of an untrammeled opinion
which seems to fill the air with its suggestions of
duty; and those who stand at the head of affairs have
it as their bounden obligation to endeavor to express
in their own actions those things that seem to rise
out of the conscience and hope and purpose of the
great body of the people themselves.

America, I have said, was reborn by the struggle
of the Civil War, but America is reborn every day
of her life by the purposes we form, the conceptions
we entertain, the hopes that we cherish. We live
in our visions. We live in the things that we see.
We live, and hope abounds in us as we live, in the
things that we purpose. Let us go away from this
place renewed in our devotion to daily duty and to
those ideals which keep a nation young, keep it noble,
keep it rich in enterprise and achievement; make it
to lead the nations of the world in those things that
make for hope and for the benefit of mankind.

DEMOCRACY NO LONGER AN EXPERIMENT

ADDRESS TO THE GRAND ARMY OF THE REPUBLIC, WASH-
INGTON, SEPTEMBER 28, 1915. FROM OFFICIAL PUB-
LICATION IN MR. WILSON'S FILES.

IT is a singular thing that men of a single generation should have witnessed what you have witnessed in the crowded fifty years which you celebrate
tonight. You took part when you were young men
in a struggle the meaning of which, I dare say, you
thought would not be revealed during your lifetime,
and yet more has happened in the making of this
Nation in your lifetime than has ever happened in
the making of any other nation in the lifetime of a
dozen generations.

The Nation in which you now live is not the Nation for whose union you fought. You have seen
many things come about which have made this Nation
one of the representative nations of the world with
regard to the modern spirit of that world, and you
have the satisfaction, which, I dare say few soldiers
have ever had, of looking back upon a war absolutely
unique in this, that, instead of destroying, it healed;
that, instead of making a permanent division, it
made a permanent union. * * * *

This Nation was from the beginning a spiritual
enterprise, and you have seen the spirits of the two
once-divided sections of this country absolutely

united. A war which seemed as if it had the seed
of every kind of bitterness in it has seen a single
generation put bitterness absolutely out of its heart
and you feel, as I am sure the men who fought
against you feel, that you were comrades even then,
though you did not know it, and that now you know
that you are comrades in a common love for a country which you are equally eager to serve.

This is a miracle of the spirit, so far as national
history is concerned. This is one of the very few
wars in which in one sense everybody engaged may
take pride. Some wars are to be regretted, some
wars mar the annals of history, but some wars, contrasted with those, make those annals distinguished,
show that the spirit of man sometimes springs to
great enterprises that are even greater than his own
mind had conceived. * * * *

You set the Nation free for that greater career
of development, of unhampered development, which
the world has witnessed since the Civil War; but,
for my part, I would not be proud of the extraordinary physical development of this country, of its
extraordinary development in material wealth and
financial power, did I not believe that the people
of the United States wished all of this power devoted
to ideal ends.

There have been other nations as rich as we, there
have been other nations as powerful, there have been
other nations as spirited; but I hope we shall never
forget that we created this Nation, not to serve ourselves, but to serve mankind. * * * * *

I hope I may say without even an implication of

criticism upon any other great people in the world that it has always seemed to me that the people of the United States wished to be regarded as devoted to the promotion of particular principles of human right. The United States were founded, not to provide free homes, but to assert human rights. This flag meant a great enterprise of the human spirit.

Nobody, no large bodies of men, in the time that flag was first set up believed with a very firm belief in the efficacy of democracy. Do you realize that only so long ago as the time of the American Revolution democracy was regarded as an experiment in the world and we were regarded as rash experimenters? But we not only believed in it, we showed that our belief was well founded, and that a nation as powerful as any in the world could be erected upon the will of the people; that, indeed, there was a power in such a nation that dwelt in no other nation, unless also in that other nation the spirit of the people prevailed.

Democracy is the most difficult form of government, because it is the form under which you have to persuade the largest number of persons to do anything in particular. But I think we were the more pleased to undertake it because it is difficult. Anybody can do what is easy. We have shown that we could do what was hard, and the pride that ought to dwell in your hearts tonight is that you saw to it that that experiment was brought to the day of its triumphant demonstration. We now know and the world knows that the thing that we then undertook, rash as it seemed, has been practicable, and that we

have set up in the world a government maintained
and promoted by the general conscience and the
general conviction. So I stand here not to welcome
you to the Nation's Capital as if I were your host,
but merely to welcome you to your own Capital, because I am, and am proud to be, your servant. I
hope I shall catch, as I hope we shall all catch, from
the spirit of this occasion a new consecration to the
high duties of American citizenship.

BE NOT AFRAID OF OUR FOREIGN-BORN CITIZENS

ADDRESS TO THE DAUGHTERS OF THE AMERICAN REVOLU-
TION, WASHINGTON, OCTOBER 11, 1915. FROM THE
WHITE HOUSE FILES.

AGAIN it is my very great privilege to welcome
you to the City of Washington and to the hos-
pitalities of the Capitol. May I admit a point of
ignorance? I was surprised to learn that this association is so young, and that an association so
young should devote itself wholly to memory I cannot believe. For to me the duties to which you are
consecrated are more than the duties and the pride
of memory.

There is a very great thrill to be had from the
memories of the American Revolution, but the American Revolution was a beginning, not a consummation, and the duty laid upon us by that beginning
is the duty of bringing the things then begun to a
noble triumph of completion. For it seems to me
that the peculiarity of patriotism in America is that
it is not a mere sentiment. It is an active principle
of conduct. It is something that was born into the
world, not to please it, but to regenerate it. It is
something that was born into the world to replace
systems that had preceded it and to bring men out
upon a new plane of privilege. The glory of the

men whose memories you honor and perpetuate is that they saw this vision, and it was a vision of the future. It was a vision of great days to come when a little handful of three million people upon the borders of a single sea should have become a great multitude of free men and women spreading across a great continent, dominating the shores of two oceans, and sending West as well as East the influences of individual freedom. These things were consciously in their minds as they framed the great Government which was born out of the American Revolution; and every time we gather to perpetuate their memories it is incumbent upon us that we should be worthy of recalling them and that we should endeavor by every means in our power to emulate their example.

The American Revolution was the birth of a nation; it was the creation of a great free republic based upon traditions of personal liberty which theretofore had been confined to a single little island, but which it was purposed should spread to all mankind. And the singular fascination of American history is that it has been a process of constant re-creation, of making over again in each generation the thing which was conceived at first. You know how peculiarly necessary that has been in our case, because America has not grown by the mere multiplication of the original stock. It is easy to preserve tradition with continuity of blood; it is easy in a single family to remember the origins of the race and the purposes of its organization; but it is not so easy when that race is constantly being renewed and augmented from other sources, from stocks that did not carry or originate the same principles. So from generation to generation strangers have had to be indoctrinated with the principles of the American family, and the wonder and the beauty of it all has been that the infection has been so generously easy. For the principles of liberty are united with the principles of hope. Every individual, as well as every Nation, wishes to realize the best thing that is in him, the best thing that can be conceived out of the materials of which his spirit is constructed. It has happened in a way that fascinates the imagination that we have not only been augmented by additions from outside, but that we have been greatly stimulated by those additions. Living in the easy prosperity of a free people, knowing that the sun had always been free to shine upon us and prosper our undertakings, we did not realize how hard the task of liberty is and how rare the privilege of liberty is; but men were drawn out of every climate and out of every race because of an irresistible attraction of their spirits to the American ideal. They thought of America as lifting, like that great statue in the harbor of New York, a torch to light the pathway of men to the things that they desire, and men of all sorts and conditions struggled toward that light and came to our shores with an eager desire to realize it, and a hunger for it such as some of us no longer felt, for we were as if satiated and satisfied and were indulging ourselves after a fashion that did not belong to the ascetic devotion of the early devotees of those great principles. Strangers came to remind us of what we had promised ourselves and through ourselves had promised mankind. All men came to us and said, "Where is the bread of life with which you promised to feed us, and have you partaken of it yourselves?" For my part, I believe that the constant renewal of this people out of foreign stocks has been a constant source of reminder to this people of what the inducement was that was offered to men who would come and be of our number.

Now we have come to a time of special stress and test. There never was a time when we needed more clearly to conserve the principles of our own patriotism than this present time. The rest of the world from which our politics were drawn seems for the time in the crucible and no man can predict what will come out of that crucible. We stand apart, unembroiled, conscious of our own principles, conscious of what we hope and purpose, so far as our powers permit, for the world at large, and it is necessary that we should consolidate the American principle. Every political action, every social action, should have for its object in America at this time to challenge the spirit of America; to ask that every man and woman who thinks first of America should rally to the standards of our life. There have been some among us who have not thought first of America, who have thought to use the might of America in some matter not of America's origination. They have forgotten that the first duty of a nation is to express its own individual principles in the action of the family of nations and not to seek to aid and abet any rival or contrary ideal.

Neutrality is a negative word. It is a word that does not express what America ought to feel. America has a heart and that heart throbs with all sorts of intense sympathies, but America has schooled its heart to love the things that America believes in and it ought to devote itself only to the things that America believes in; and, believing that America stands apart in its ideals, it ought not to allow itself to be drawn, so far as its heart is concerned, into anybody's quarrel. Not because it does not understand the quarrel, not because it does not in its head assess the merits of the controversy, but because America has promised the world to stand apart and maintain certain principles of action which are grounded in law and in justice. We are not trying to keep out of trouble; we are trying to preserve the foundations upon which peace can be rebuilt. Peace can be rebuilt only upon the ancient and accepted principles of international law, only upon those things which remind nations of their duties to each other, and, deeper than that, of their duties to mankind and to humanity.

America has a great cause which is not confined to the American continent. It is the cause of humanity itself. I do not mean in anything that I say even to imply a judgment upon any nation or upon any policy, for my object here this afternoon is not to sit in judgment upon anybody but ourselves and to challenge you to assist all of us who are trying to make America more than even conscious of her own principles and her own duty. I looked forward to the necessity in every political agitation in the years which are immediately at hand of calling upon every man to declare himself, where he stands. Is it America first or is it not?

We ought to be very careful about some of the impressions that we are forming just now. There is too general an impression, I fear, that very large numbers of our fellow-citizens born in other lands have not entertained with sufficient intensity and affection the American ideal. But the number of such is, I am sure, not large. Those who would seek to represent them are very vocal, but they are not very influential. Some of the best stuff of America has come out of foreign lands, and some of the best stuff in America is in the men who are naturalized citizens of the United States. I would not be afraid upon the test of "America first" to take a census of all the foreign-born citizens of the United States, for I know that the vast majority of them came here because they believed in America; and their belief in America has made them better citizens than some people who were born in America. They can say that they have bought this privilege with a great price. They have left their homes, they have left their kindred, they have broken all the nearest and dearest ties of human life in order to come to a new land, take a new rootage, begin a new life, and so by self-sacrifice express their confidence in a new principle; whereas, it cost us none of these things. We were born into this privilege; we were rocked and cradled in it; we did nothing to create it; and it is, therefore, the greater duty on our part to do a great deal to enhance it and preserve it. I am not deceived

as to the balance of opinion among the foreign-born
citizens of the United States, but I am in a hurry
for an opportunity to have a line-up and let the men
who are thinking first of other countries stand on
one side and all those that are for America first, last,
and all the time on the other side.

Now, you can do a great deal in this direction.
When I was a college officer I used to be very much
opposed to hazing; not because hazing is not wholesome, but because sophomores are poor judges. I
remember a very dear friend of mine, a professor
of ethics on the other side of the water, was asked
if he thought it was ever justifiable to tell a lie. He
said Yes, he thought it was sometimes justifiable to
lie; "but," he said, "it is so difficult to judge of
the justification that I usually tell the truth." I
think that ought to be the motto of the sophomore.
There are freshmen who need to be hazed, but the
need is to be judged by such nice tests that a sophomore is hardly old enough to determine them. But
the world can determine them. We are not freshmen at college, but we are constantly hazed. I would
a great deal rather be obliged to draw pepper up
my nose than to observe the hostile glances of my
neighbors. I would a great deal rather be beaten
than ostracized. I would a great deal rather endure
any sort of physical hardship if I might have the
affection of my fellow-men. We constantly discipline
our fellow-citizens by having an opinion about them.
That is the sort of discipline we ought now to administer to everybody who is not to the very core
of his heart an American. Just have an opinion

about him and let him experience the atmospheric
effects of that opinion! And I know of no body of
persons comparable to a body of ladies for creating
an atmosphere of opinion! I have myself in part
yielded to the influences of that atmosphere, though
it took me a long time to determine how I was going
to vote in New Jersey.

So it has seemed to me that my privilege this
afternoon was not merely a privilege of courtesy,
but the real privilege of reminding you—for I am
sure I am doing nothing more—of the great principles which we stand associated to promote. I for
my part rejoice that we belong to a country in which
the whole business of government is so difficult. We
do not take orders from anybody; it is a universal
communication of conviction, the most subtle, delicate, and difficult of processes. There is not a single
individual's opinion that is not of some consequence
in making up the grand total, and to be in this great
co operative effort is the most stimulating thing in
the world. A man standing alone may well misdoubt
his own judgment. He may mistrust his own intellectual processes; he may even wonder if his own
heart leads him right in matters of public conduct;
but if he finds his heart part of the great throb of
a national life, there can be no doubt about it. If
that is his happy circumstance, then he may know
that he is part of one of the great forces of the world.

I would not feel any exhilaration in belonging to
America if I did not feel that she was something
more than a rich and powerful nation. I should
not feel proud to be in some respects and for a little

while her spokesman if I did not believe that there
was something else than physical force behind her.
I believe that the glory of America is that she is a
great spiritual conception and that in the spirit of
her institutions dwells not only her distinction but
her power. The one thing that the world cannot
permanently resist is the moral force of great and
triumphant convictions.

A NEW KIND OF CHURCH LIFE

ADDRESS BEFORE THE FEDERAL COUNCIL OF CHURCHES,
COLUMBUS, OHIO, DECEMBER 10, 1915. FROM THE
"CONGRESSIONAL RECORD," 64TH CONGRESS, 1ST SES-
SION, VOL. 53, PP. 15751-15753.

I FEEL an unaffected diffidence in coming into this conference without having participated in its deliberations. I wish that I might have been here to learn the many things that I am sure have been learned by those who have attended these conferences. I feel confident that nothing that I say about the rural church will be new to you. I am here simply because I wished to show my profound interest in the subject which you have been considering and not because I thought I had anything original to contribute to your thought.

I think that as we have witnessed the processes of our civilization in recent years we have more and more realized how our cities were tending to draw the vitality from the countryside, how much less our life centered upon country districts and how much more upon crowded cities. There was a time when America was characteristically rural, when practically all her strength was drawn from quiet countrysides, where life ran upon established lines and where men and women and children were familiar with each other in a long-established neighborliness;

but our rural districts are not now just what they used to be and have partaken in recent years of something of the fluidity that has characterized our general life. So that we have again and again been called upon from one point of view or another to study the revitalization of the countryside. There was a time, no longer ago than the youth of my own father, for example, when pastors found some of their most vital work in the country churches. I remember my dear father used to ride from church to church in a thickly populated country region and minister to several churches with a sense of ministering to the most vital interests of the part of the country in which he lived.

After all, the most vitalizing thing in the world is Christianity. The world has advanced, advanced in what we regard as real civilization, not by material but by spiritual means, and one nation is distinguished from another nation by its ideals, not by its possessions; by what it believes in, by what it lives by, by what it intends, by the visions which its young men dream and the achievements which its mature men attempt. So that each nation when it writes its poetry or writes its memoirs, exalts the character of its people and of those who spring from the loins of its people.

There is an old antithesis upon which I do not care to dwell, because there is not a great deal to be got from dwelling on it, between life and doctrine. Here is no real antithesis. A man lives as he believes he ought to live as he believes that it is to his advantage to live. He lives upon a doctrine, upon a principle, upon an idea—sometimes a very low principle, sometimes a very exalted principle. I used to be told when I was a youth that some of the old casuists reduced all sin to egotism, and I have thought as I watched the career of some individuals that the analysis had some vital point to it. An egotist is a man who has got the whole perspective of life wrong. He conceives of himself as the center of affairs. He conceives of himself as the center of affairs even as affects the providence of God. He has not related himself to the great forces which dominate him with the rest of us, and therefore has set up a little kingdom all his own in which he reigns with unhonored sovereignty. So there are some men who set up the principle of individual advantage as the principle, the doctrine, of their life, and live by that, and live generally a life that leads to all sorts of shipwreck. Whatever our doctrine be, our life is conformed to it.

But what I want to speak of is not the contrast between doctrine and life, but the translation of doctrine into life. After all, Christianity is not important to us because it is a valid body of conceptions regarding God and man, but because it is a vital body of conceptions which can be translated into life for us, life in this world and a life still greater in the next. Except as Christianity changes and inspires life, it has failed of its mission. That is what Christ came into the world for, to save our spirits, and you cannot have your spirit altered without having your life altered.

When I think of the rural church, therefore, I wonder how far the rural church is vitalizing the lives

of the communities in which it exists. We have had
a great deal to say recently, and it has been very
profitably said, about the school as a social center,
by which is meant the schoolhouse as a social center;
about making the house which in the daytime is used
for the children a place which their parents may use
in the evenings and at other disengaged times for the
meetings of the community, where they will be privileged to come together and talk about anything that
is of community interest and talk about it with the
utmost freedom. Some people have been opposed to
it because there are some things that they do not
want talked about. Some boards of education have
been opposed to it because they realized that it might
not be well for the board of education to be talked
about. Talk is a very dangerous thing, community
comparisons of views are a very dangerous thing,
to the men who are doing wrong, but I, for my part,
believe in making the schoolhouse the social center,
the place that the community can use for any kind of
coordinating that it wants to do in its life. But I believe that where the school is inadequate, and even
where it is adequate, the most vital social center
should be the church itself, and that not by way of
organizing the church for social service—that is not
my topic to-night; that is another topic—but of making the community realize that that congregation,
and particularly that pastor, is interested in everything that is important for that community, and that
the members of that church are ready to co-operate
and the pastor ready to lend his time and his energy
to the kind of organization which is necessary out-

side the church, as well as within it, for the benefit of
the community.

It seems to me that the country pastor has an unparalleled opportunity to be a country leader, to
make everybody realize that he, as the representative
of Christ, believes himself related to everything
human, to everything human that has as its object
the uplift and instruction and inspiration of the
community or the betterment of any of its conditions; and that if any pastor will make it felt
throughout the community that that is his spirit, that
his interest, and that he is ready to draw his elders
or his deacons or his vestrymen along with him as
active agents in the betterment of the community, the
church will begin to have a dominating influence in
the community such as it has lost for the time being
and we must find it means to regain.

For example, in a farming community one of the
things that the Department of Agriculture at Washington is trying to do is to show the farmers of the
country the easiest and best methods of co-operation
with regard to marketing their crops—helping in
their effort to learn how to handle their crops in a co-
operative fashion so that they can get the best service from the railroads; to learn how to find the pre-
vailing market prices in the accessible market so as to
know where it will be best and most profitable to
send their farm products; and to draw them together
into co-operative association with these objects in
view. The church ought to lend its hand in that.
The pastor ought to say, "If you want somebody to
look after this for you, I will give part of my time

and I will find other men in my congregation who
will help you in the work and help you without
charging you anything for it. We want you to realize that this church is interested in the lives of the
people of this community and that it will lend itself
to any legitimate project that advances the life and
interest of this community.''

Let the rural church find that road and then discover, as it will discover, that men begin to swing
their thoughts to those deeper meanings of the church
in which we wish to draw their attention; that this
is a spiritual brotherhood; that the pastor and his
associates are interested in them because they are
interested in the souls of men and the prosperity of
men as it lies deep in their hearts. There are a great
many ways by which leadership can be exercised.
The church has too much depended upon individual
example. ''So let your light shine before men'' has
been interpreted to mean, ''Put your individual self
on a candlestick and shine.'' Now, the trouble is that
some people cannot find a candlestick, but the greater
trouble is that they are very poor candles and the
light is very dim. It does not dispel much of the
darkness for me individually to sit on top of a candlestick, but if I can lend such little contribution of
spiritual force as I have to my neighbor and to my
comrade and to my friend, and we can draw a circle
of friends together and unite our spiritual forces,
then we have something more than example: we have
co-operation.

Co-operation ladies and gentlemen, is the vital
principle of social life; not organization merely. I

think I know something about organization. I can make an organization, but it is one thing to have an organization and another thing to fill it with life. And then it is a very important matter what sort of life you fill it with. If the object of the organization is what the object of some business organizations is and the object of many political organizations is, to absorb the life of the community and run the community for its own benefit, then there is nothing beneficial in it. But if the object of the organization is to afford a mechanism by which the whole community can co-operatively use its life, then there is a great deal in it. An organization without the spirit of co-operation is dead and may be dangerous. The vital principle is co-operation, and organization is secondary. I have been a member of one or two churches that were admirably organized and they were accomplishing nothing. You know some people dearly love organization. They dearly love to sit in a chair and preside. They pride themselves upon their knowledge of parliamentary practice. They love to concoct and write minutes. They love to appoint committees. They boast of the number of committees that their organization has and they like the power and the social influence of distributing their friends among the committees, and then when the committees are formed there is nothing to commit to them.

This is a Nation which loves to go through the motions of public meeting whether there is anything particularly important to consider or not. It is an interesting thing to me how the American is born knowing how to conduct a public meeting. I remember that when I was a lad I belonged to an organization which at that time seemed to me very important, which was known as the Lightfoot Baseball Club. Our clubroom was a corner, an unoccupied corner, of the loft of my father's barn, the part that the hay had not encroached upon, and I distinctly remember how we used to conduct orderly meetings of the club in that corner of the loft. I had never seen a public meeting and I do not believe any of the other lads with whom I was associated had ever seen a public meeting, but we somehow knew how to conduct one. We knew how to make motions and second them; we knew that a motion could not have more than two amendments offered at the same time; and we knew the order in which the amendments had to be put, the second amendment before the first. How we knew it I do not know. We were born that way, I suppose. But nothing very important happened at those meetings, and I have been present at some church organization meetings at which nothing more important happened than happened with the Lightfoot Baseball Club. I remember distinctly that my delight and interest was in the meetings, not in what they were for; just the sense of belonging to an organization and doing something with the organization, it did not very much matter what. Some churches are organized that way. They are exceedingly active about nothing. Now, why not lend that organizing instinct, that acting instinct, to the real things that are happening in the community, whether they have anything to do with the church or not?

We look back to the time of the early settlements
in this country and remember that in old New England the church and the school were the two sources
of the life of the community. Everything centered
in them. Everything emanated from them. The
school fed the church and the church ran the community. It sometimes did not run it very liberally,
and I for my part would not wish to see any church
run any community, but I do wish to see every
church assist the community in which it is established
to run itself, to show that the spirit of Christianity
is the spirit of assistance, of counsel, of vitalization,
of intense interest in everything that affects the lives
of men and women and children. So that I am
hoping that the outcome of these conferences, of all
that we say and do about this very important matter, may be to remind the church that it is put into
this world not only to serve the individual soul but
to serve society also. And it has got to go to work on
society with a greater sense of the exigency of the
thing than in the case of the individual, because you
have got to save society in this world, not in the next.
I hope that our society is not going to exist in the
next. It needs amendment in several particulars, I
venture to say, and I hope that the society in the next
world will be amended in those particulars—I will
not mention them. But we have nothing to do with
society in the next world. We may have something
to do with the individual soul in the next world by
getting it started straight for the next world, but we
have got nothing to do with the organization of society in the next world. We have got to save society,

so far as it is saved by the instrumentality of Christianity in this world. It is a job, therefore, that you have got to undertake immediately and work at all the time, and it is the business of the church.

Legislation can not save society. Legislation can not even rectify society. The law that will work is merely the summing up in legislative form of the moral judgment that the community has already reached. Law records how far society has got, and there have got to be instrumentalities preceding the law that get society up to that point where it will be ready to record. Try the experiment. Enact a law that is the moral judgment of a very small minority of the community, and it will not work. Most people will not understand it, and if they do understand they will resent it, and whether they understand it and resent it or not they will not obey it. Law is a record of achievement. It is not a process of regeneration. Our wills have to be regenerated, and our purposes rectified before we are in a position to enact laws that record those moral achievements. And that is the business, primarily, it seems to me, of the Christian.

There are a great many arguments about Christianity. There are a great many things which we spiritually assert which we can not prove in the ordinary, scientific sense of the word "prove"; but there are some things which we can show. The proof of Christianity is written in the biography of the saints, and by the saints I do not mean the technical saints, those whom the church or the world has picked out to label "saints," for they are not very numerous, but the people whose lives, whose individual lives, have been transformed by Christianity. It is the only force in the world that I have ever heard of that does actually transform the life, and the proof of that transformation is to be found all over the Christian world and is multiplied and repeated as Christianity gains fresh territory in the heathen world. Men begin suddenly to erect great spiritual standards over the little personal standards which they theretofore professed and will walk smilingly to the stake in order that their souls may be true to themselves. There is nothing else that does that. There is something that is analogous to it, and that is patriotism. Men will go into the fire of battle and freely give their lives for something greater than themselves, their duty to their country; and there is a pretty fine analogy between patriotism and Christianity. It is the devotion of the spirit to something greater and nobler than itself. These are the transforming influences. All the transforming influences in the world are unselfish. There is not a single selfish force in the world that is not touched with sinister power, and the church is the only embodiment of the things that are entirely unselfish, the principles of self-sacrifice and devotion. Surely this is the instrumentality by which rural communities may be transformed and led to the things that are great; and surely there is nothing in the rural community in which the rural church ought not to be the leader and of which it ought not to be the vital actual center.

That is the simple message that I came to utter to-

night, and, as I began by saying, I dare say it is no
message; I dare say it has been repeatedly said in
this conference; I merely wanted to add my testimony to the validity and power of that conception.
Because, ladies and gentlemen, we are in the world
to do something more than look after ourselves.

The reason that I am proud to be an American is
because America was given birth to by such conceptions as these; that its object in the world, its only
reason for existence as a Government, was to show
men the paths of liberty and of mutual serviceability,
to lift the common man out of the paths, out of the
sloughs of discouragement and even despair; set his
feet upon firm ground; tell him, "Here is the high
road upon which you are as much entitled to walk as
we are, and, we will see that there is a free field and
no favor, and that as your moral qualities are and
your physical powers so will your success be. We
will not let any man make you afraid, and we will
not let any man do you an injustice."

Those are the ideals of America. We have not always lived up to them. No community has always
lived up to them, but we are dignified by the fact
that those are the things we live for and sail by;
America is great in the world, not as she is a successful Government merely, but as she is the successful
embodiment of a great ideal of unselfish citizenship.
That is what makes the world feel America draw it
like a lodestone. That is the reason why the ships
that cross the sea have so many hopeful eyes lifted
from their humbler quarters towards the shores of
the new world. That is the reason why men, after

they have been for a little while in America and go back for a visit to the old country, have a new light in their faces—the light that has kindled there in the country where they have seen some of their objects fulfilled. That is the light that shines from America. God grant that it may always shine and that in many a humble hearth, in quiet country churches, the flames may be lighted by which this great light is kept alive.

"YOU CANNOT FOOL ALL THE PEOPLE ALL THE TIME"

ADDRESS AT THE FIRST ANNUAL BANQUET OF THE MOTION PICTURE BOARD OF TRADE, HOTEL BILTMORE, NEW YORK, JANUARY 27, 1916. FROM THE WHITE HOUSE FILES.

I WONDERED when I was on my way here what would be expected of me. It occurred to me that perhaps I would only be expected to go through the motions of a speech, and then I reflected that, never having seen myself speak and generally having my thoughts concentrated upon what I had to say, I had not the least notion what my motions were when I made a speech. Because it has never occurred to me in my simplicity to make a speech before a mirror. If you will give me time, I will rehearse this difficult part and return and perform it for you.

I have sometimes been very much chagrined in seeing myself in a motion picture. I have wondered if I really was that kind of a "guy." The extraordinary rapidity with which I walked, for example, the instantaneous and apparently automatic nature of my motion, the way in which I produce uncommon grimaces, and altogether the extraordinary exhibition I make of myself sends me to bed very unhappy. And I often think to myself that, although all the world is a stage and men and women but actors upon it, after all the external appearances of things are very superficial indeed. I am very much more interested in what my fellow-men are thinking about than in the motions through which they are going. While we unconsciously display a great deal of human nature in our visible actions, there are some very deep waters which no picture can sound.

When you think of a great nation you are not thinking of a visible thing; you are thinking of a spiritual thing. I suppose a man in public office feels this with a peculiar poignancy, because what it is important for him to know is the real, genuine sentiments and emotions of the people that make up the nation. I found out what was going on in Mexico in a very singular way,—by hearing a sufficiently large number of liars talk about it. I think the psychological explanation will interest you.

You know that the truth is consistent with itself; one piece matches another. Now no man is an inventive enough liar not to bring in large sections of truth in what he says, and after all the liars are done talking to you about the same subject it will come to your consciousness that long and large pieces of what they said matched; that in that respect they all said the same thing; that the variations are lies and the consistencies are the truth. They will not all tell you the same piece of the truth, so that if you hear enough of them, you may get the whole of the truth. And yet it is very tedious to hear men lie, particularly when you know they are lying. You feel like reminding them that really your time is important to you and that you wish they would get down to business and tell you what is really so, but they do not. They want this adventure of their invention; they want to give an excursion to their minds before they get down to business. What I particularly object to is a very able man with a lot of inventions coming to me and lying to me, because then the interview is very tedious and long before we get down to business. I got to know that story so by heart that the last time a deputation visited me about Mexico I thought I would save time and I told them exactly what they were going to say to me. They went away very much confused; they wondered how I had heard it, because they knew it was not so.

Yet underneath all of this are those great pulses which throb in great bodies of men and drive the great affairs of state, and I wonder how men venture to try to deceive a great nation. There never was a profounder saying than that of Lincoln that you can fool all the people some of the time and some of the people all of the time, but you cannot fool all the people all of the time, and the best way in which to silence any friend of yours whom you know to be a fool is to induce him to hire a hall. Nothing chills pretense like exposure. Nothing will bear the tests of examination for a shorter length of time than pretense. At least so I try to persuade myself, and yet there are some humbugs that have been at large a long time. I suppose that there is always a rising generation whom they can fool, but the older heads ought not to permit themselves to be fooled.

I should think that in a year like the year 1916, when there is to be a common reckoning for everybody, men would hurry up and begin to tell the truth. They are not hurrying about it; they are taking their time, but the American people are going to insist upon it before this year is over that everybody comes up and is counted on the great questions of the day. They are not going to take any excuses, they are not going to take any pretenses; they are going to insist upon the goods being delivered on the spot, and anybody that declines to deliver them is going to go bankrupt, and ought to go bankrupt. Everybody ought to get what is coming to him.

But I came here to say that I hoped you would not believe that I am what I appear to be in the pictures you make of me. I really am a pretty decent fellow! And I have a lot of emotions that do not show on the surface, and the things that I do not say would fill a library. The great curse of public life is that you are not allowed to say all the things that you think. Some of my opinions about some men are extremely picturesque, and if you could only take a motion picture of them, you would think it was Vesuvius in eruption. Yet all these volcanic forces, all these things that are going on inside of me, have to be concealed under a most grave and reverend exterior, and I have to make believe that I have nothing but respectable and solemn thoughts all the time. There is a lot going on inside of me that would be entertaining to any audience anywhere.

I am very much complimented that you should have allowed me to come in at this late hour in your feast and, without partaking of the pleasures of conversation, to make you all, whether you would or not, listen to me talk. My object in life is not talking. I wish there were less talking to do. I wish that not everybody had to be persuaded to do the right thing. I wish that the things that are obvious did not have to be explained. I wish that principles did not have to be re-expounded. We all in our hearts agree upon the fundamental principles of our lives and of our life as a nation; now we ought to tax ourselves with the duty of seeing that those principles are realized in action and no fooling about it. The only difficult things in life, ladies and gentlemen, are the applications of the principles of right and wrong. I can set forth the abstract principles of right and wrong, and so can you, but when it comes down to an individual item of conduct, whether in public affairs or in private affairs, there comes the pinch,—in the first place, to see the right way to do it; and, in the second place, to do it that way. If we could only agree that in all matters of public concern we would adjourn our private interests, look each other frankly in the face and say, "We are all ready at whatever sacrifice of our own interest to do in common the thing that the common weal demands," what an irresistible force America would be! I can point out to you a few men,—of course, I am not going to name them now,—whom every man ought to be afraid of, because nothing but the truth resides in them. I have one in particular in mind whom I have never caught thinking about himself. I would not dare make a pretense in the presence of that man even if I wanted to. His eyes contain the penetrating light of truth before which all disguises fall away.

Suppose we were all like that! It would hasten the millennium immensely. And if Americans were always to do what when the real temper of America is aroused they do, the world would always turn to America for guidance and America would be the most potent and influential force in all the world. So that when I look at pictures, whether they move or whether they do not move, I think of all the deep sources of happiness and of pain, of joy and of misery, that lie beneath that surface, and I am interested chiefly in the heart that beats underneath it all. For I know that there is the pulse and the machinery of all the great forces of the world.

PUBLIC OFFICIALS SWELL UP

ADDRESS TO THE NATIONAL PRESS CLUB, MAY 15, 1916.
FROM THE WHITE HOUSE FILES.

I AM both glad and sorry to be here; glad because I am always happy to be with you, and know and like so many of you, and sorry because I have to make a speech. One of the leading faults of you gentlemen of the press is your inordinate desire to hear other men talk, to draw them out upon all occasions, whether they wish to be drawn out or not. I remember being in this Press Club once before, making many unpremeditated disclosures of myself, and then having you with your singular instinct for publicity insist that I should give it away to everybody else.

I was thinking as I was looking forward to coming here this evening of that other occasion when I stood very nearly at the threshold of the duties that I have since been called upon to perform, and I was going over in my mind the impressions that I then had by way of forecast of the duties of President and comparing them with the experiences that had followed. I must say that the forecast has been very largely verified, and that the impressions I had then had been deepened rather than weakened.

You may recall that I said then that I felt constantly a personal detachment from the Presidency;

that one thing that I resented when I was not performing the duties of the office was being reminded that I was the President of the United States. I felt toward it as a man feels toward a great function which, in working hours, he is obliged to perform, but which, out of working hours, he is glad to get away from and almost forget and resume the quiet course of his own thoughts. I am constantly reminded as I go about, as I do sometimes at the week end, of the personal inconvenience of being President of the United States. If I want to know how many people live in a small town all I have to do is to go there and they at once line up to be counted. I might, in a census-taking year, save the census takers a great deal of trouble by asking them to accompany me and count the people on the spot. Sometimes, when I am most beset, I seriously think of renting a pair of whiskers or of doing something else that will furnish me with an adequate disguise, because I am sorry to find that the cut of my jib is unmistakable and that I must sail under false colors if I am going to sail incognito.

Yet as I have matched my experiences with my anticipations, I, of course, have been aware that I was taken by surprise because of the prominence of many things to which I had not looked forward. When we are dealing with domestic affairs, gentlemen, we are dealing with things that to us as Americans are more or less calculable. There is a singular variety among our citizenship, it is true, a greater variety even than I had anticipated; but, after all, we are all steeped in the same atmosphere, we are all sur-

rounded by the same environment, we are all more
or less affected by the same traditions, and, moreover,
we are working out something that has to be worked
out among ourselves, and the elements are there to
be dealt with at first hand. But when the fortunes
of your own country are, so to say, subject to the in-
calculable winds of passion that are blowing through
other parts of the world, then the strain is of a singular and unprecedented kind, because you do not
know by what turn of the wheel of fortune the control of things is going to be taken out of your hand;
it makes no difference how deep the passion of the
Nation lies, that passion may be so overborne by the
rush of fortune in circumstances like those which now
exist that you feel the sort of—I had almost said resentment that a man feels when his own affairs are
not within his own hands. You can imagine the
strain upon the feeling of any man who is trying to
interpret the spirit of his country when he feels that
that spirit cannot have its own way beyond a certain
point. And one of the greatest points of strain upon
me, if I may be permitted to point it out, was this:

There are two reasons why the chief wish of America is for peace. One is that they love peace and
have nothing to do with the present quarrel; and the
other is that they believe the present quarrel has
carried those engaged in it so far that they cannot
be held to ordinary standards of responsibility, and
that, therefore, as some men have expressed it to me,
since the rest of the world is mad, why should we not
simply refuse to have anything to do with the rest
of the world in the ordinary channels of action?

Why not let the storm pass, and then, when it is all over, have the reckonings? Knowing that from both these two points of view the passion of America was for peace, I was, nevertheless, aware that America is one of the nations of the world, not only, but one of the chief nations of the world—a Nation that grows more and more powerful almost in spite of herself; that grows morally more and more influential even when she is not aware of it; and that if she is to play the part which she most covets, it is necessary that she should act more or less from the point of view of the rest of the world. If I cannot retain my moral influence over a man except by occasionally knocking him down, if that is the only basis upon which he will respect me, then for the sake of his soul I have got occasionally to knock him down. You know how we have read in—isn't it in Ralph Connor's stories of western life in Canada?—that all his sky pilots are ready for a fracas at any time, and how the ultimate salvation of the souls of their parishioners depends upon their using their fists occasionally. If a man will not listen to you quietly in a seat, sit on his neck and make him listen; just as I have always maintained, particularly in view of certain experiences of mine, that the shortest road to a boy's moral sense is through his cuticle. There is a direct and, if I may be permitted the pun, a fundamental connection between the surface of his skin and his moral consciousness. You arrest his attention first in that way, and then get the moral lesson conveyed to him in milder ways that, if he were grown up, would be the only ways you would use.

So I say that I have been aware that in order to do the very thing that we are proudest of the ability to do, there might come a time when we would have to do it in a way that we would prefer not to do it; and the great burden on my spirits, gentlemen, has been that it has been up to me to choose when that time came. Can you imagine a thing more calculated to keep a man awake at nights than that? Because, just because I did not feel that I was the whole thing and was aware that my duty was a duty of interpretation, how could I be sure that I had the right elements of information by which to interpret truly?

What we are now talking about is largely spiritual. You say, "All the people out my way think so and so." Now, I know perfectly well that you have not talked with all the people out your way. I find that out again and again. And so you are taken by surprise. The people of the United States are not asking anybody's leave to do their own thinking, and are not asking anybody to tip them off what they ought to think. They are thinking for themselves, every man for himself; and you do not know, and, the worst of it is, since the responsibility is mine, I do not know what they are thinking about. I have the most imperfect means of finding out, and yet I have got to act as if I knew. That is the burden of it, and I tell you, gentlemen, it is a pretty serious burden, particularly if you look upon the office as I do—that I am not put here to do what I please. If I were, it would have been very much more interesting than it has been. I am put here to interpret, to register, to suggest, and, more than that, and much greater than that, to be suggested to.

Now, that is where the experience that I forecast has differed from the experience that I have had. In domestic matters I think I can in most cases come pretty near a guess where the thought of America is going, but in foreign affairs the chief element is where action is going on in other quarters of the world and not where thought is going in the United States. Therefore, I have several times taken the liberty of urging upon you gentlemen not yourselves to know more than the State Department knows about foreign affairs. Some of you have shown a singular range of omniscience, and certain things have been reported as understood in administrative circles which I never heard of until I read the newspapers. I am constantly taken by surprise in regard to decisions which are said to be my own, and this gives me an uncomfortable feeling that some providence is at work with which I have had no communication at all. Now, that is pretty dangerous, gentlemen, because it happens that remarks start fires. There is tinder lying everywhere, not only on the other side of the water, but on this side of the water, and a man that spreads sparks may be responsible for something a great deal worse than burning a town on the Mexican border. Thoughts may be bandits. Thoughts may be raiders. Thoughts may be invaders. Thoughts may be disturbers of international peace; and when you reflect upon the importance of this country keeping out of the present war, you will know what tremendous elements we are all dealing with. We are all in the same boat. If some-

body does not keep the processes of peace going, if
somebody does not keep their passions disengaged, by
what impartial judgment and suggestion is the world
to be aided to a solution when the whole thing is
over? If you are in a conference in which you know
nobody is disinterested, how are you going to make
a plan? I tell you this, gentlemen, the only thing
that saves the world is the little handful of disinterested men that are in it.

Now, I have found a few disinterested men. I wish
I had found more. I can name two or three men with
whom I have conferred again and again and again,
and I have never caught them by an inadvertence
thinking about themselves for their own interests,
and I tie to those men as you would tie to an anchor.
I tie to them as you would tie to the voices of conscience if you could be sure that you always heard
them. Men who have no axes to grind! Men who
love America so that they would give their lives for
it and never care whether anybody heard that they
had given their lives for it; willing to die in obscurity
if only they might serve! Those are the men, and
nations like those men are the nations that are going
to serve the world and save it. There never was a
time in the history of the world when character, just
sheer character all by itself, told more than it does
now. A friend of mine says that every man who
takes office in Washington either grows or swells, and
when I give a man an office, I watch him carefully to
see whether he is swelling or growing. The mischief
of it is that when they swell they do not swell enough
to burst. If they would only swell to the point where

you might insert a pin and let the gases out, it would
be a great delight. I do not know any pastime that
would be more diverting, except that the gases are
probably poisonous so that we would have to stand
from under. But the men who grow, the men who
think better a year after they are put in office than
they thought when they were put in office, are the
balance wheel of the whole thing. They are the bal-
last that enables the craft to carry sail and to make
port in the long run, no matter what the weather is.

So I have come willing to make this narrative of
experience to you. I have come through the fire since
I talked to you last. Whether the metal is purer
than it was, God only knows; but the fire has been
there, the fire has penetrated every part of it, and
if I may believe my own thoughts I have less partisan feeling, more impatience of party maneuver,
more enthusiasm for the right thing, no matter whom
it hurts, than I ever had before in my life. And I
have something that it is no doubt dangerous to
have, but that I cannot help having. I have a profound intellectual contempt for men who cannot see
the signs of the times. I have to deal with some men
who know no more of the modern processes of politics
than if they were living in the eighteenth century,
and for them I have a profound and comprehensive
intellectual contempt. They are blind. They are
hopelessly blind; and the worst of it is I have to
spend hours of my time talking to them when I know
before I start as much as after I have finished that
it is absolutely useless to talk to them. I am talking
in vacuo.

The business of every one of us, gentlemen, is to realize that if we are correspondents of papers who have not yet heard of modern times we ought to send them as many intimations of modern movements as they are willing to print. There is a simile that was used by a very interesting English writer that has been much in my mind. Like myself, he had often been urged not to try to change so many things. I remember when I was president of a university a man said to me, "Good heavens, man, why don't you leave something alone and let it stay the way it is?" And I said, "If you will guarantee to me that it will stay the way it is I will let it alone; but if you knew anything you would know that if you leave a live thing alone it will not stay where it is. It will develop and will either go in the wrong direction or decay." I reminded him of this thing that the English writer said, that if you want to keep a white post white you cannot let it alone. It will get black. You have to keep doing something to it. In that instance you have got to keep painting it white, and you have got to paint it white very frequently in order to keep it white, because there are forces at work that will get the better of you. Not only will it turn black, but the forces of moisture and the other forces of nature will penetrate the white paint and get at the fiber of the wood, and decay will set in, and the next time you try to paint it you will find that there is nothing but punk to paint. Then you will remember the Red Queen in "Alice in Wonderland," or "Alice Through the Looking Glass"—I forget which, it has been so long since I read them—who takes Alice by the hand and they rush along at a great pace, and then when they stop Alice looks around and says, "But we are just where we were when we started." "Yes," says the Red Queen, "you have to run twice as fast as that to get anywhere else."

That is also true, gentlemen, of the world and of affairs. You have got to run fast merely to stay where you are, and in order to get anywhere, you have got to run twice as fast as that. That is what people do not realize. That is the mischief of these hopeless dams against the stream known as reactionaries and standpatters, and other words of obloquy. That is what is the matter with them; they are not even staying where they were. They are sinking further and further back in what will sometime comfortably close over their heads as the black waters of oblivion. I sometimes imagine that I see their heads going down, and I am not inclined even to throw them a life preserver. The sooner they disappear, the better. We need their places for people who are awake; and we particularly need now, gentlemen, men who will divest themselves of party passion and of personal preference and will try to think in the terms of America. If a man describes himself to me now in any other terms than those terms, I am not sure of him; and I love the fellows that come into my office sometimes and say, "Mr. President, I am an American." Their hearts are right, their instinct true, they are going in the right direction, and will take the right leadership if they believe that the leader is also a man who thinks first of America.

You will see, gentlemen, that I did not premedi-

tate these remarks, or they would have had some
connection with each other. They would have had
some plan. I have merely given myself the pleasure
of telling you what has really been in my heart, and
not only has been in my heart but is in my heart
every day of the week. If I did not go off at week
ends occasionally and throw off, as much as it is possible to throw off, this burden, I could not stand it.
This week I went down the Potomac and up the
James and subsituted history for politics, and there
was an infinite, sweet calm in some of those old places
that reminded me of the records that were made in
the days that are past; and I comforted myself with
the recollection that the men we remember are the
disinterested men who gave us the deeds that have
covered the name of America all over with the luster
of imperishable glory.

FIRST COMMITMENT TO THE IDEA OF A LEAGUE OF NATIONS

ADDRESS BEFORE THE LEAGUE TO ENFORCE PEACE, WASHINGTON, MAY 27, 1916. FROM OFFICIAL PUBLICATION IN MR. WILSON'S FILES.

WHEN the invitation to be here to-night came to me, I was glad to accept it—not because it offered me an opportunity to discuss the programme of the League—that you will, I am sure, not expect of me—but because the desire of the whole world now turns eagerly, more and more eagerly, towards the hope of peace, and there is just reason why we should 'take our part in counsel upon this great theme. It is right that I, as spokesman of our Government, should attempt to give expression to what I believe to be the thought and purpose of the people of the United States in this vital matter.

This great war that broke so suddenly upon the world two years ago, and which has swept within its flame so great a part of the civilized world, has affected us very profoundly, and we are not only at liberty, it is perhaps our duty, to speak very frankly of it and of the great interests of civilization which it affects.

With its causes and its objects we are not concerned. The obscure fountains from which its stupendous flood has burst forth we are not interested to search for or explore. But so great a flood, spread far and wide to every quarter of the globe, has of necessity engulfed many a fair province of right that lies very near to us. Our own rights as a Nation, the liberties, the privileges, and the property of our people have been profoundly affected. We are not mere disconnected lookers-on. The longer the war lasts, the more deeply do we become concerned that it should be brought to an end and the world be permitted to resume its normal life and course again. And when it does come to an end we shall be as much concerned as the nations at war to see peace assume an aspect of permanence, give promise of days from which the anxiety of uncertainty shall be lifted, bring some assurance that peace and war shall always hereafter be reckoned part of the common interest of mankind. We are participants, whether we would or not, in the life of the world. The interests of all nations are our own also. We are partners with the rest. What affects mankind is inevitably our affair as well as the affair of the nations of Europe and of Asia.

One observation on the causes of the present war we are at liberty to make, and to make it may throw some light forward upon the future, as well as backward upon the past. It is plain that this war could have come only as it did, suddenly and out of secret counsels, without warning to the world, without discussion, without any of the deliberate movements of counsel with which it would seem natural to approach so stupendous a contest. It is probable that if it had been foreseen just what would happen, just what alliances would be formed, just what forces arrayed against one another, those who brought the great contest on would have been glad to substitute conference for force. If we ourselves had been afforded some opportunity to apprise the belligerents of the attitude which it would be our duty to take, of the policies and practices against which we would feel bound to use all our moral and economic strength, and in certain circumstances even our physical strength also, our own contribution to the counsel which might have averted the struggle would have been considered worth weighing and regarding.

And the lesson which the shock of being taken by surprise in a matter so deeply vital to all the nations of the world has made poignantly clear is, that the peace of the world must henceforth depend upon a new and more wholesome diplomacy. Only when the great nations of the world have reached some sort of agreement as to what they hold to be fundamental to their common interest, and as to some feasible method of acting in concert when any nation or group of nations seeks to disturb those fundamental things, can we feel that civilization is at last in a way of justifying its existence and claiming to be finally established. It is clear that nations must in the future be governed by the same high code of honor that we demand of individuals.

We must, indeed, in the very same breath with which we avow this conviction admit that we have ourselves upon occasion in the past been offenders against the law of diplomacy which we thus forecast; but our conviction is not the less clear, but rather the more clear, on that account. If this war has accomplished nothing else for the benefit of the world, it has at least disclosed a great moral necessity and set forward the thinking of the statesmen of the world by a whole age. Repeated utterances of the leading statesmen of most of the great nations now engaged in war have made it plain that their thought has come to this, that the principle of public right must henceforth take precedence over the individual interests of particular nations, and that the nations of the world must in some way band themselves together to see that that right prevails as against any sort of selfish aggression; that henceforth alliance must not be set up against alliance, understanding against understanding, but that there must be a common agreement for a common object, and that at the heart of that common object must lie the inviolable rights of peoples and of mankind. The nations of the world have become each other's neighbors. It is to their interest that they should understand each other. In order that they may understand each other, it is imperative that they should agree to cooperate in a common cause, and that they should so act that the guiding principle of that common cause shall be even-handed and impartial justice.

This is undoubtedly the thought of America. This is what we ourselves will say when there comes proper occasion to say it. In the dealings of nations with one another arbitrary force must be rejected and we must move forward to the thought of the modern world, the thought of which peace is the very atmosphere. That thought constitutes a chief part of the passionate conviction of America. We believe these fundamental things: First, that every people has a right to choose the sovereignty under which they shall live. Like other nations, we have ourselves no doubt once and again offended against that principle when for a little while controlled by selfish passion as our franker historians have been honorable enough to admit; but it has become more and more our rule of life and action. Second, that the small states of the world have a right to enjoy the same respect for their sovereignty and for their territorial integrity that great and powerful nations expect and insist upon. And, third, that the world has a right to be free from every disturbance of its peace that has its origin in aggression and disregard of the rights of peoples and nations.

So sincerely do we believe in these things that I am sure that I speak the mind and wish of the people of America when I say that the United States is willing to become a partner in any feasible association of nations formed in order to realize these objects and make them secure against violation.

There is nothing that the United States wants for itself that any other nation has. We are willing, on the contrary, to limit ourselves along with them to a prescribed course of duty and respect for the rights of others which will check any selfish passion of our own, as it will check any aggressive impulse of theirs.

If it should ever be our privilege to suggest or initiate a movement for peace among the nations now at war, I am sure that the people of the United

States would wish their Government to move along
these lines: First, such a settlement with regard to
their own immediate interests as the belligerents may
agree upon. We have nothing material of any kind
to ask for ourselves, and are quite aware that we are
in no sense or degree parties to the present quarrel.
Our interest is only in peace and its future guarantees. Second, an universal association of the nations
to maintain the inviolate security of the highway of
the seas for the common and unhindered use of all
the nations of the world, and to prevent any war
begun either contrary to treaty covenants or without
warning and full submission of the causes to the
opinion of the world—a virtual guarantee of territorial integrity and political independence.

But I did not come here, let me repeat, to discuss
a programme. I came only to avow a creed and
give expression to the confidence I feel that the world
is even now upon the eve of a great consummation,
when some common force will be brought into existence which shall safeguard right as the first and most
fundamental interest of all peoples and all governments, when coercion shall be summoned not to the
service of political ambition or selfish hostility, but
to the service of a common order, a common justice,
and a common peace. God grant that the dawn of
that day of frank dealing and of settled peace, concord, and co-operation may be near at hand!

I AM ALL SORTS OF A DEMOCRAT

ADDRESS BEFORE THE ASSOCIATED ADVERTISING CLUBS, PHILADELPHIA, JUNE 29, 1916. FROM THE WHITE HOUSE FILES.

YOU will understand that I have not come here to make you an extended address. I do not need to explain to you the circumstances which have made it impossible that I should prepare an extended address, but I count myself very fortunate to be able to leave my duties at Washington long enough to face this interesting company of men who have the very fine conception that it is their duty to lift the standards and ideals of their profession.

I understand, gentlemen, that you have associated yourselves together in order to promote candor and truth in the advertisement of your business. I wish very much, gentlemen, that candor and truth might always be the standard of politics as well as the standard of business. I want to challenge your attention for a moment to this aspect of your activities. I do not see how a man can devote himself to candor and truth in the promotion of a particular business without studying the life of the great nation to whom he addresses his advertising. I do not see how a man can fail, having established the horizon of his business where the great hills of truth lie, to lift his eyes to the great multitude of laboring men and

striving women who constitute a great nation like
ours, and in the very act of addressing them get in
his own consciousness some part of the impulse of
their life. You cannot commend your business to
people that you do not understand, and you cannot
understand the people of the United States without
wishing to serve them.

So I come to you with this thought: America is
at a point, gentlemen, where it is more than ever
necessary that she should understand her own ideals
not only, but be ready to put them into action at any
cost. It is one thing to entertain fine principles and
another thing to make them work. It is one thing
to entertain them in the formulæ of words like the
splendid words which were uttered and gave distinction to this ancient and historic building behind me,
but it is another thing to do what those same men
did, make those words live in the action of their
lives. And America is summoned in each new generation to renew not only the pledges that those men
made, but to renew the example which they gave to
the world.

I am not interested, and I beg that you will believe
me when I say that I never have been interested, in
fighting for myself, but I am immensely interested
in fighting for the things that I believe in, and so
far as they are concerned I am a challenger to all
comers. It is important, therefore, since I am in
fighting mood, to let you know what are some of the
things that I do believe in.

In the first place, I believe, and I summon you to
show your belief in the same thing, that it is the

duty of every American in everything that he does,
in his business and out of it, to think first, not of
himself or of any interest which he may be called
upon to sacrifice, but of the country which we serve.
"America first" means nothing until you translate
it into what you do. So I believe most profoundly
in the duty of every American to exalt the national
consciousness by purifying his own motives and exhibiting his own devotion.

I believe, in the second place, that America, the
country that we put first in our thoughts, should be
ready in every point of policy and of action to vindicate at whatever cost the principles of liberty, of
justice, and of humanity to which we have been devoted from the first. [Cheers.] You cheer the sentiment, but do you realize what it means? It means
that you have not only got to be just to your fellow
men, but that as a nation you have got to be just
to other nations. It comes high. It is not an easy
thing to do. It is easy to think first of the material
interest of America, but it is not easy to think first
of what America, if she loves justice, ought to do
in the field of international affairs. I believe that
at whatever cost America should be just to other
peoples and treat other peoples as she demands that
they should treat her. She has a right to demand
that they treat her with justice and respect, and she
has a right to insist that they treat her in that fashion, but she cannot with dignity or with self-respect
insist upon that unless she is willing to act in the
same fashion toward them. That I am ready to fight
for at any cost to myself.

Then, in the third place, touching ourselves more intimately, my fellow citizens, this is what I believe: If I understand the life of America, the central principle of it is this, that no small body of persons, no matter how influential, shall be trusted to determine the policy and development of America. You know what you want in your business. You want a fair field and no favor. You want to be given the same opportunity that other men have, not only to make known what you have to sell, but to sell it under as favorable conditions as anybody else. The principle of the life of America is that she draws her vitality, not from small bodies of men who may wish to assume the responsibility of guiding and controlling her, but from the great body of thinking and toiling and planning men from whom she draws her energy and vitality as a nation. I believe, and this is the reason I am a Democrat, not merely with a big "D" but with a little "d"—I am all kinds of a democrat, so far as I can discover—but the root of the whole business is this, that I believe in the patriotism and energy and initiative of the average man. Some men say they believe in it, but when they act, they show that they do not. They show that they think the only advice that it is safe to take is their advice. [Voice in crowd: "Oh, you Teddy!"]

I was not referring to any individual, but I could give you an interesting and a very short list of a group of individuals who have that opinion, namely, that it is not safe for the United States to escape from their control. I feel perfectly safe in the hands

of the average body of my fellow citizens. You are
bound to feel safe in their hands. If they do not
believe in you, you cannot sell anything. If they
do not believe in you, you cannot conduct your business. Your vitality comes from them to you; it does
not go from you to them. The theory of government
which I decline to subscribe to is that the vitality
of the nation comes out of closeted councils where a
few men determine the policy of the country.

So, gentlemen, I feel at home in this company,
not because I advertise, but because I have got principles that I am perfectly willing to expose to the
public view, and because I want to express my sympathy with, not only, but my admiration for a body
of men who think it is worth while to get together
in order to tell the truth. The only thing that ever
set any man free, the only thing that ever set any
nation free, is the truth. A man that is afraid of
the truth is afraid of the law of life. A man that
does not love the truth is in the way of decay and
of failure, and I believe that if you will just let the
vitality that is in you and the enthusiasm that is in
you run beyond the confines of the businesses that
you may be interested in, you will presently feel that
infinite reward, as if the red blood of a whole nation
came surging back into your own veins.

Can you imagine, my fellow countrymen, a more
inspiring thing than to belong to a free nation and
make your way among men every one of whom has
the right and the opportunity to say what he thinks.
Criticism does not hurt anybody. I heard an old
politician once say to his son, "John, don't bother

your head about lies and slanders; they will take
care of themselves, but if you ever hear me denying
anything, you may make up your mind that it is
so.'' When you see a man wincing under criticism,
you may know that something hit him that was so.
And, therefore, when they are saying the things that
are not true, there is no credit in keeping your head
and not minding it. I have such an inveterate confidence in the ultimate triumph of the truth that I
feel, with old Doctor Oliver Wendell Holmes, that
the truth is no invalid, and you need not mind how
roughly you handle her. She has got a splendid constitution and she will survive every trial and every
labor.

I have come, therefore, as I have abundantly
shown you, not to make a formal speech—if I could
show you some of the things I have been obliged
to do before I came here, you would know that I
could not possibly make up a speech—but merely to
show my profound interest in a body of men who are
not only devoted to business but devoted to ideals.
Business is all right so long as it is not sordid, and
it cannot be sordid if it is shot through with ideals.
A man, no matter how humble his business, can hold
his head up among the princes of the world if, as
they ought to do, he will think of himself as the
servant of the people and not as their master, as
one who would serve and not as one who would
govern.

I congratulate you, my fellow citizens, upon the
ideals of a profession which can lower or exalt business, as you choose, and which you have chosen to

employ for its exaltation. I came away from Washington to look into your faces and get some of the enthusiasm which I always get when I come away from officialdom and touch hand to hand with great bodies of the free American people.

WE ARE SERVANTS OF THE RANK AND FILE OF THE PEOPLE

ADDRESS BEFORE THE PRESS CLUB, NEW YORK, JUNE 30, 1916. FROM THE "CONGRESSIONAL RECORD," 64TH CONGRESS, 1ST SESSION, VOL. 53, PP. 11925-11926.

I REALIZE that I have done a very impudent thing; I have come to address this thoughtful company of men without any preparation whatever. If I could have written as witty a speech as Mr. Pulitzer, I would have written it. If I could have written as clear an enunciation of the fundamental ideas of American patriotism as the mayor, I should have attempted it. If I could have been as appealing a person and of as feeling a heart as Mr. Cobb, I would have felt safe.

If I could have been as generous and interesting and genuine as Mr. Colby, I should have felt that I could let myself go without any preparation. But, gentlemen, as a matter of fact, I have been absorbed by the responsibilities which have been so frequently referred to here to-night, and that preoccupation has made it impossible for me to forecast even what you would like to hear me talk about.

There is something very oddly contradictory about the effect you men have on me. You are sometimes, particularly in your photographic enterprises, very brutal to me, and you sometimes invade my privacy, even to the extent of formulating my judgments

before they are formed, and yet I am tempted when
I stand face to face with you to take off all guard
and merely expose myself to you as the fallible
human being that I am.

Mr. Colby said something that was among the few
things I had forecast to say myself. He said that
there are some things which it is really useless to
debate, because they go as a matter of course.

Of course it is our duty to prepare this Nation
to take care of its honor and of its institutions. Why
debate any part of that, except the detail, except the
plan itself, which is always debatable?

Of course it is the duty of the Government, which
it will never overlook, to defend the territory and
people of this country. It goes without saying that
it is the duty of the administration to have constantly in mind with the utmost sensitiveness every
point of national honor.

But, gentlemen, after you have said and accepted
these obvious things your program of action is still
to be formed. When will you act and how will you
act?

The easiest thing is to strike. The brutal thing is
the impulsive thing. No man has to think before
he takes aggressive action; but before a man really
conserves the honor by realizing the ideals of the
Nation he has to think exactly what he will do and
how he will do it.

Do you think the glory of America would be enhanced by a war of conquest in Mexico? Do you
think that any act of violence by a powerful nation
like this against a weak and destructive neighbor

would reflect distinction upon the annals of the
United States?

Do you think that it is our duty to carry self-
defense to a point of dictation into the affairs of
another people? The ideals of America are written
plain upon every page of American history.

And I want you to know how fully I realize whose
servant I am. I do not own the Government of the
United States, even for the time being. I have no
right in the use of it to express my own passions.

I have no right to express my own ambitions for
the development of America if those ambitions are
not coincident with the ambitions of the Nation itself.

And I have constantly to remind myself that I am
not the servant of those who wish to enhance the value
of their Mexican investments, that I am the servant of
the rank and file of the people of the United States.

I get a great many letters, my fellow citizens, from
important and influential men in this country, but
I get a great many other letters. I get letters from
unknown men, from humble women, from people
whose names have never been heard and never will
be recorded, and there is but one prayer in all of
these letters: "Mr. President, do not allow anybody
to persuade you that the people of this country want
war with anybody."

I got off a train yesterday and as I was bidding
good-by to the engineer he said, in an undertone,
"Mr. President, keep out of Mexico." And if one
man has said that to me a thousand have said it
to me as I have moved about the country.

If I have opportunity to engage them further in

conversation, they say, "Of course, we know that
you can not govern the circumstances of the case
altogether, and it may be necessary; but for God's
sake do not do it unless it is necessary."

I am for the time being the spokesman of such
people, gentlemen. I have not read history without
observing that the greatest forces in the world and
the only permanent forces are the moral forces.

We have the evidence of a very competent witness,
namely, the first Napoleon, who said that as he
looked back in the last days of his life upon so much
as he knew of human history he had to record the
judgment that force had never accomplished anything that was permanent.

Force will not accomplish anything that is permanent, I venture to say, in the great struggle which
is going on on the other side of the sea. The permanent things will be accomplished afterwards, when
the opinion of mankind is brought to bear upon the
issues, and the only thing that will hold the world
steady is this same silent, insistent, all-powerful opinion of mankind.

Force can sometimes hold things steady until opinion has time to form, but no force that was ever ex-
erted, except in response to that opinion, was ever a
conquering and predominant force.

I think the sentence in American history that I
myself am proudest of is that in the introductory
sentences of the Declaration of Independence, where
the writers say that a due respect for the opinion
of mankind demands that they state the reasons for
what they are about to do.

I venture to say that a decent respect for the opinions of mankind demanded that those who started the present European war should have stated their reasons; but they did not pay any heed to the opinion of mankind, and the reckoning will come when the settlement comes.

So, gentlemen, I am willing, no matter what my personal fortunes may be, to play for the verdict of mankind. Personally, it will be a matter of indifference to me what the verdict on the 7th of November is, provided I feel any degree of confidence that when a later jury sits I shall get their judgment in my favor. Not my favor personally—what difference does that make?—but in my favor as an honest and conscientious spokesman of a great national convention.

There are some gentlemen who are under the delusion that the power of a nation comes from the top. It does not. It comes from the bottom.

Power and virtue of the tree does not come from the blossoms and fruit down into the roots, but it comes from the roots in the obscure passage of the earth where the power is derived, which displays itself in the blossoms and the fruit; and I know that among the silent, speechless masses of the American people is slowly coming up the sap of moral purpose and love of justice and reverence for humanity which constitutes the only virtue and distinction of the American people.

Look for your rulers of the future! Can you pick out the families that are to produce them? Can you pick out the localities that are going to produce them?

You have heard what has been said about Abraham Lincoln. It is singular how touching every reference to Abraham Lincoln is. It always makes you feel that you wish you had been there to help him in some fashion to fight the battles that he was fighting, sometimes almost alone.

Could you have predicted, if you had seen Abraham Lincoln's birth and boyhood, where that great ruling figure of the world was going to spring from?

I have presided over a university, but I never deceived myself by supposing that by university processes you were producing the ruling forces of the world.

I knew that all a university could do if it knew its business was to interpret the moral forces of the world and let the young man, who sat under its influence, know the very truth of truths about where it came from, and that no man could produce it unless he felt in his blood every corpuscle spring into delightful life with the mention of ideals which have lifted men slowly, oh, so slowly, up the arduous grades, which have resisted the progress since the world began.

So, gentlemen, I have not come here to-night to do anything but to remind that you do not constitute the United States; that I do not constitute the United States; that it is something bigger and greater and finer than any of us; that it was born in an ideal, and only by pursuing an ideal in the face of every adverse circumstance will it continue to deserve the beloved name which we love and for which we are ready to die, the name ''America.''

LOYALTY MEANS SELF-SACRIFICE

ADDRESS ON CITIZENSHIP DELIVERED AT WASHINGTON
BEFORE THE CONFERENCE ON AMERICANIZATION,
JULY 13, 1916. FROM THE WHITE HOUSE FILES.

I HAVE come here for the simple purpose of expressing my very deep interest in what these conferences are intended to attain. It is not fair to the great multitudes of hopeful men and women who press into this country from other countries that we should leave them without that friendly and intimate instruction which will enable them very soon after they come to find out what America is like at heart and what America is intended for among the nations of the world.

I believe that the chief school that these people must attend after they get here is the school which all of us attend, which is furnished by the life of the communities in which we live and the Nation to which we belong. It has been a very touching thought to me sometimes to think of the hopes which have drawn these people to America. I have no doubt that many a simple soul has been thrilled by that great statue standing in the harbor of New York and seeming to lift the light of liberty for the guidance of the feet of men; and I can imagine that they have expected here something ideal in the treatment that they will receive, something ideal in the laws which they would have to live under, and it has caused me many a time to turn upon myself the eye of examination to see whether there burned in me the true light of the American spirit which they expected to find here. It is easy, my fellow citizens, to communicate physical lessons, but it is very difficult to communicate spiritual lessons. America was intended to be a spirit among the nations of the world, and it is the purpose of conferences like this to find out the best way to introduce the newcomers to this spirit, and by that very interest in them to enhance and purify in ourselves the thing that ought to make America great and not only ought to make her great, but ought to make her exhibit a spirit unlike any other nation in the world.

I have never been among those who felt comfortable in boasting of the superiority of America over other countries. The way to cure yourself of that is to travel in other countries and find out how much of nobility and character and fine enterprise there is everywhere in the world. The most that America can hope to do is to show, it may be, the finest example, not the only example, of the things that ought to benefit and promote the progress of the world.

So my interest in this movement is as much an interest in ourselves as in those whom we are trying to Americanize, because if we are genuine Americans they cannot avoid the infection; whereas, if we are not genuine Americans, there will be nothing to infect them with, and no amount of teaching, no amount of exposition of the Constitution—which I find very few persons understand—no amount of dwelling upon the idea of liberty and of justice will

accomplish the object we have in view, unless we ourselves illustrate the idea of justice and of liberty.
My interest in this movement is, therefore, a two-
fold interest. I believe it will assist us to become
self-conscious in respect of the fundamental ideas of
American life.

When you ask a man to be loyal to a government,
if he comes from some foreign countries, his idea is
that he is expected to be loyal to a certain set of
persons like a ruler or a body set in authority over
him, but that is not the American idea. Our idea
is that he is to be loyal to certain objects in life,
and that the only reason he has a President and a
Congress and a Governor and a State Legislature
and courts is that the community shall have instrumentalities by which to promote those objects. It is
a coöperative organization expressing itself in this
Constitution, expressing itself in these laws, intending to express itself in the exposition of those laws
by the courts; and the idea of America is not so much
that men are to be restrained and punished by the
law as instructed and guided by the law. That is
the reason so many hopeful reforms come to grief.
A law cannot work until it expresses the spirit of
the community for which it is enacted, and if you
try to enact into law what expresses only the spirit
of a small coterie or of a small minority, you know,
or at any rate you ought to know, beforehand that
it is not going to work.

The object of the law is that there, written upon
these pages, the citizen should read the record of the
experience of this state and Nation; what they have

concluded it is necessary for them to do because of the life they have lived and the things that they have discovered to be elements in that life.

So that we ought to be careful to maintain a government at which the immigrant can look with the closest scrutiny and to which he should be at liberty to address this question: "You declare this to be a land of liberty and of equality and of justice; have you made it so by your law?" We ought to be able in our schools, in our night schools and in every other method of instructing these people, to show them that that has been our endeavor. We cannot conceal from them long the fact that we are just as human as any other nation, that we are just as selfish, that there are just as many mean people amongst us as anywhere else, that there are just as many people here who want to take advantage of other people as you can find in other countries, just as many cruel people, just as many people heartless when it comes to maintaining and promoting their own interest; but you can show that our object is to get these people in harness and see to it that they do not do any damage and are not allowed to indulge the passions which would bring injustice and calamity at last upon a Nation whose object is spiritual and not material.

America has built up a great body of wealth. America has become, from the physical point of view, one of the most powerful nations in the world, a nation which if it took the pains to do so, could build that power up into one of the most formidable instruments in the world, one of the most formidable instruments of force, but which has no other idea than to use its force for ideal objects and not for self-aggrandizement.

We have been disturbed recently, my fellow citizens, by certain symptoms which have showed themselves in our body politic. Certain men—I have never believed a great number—born in other lands, have in recent months thought more of those lands than they have of the honor and interest of the government under which they are now living. They have even gone so far as to draw apart in spirit and in organization from the rest of us to accomplish some special object of their own. I am not here going to utter any criticism of these people, but I want to say this, that such a thing as that is absolutely incompatible with the fundamental idea of loyalty, and that loyalty is not a self-pleasing virtue. I am not bound to be loyal to the United States to please myself. I am bound to be loyal to the United States because I live under its laws and am its citizen, and whether it hurts me or whether it benefits me, I am obliged to be loyal. Loyalty means nothing unless it has at its heart the absolute principle of self-sacrifice. Loyalty means that you ought to be ready to sacrifice every interest that you have, and your life itself, if your country calls upon you to do so, and that is the sort of loyalty which ought to be inculcated into these newcomers, that they are not to be loyal only so long as they are pleased, but that, having once entered into this sacred relationship, they are bound to be loyal whether they are pleased or not; and that loyalty which is merely self-pleasing is only self-indulgence and selfishness. No man has ever risen to the real stature of spiritual manhood until he has found that it is finer to serve somebody else than it is to serve himself.

These are the conceptions which we ought to teach the newcomers into our midst, and we ought to realize that the life of every one of us is part of the schooling, and that we cannot preach loyalty unless we set the example, that we cannot profess things with any influence upon others unless we practice them also. This process of Americanization is going to be a process of self-examination, a process of purification, a process of rededication to the things which America represents and is proud to represent. And it takes a great deal more courage and steadfastness, my fellow citizens, to represent ideal things than to represent anything else.

It is easy to lose your temper, and hard to keep it. It is easy to strike and sometimes very difficult to refrain from striking and I think you will agree with me that we are most justified in being proud of doing the things that are hard to do and not the things that are easy. You do not settle things quickly by taking what seems to be the quickest way to settle them. You may make the complication just that much the more profound and inextricable, and, therefore, what I believe America should exalt above everything else is the sovereignty of thoughtfulness and sympathy and vision as against the grosser impulses of mankind. No nation can live without vision, and no vision will exalt a nation except the vision of real liberty and real justice and purity of conduct.

ABRAHAM LINCOLN

ACCEPTANCE OF THE LINCOLN MEMORIAL, HODGENVILLE, KENTUCKY. SEPTEMBER 4, 1916. FROM THE "CONGRESSIONAL RECORD," 64TH CONGRESS, 1ST SESSION. VOL. 53, APPENDIX, P. 2160.

NO more significant memorial could have been presented to the nation than this. It expresses so much of what is singular and noteworthy in the history of the country; it suggests so many of the things that we prize most highly in our life and in our system of government. How eloquent this little house within this shrine is of the vigor of democracy! There is nowhere in the land any home so remote, so humble, that it may not contain the power of mind and heart and conscience to which nations yield and history submits its processes. Nature pays no tribute to aristocracy, subscribes to no creed of caste, renders fealty to no monarch or master of any name or kind. Genius is no snob. It does not run after titles or seek by preference the high circles of society. It affects humble company as well as great. It pays no special tribute to universities or learned societies or conventional standards of greatness, but serenely chooses its own comrades, its own haunts, its own cradle even, and its own life of adventure and of training. Here is proof of it. This little hut was the cradle of one of the great sons of men, a man

of singular, delightful, vital genius who presently
emerged upon the great stage of the nation's history,
gaunt, shy, ungainly, but dominant and majestic, a
natural ruler of men, himself inevitably the central
figure of the great plot. No man can explain this,
but every man can see how it demonstrates the vigor
of democracy, where every door is open, in every
hamlet and countryside, in city and wilderness alike,
for the ruler to emerge when he will and claim his
leadership in the free life. Such are the authentic
proofs of the validity and vitality of democracy.

Here, no less, hides the mystery of democracy.
Who shall guess this secret of nature and providence
and a free polity? Whatever the vigor and vitality
of the stock from which he sprang, its mere vigor
and soundness do not explain where this man got
his great heart that seemed to comprehend all mankind in its catholic and benignant sympathy, the
mind that sat enthroned behind those brooding,
melancholy eyes, whose vision swept many an horizon
which those about him dreamed not of, that mind
that comprehended what it had never seen, and understood the language of affairs with the ready ease
of one to the manner born—or that nature which
seemed in its varied richness to be the familiar of
men of every way of life. This is the sacred mystery of democracy, that its richest fruits spring up
out of soils which no man has prepared and in circumstances amidst which they are the least expected.
This is a place alike of mystery and of reassurance.

It is likely that in a society ordered otherwise than
our own Lincoln could not have found himself or

the path of fame and power upon which he walked serenely to his death. In this place it is right that we should remind ourselves of the solid and striking facts upon which our faith in democracy is founded. Many another man besides Lincoln has served the nation in its highest places of counsel and of action whose origins were as humble as his. Though the greatest example of the universal energy, richness, stimulation, and force of democracy, he is only one example among many. The permeating and all-pervasive virtue of the freedom which challenges us in America to make the most of every gift and power we possess every page of our history serves to emphasize and illustrate. Standing here in this place, it seems almost the whole of the stirring story.

Here Lincoln had his beginnings. Here the end and consummation of that great life seem remote and a bit incredible. And yet there was no break anywhere between beginning and end, no lack of natural sequence anywhere. Nothing really incredible happened. Lincoln was unaffectedly as much at home in the White House as he was here. Do you share with me the feeling, I wonder, that he was permanently at home nowhere? It seems to me that in the case of a man—I would rather say of a spirit—like Lincoln the question *where* he was is of little significance, that it is always *what* he was that really arrests our thought and takes hold of our imagination. It is the spirit always that is sovereign. Lincoln, like the rest of us, was put through the discipline of the world—a very rough and exacting discipline for him, an indispensable discipline for every

man who would know what he is about in the midst
of the world's affairs; but his spirit got only its
schooling there. It did not derive its character or
its vision from the experiences which brought it to
its full revelation. The test of every American must
always be, not where he is, but what he is. That, also,
is of the essence of democracy, and is the moral of
which this place is most gravely expressive.

We would like to think of men like Lincoln and
Washington as typical Americans, but no man can
be typical who is so unusual as these great men were.
It was typical of American life that it should produce such men with supreme indifference as to the
manner in which it produced them, and as readily
here in this hut as amidst the little circle of cultivated
gentlemen to whom Virginia owed so much in leadership and example. And Lincoln and Washington
were typical Americans in the use they made of their
genius. But there will be few such men at best, and
we will not look into the mystery of how and why
they come. We will only keep the door open for
them always, and a hearty welcome— after we have
recognized them.

I have read many biographies of Lincoln; I have
sought out with the greatest interest the many intimate stories that are told of him, the narratives of
nearby friends, the sketches at close quarters, in
which those who had the privilege of being associated
with him have tried to depict for us the very man
himself "in his habit as he lived;" but I have nowhere found a real intimate of Lincoln's. I nowhere
get the impression in any narrative or reminiscence

that the writer had in fact penetrated to the heart
of his mystery, or that any man could penetrate to
the heart of it. That brooding spirit had no real
familiars. I get the impression that it never spoke
out in complete self-revelation, and that it could not
reveal itself completely to anyone. It was a very
lonely spirit that looked out from underneath those
shaggy brows and comprehended men without fully
communing with them, as if, in spite of all its genial
efforts at comradeship, it dwelt apart, saw its visions
of duty where no man looked on. There is a very
holy and very terrible isolation for the conscience
of every man who seeks to read the destiny in affairs
for others as well as for himself, for a nation as well
as for individuals. That privacy no man can intrude
upon. That lonely search of the spirit for the right
perhaps no man can assist. This strange child of
the cabin kept company with invisible things, was
born into no intimacy but that of its own silently as-
sembling and deploying thoughts.

I have come here to-day, not to utter a eulogy on
Lincoln; he stands in need of none, but to endeavor
to interpret the meaning of this gift to the nation
of the place of his birth and origin. Is not this an
altar upon which we may forever keep alive the vestal
fire of democracy as upon a shrine at which some of
the deepest and most sacred hopes of mankind may
from age to age be rekindled? For these hopes must
constantly be rekindled, and only those who live can
rekindle them. The only stuff that can retain the
life-giving heat is the stuff of living hearts. And
the hopes of mankind cannot be kept alive by words

merely, by constitutions and doctrines of right and
codes of liberty. The object of democracy is to trans-
mute these into the life and action of society, the
self-denial and self-sacrifice of heroic men and women
willing to make their lives an embodiment of right
and service and enlightened purpose. The commands
of democracy are as imperative as its privileges and
opportunities are wide and generous. Its compulsion
is upon us. It will be great and lift a great light
for the guidance of the nations only if we are great
and carry that light high for the guidance of our own
feet. We are not worthy to stand here unless we ourselves be in deed and in truth real democrats and
servants of mankind, ready to give our very lives for
the freedom and justice and spiritual exaltation of
the great Nation which shelters and nurtures us.

LABOR AND CAPITAL

ADDRESS DELIVERED AT SHADOW LAWN, SEPTEMBER 23, 1916. FROM THE NEW YORK "TIMES," SEPTEMBER 24, 1916.

I NEED not tell you what a sense of gratification it gives me that you should come bearing this generous message which I have just heard from your chairman. There is a sense in which the business men of America represent America, because America has devoted herself time out of mind to the arts and achievements of peace, and business is the organization of the energies of peace.

No one who looks about upon the field of American business at the present moment can fail to realize that a new breath and spirit have come into the business of America. There have been times when it looked as if America were interested only in herself, but in these recent years American business men have lifted their eyes to more distant horizons and have seen how the markets of the world were waiting for their service, and as they have sought and obtained entrance into these markets a new vision has come to them of what the development of the resources of America means; of what the organization of American efficiency means; of why it was that American merchants and American manufacturers and American miners, and all the multitude of men who have developed the peaceful industries of America were planted under this free polity in order that they might look out upon the service of mankind and perform it.

There never was a time when the pulse of energy and success beat so strongly in the veins of American business as it beats to-day. And yet I hope that all business men in America realize that we are only at the beginning of a new era. America has not played its proportionate part in the development of the trade of the world. I mean that it has not played a part proportionate to the gifts of Americans and the resources of America, and that in the times to come, partly because of the unhappy circumstances of recent years, but chiefly because America is now about to release her energies, the scope of American business will be what men have hitherto not dreamed of, if American men know how to take advantage of the opportunity.

The problems that are before American business are world problems rather than American, domestic problems. America must understand the world in order to subject it to its peaceful service. And yet, when we look upon the field of American business there are some things that disturb us. Some men think that the way to advance American business is to walk backward and to attempt again the provincial policies which have characterized an age when we shut our doors against the influences of the world. But the chief cloud that is upon the domestic horizon is the unsatisfactory relations of capital and labor. There is only one way, gentlemen, in which the relations of capital and labor can be rendered satisfactory. That is by, in the first place, regarding labor as a human relationship of men with men; and, in the second place, to regard labor as part of the general partnership of energy which is going to make for the success of business men and business enterprises in this country. So long as labor and capital stand antagonistic, the interests of both are injured and the prosperity of America is held back from the triumphs which are legitimately its own.

You know that we have been a legalistic people. I say with all due respect to some men for whom I have a high esteem that we have been too much under the guidance of the lawyers, and that the lawyer has always regarded the relations between the employer and the employee as merely a contractual relationship, whereas it is, while based upon contract, very much more than contractual relationship. It is a relationship between one set of men and another set of men with hearts under their jackets and with interests that they ought to serve in common and with persons whom they love and must support on the one side and on the other. Labor is not a commodity. It is a form of co-operation, and if I can make a man believe in me, know that I am just, know that I want to share the profits of success with him, I can get ten times as much out of him as if he thought I were his antagonist. And his labor is cheap at any price. That is the human side of it, and the human side extends to this conception, that that laboring man is a partner of his employer. If he is a mere tool of his employer, he is only as serviceable as the tool.

His enthusiasm does not go into it. He does not plan how the work shall be better done. He does not look upon the aspect of the business or enterprise as a whole and wish to co-operate the advantage of his brain and his invention to the success of it as a whole. Human relationships, my fellow-citizens, are governed by the heart, and if the heart is not in it nothing is in it.

I have recently been through an experience which distressed me. I tried to accommodate a difference between some of the employes of the American railways and the executives of the American railways, and the distressing thing I discovered was that on the one hand there was unlimited suspicion and distrust of the other side, and that that suspicion and distrust was returned by the other side in full measure. The executives did not believe in the sincerity of the men, and the men did not believe in the sincerity and fairness of the executives, and while arbitration was being discussed, I had this sad thought: Arbitration is a word associated with the dealings of hostile interests. It is an alternative of war. There ought to be no such thing as the contemplation of hostility between men whose interests are the same and who should co-operate together.

And, therefore, it came upon me with a force that it had never had before that the real problem of capital and labor was to bring the two sides to understand and believe in one another; that the problem of the next generation, if America were really to release her energy, was to be this real, genuine, fundamental reconciliation between capital and

labor. I did not realize until I held those conferences just how far apart they were in that particular
and indispensable part of our national life, the transportation of the country, and when I did realize it,
I saw that there was a great task that was worth
any man's while ahead of us, to bring the minds of
the country together, to see that men understood one
another, to see that they had some assurance that
they were speaking the truth to one another. I never
had franker conferences in my life than I had with
the representatives of the two sides.

You know that when the public began to notice
this controversy it had already been going on for
some time. I had been watching it with great anxiety, and when it became evident that an accommodation was not going to be reached I thought it my
duty to try my hand at the difficult task of accommodation, because I knew how much was involved,
not only in the immediate effects of a great strike
such as was threatened, but also in the ultimate effects, the soreness left, the resentment that would
remain, the feelings of hostility that would be accen-
tuated; and so I asked the privilege of consulting
with them. Before I consulted with them, I, of
course, made myself acquainted with the points at
controversy, and I learned that they were very simple indeed; that the men demanded an eight-hour
day, and that, in order to make the eight-hour day
work they demanded that the railroads pay them
one-half more for overtime than they paid them for
the time in the regular day, the men alleging that
that was the only way in which they could obtain a

genuine eight-hour day, by making the railroads pay more for the time beyond the eight hours than they paid for the time within the eight hours. I saw at once that there was one part of this that was arbitrable, but that in my opinion there was another part that was not arbitrable. I do not regard the question of the principle of the eight-hour day as arbitrable.

The first thing I told both sides before I requested their opinion was that I stood for the eight-hour day. I received no suggestion of any kind from either side as to what the basis of settlement was to be, except that the railroad executives did suggest that Congress give them some sort of assurance that if the eight-hour day went into operation, they would get increased rates for the carriage of their freight. I pointed out to them that it was impossible to tell whether they would need increased rates for the carriage of their freights. We believe in the eight-hour day because a man does better work within eight hours than he does within a more extended day, and that the whole theory of it, a theory which is sustained now by abundant experience, is that his efficiency is increased, his spirit in his work is improved, and the whole moral and physical vigor of the man is added to. This is no longer conjectural. Where it has been tried, it has been demonstrated. The judgment of society, the vote of every legislature in America that has voted upon it is a verdict in favor of the eight-hour day. And, therefore, I said to these gentlemen on both sides at the very beginning, "The eight-hour day ought to be conceded." But they said, "It will cost us an immense sum of money."

"How do you know how much it will cost you?" You remember there was a case decided by the Supreme Court of the United States. It was known as the "Eighty-Cent Gas Case," where, by legislation in the State of New York, 80 cents was established as the charge for the unit of the supply of gas, and the law was contested upon the ground that it was confiscatory, and therefore unconstitutional. And when the appeal reached the Supreme Court of the United States it said: "Nobody can tell until you try to manufacture gas at 80 cents whether it is confiscatory or not. Go ahead and manufacture gas and sell it for 80 cents, and then, if it proves impossible to conduct your business upon that charge, come back and discuss with us the confiscatory character of this act." And it may be remarked in passing that the company never went back to discuss it.

I said to the railroad executives, "You are asking that the results of the eight-hour day be predicted and the prediction be arbitrated. You are asking for the arbitration of a conjecture, of an opinion, of a forecast of the figures of experts based upon an entirely different experience, and if you were to ask me personally to arbitrate such a question, I would say I am not competent to arbitrate it. The reasonable thing to do is to grant the eight-hour day, not because the men demand it, but because it is right, and let me get authority from Congress to appoint a commission of as impartial nature as I can choose to observe the results and report upon the results in order that justice may in the event be done the railroads in respect of the cost of the experiment.'' That was the proposal which they rejected and which Congress put into law, a proposal which I made to them before I conferred with it which I urged upon them at every conference, and which, when the one side rejected and the other side accepted, I went to Congress and asked Congress to enact. I did not ask neither side whether it suited them, and I requested my friends in Congress not to ask either side whether it suited them. I learned before the controversy began, so far as I was concerned in it, that the whole temper of the legislative body of the United States was in favor of the eight-hour day.

When I carried it to Congress some very interesting things happened. In the House of Representatives the plan was passed, was sanctioned by a vote which included, I am told, about seventy Republicans, as against fifty-four Republicans, and in the Senate, I am informed that the Republican members of the Senate held a conference in which they determined to put no obstacle in the way of the passage of the bill. Now this was because the proposal was reasonable and was based upon right. But, ladies and gentlemen, that is not the end of the story. This thing ought to have been done, and it had to be done at the time that it was done, so as to bring about a reasonable trial of the eight-hour day and a careful examination of the results of the eight-hour day. But that does not finish the matter. Let me call your attention to what I believe we ought all to be thinking about so as to set the stage for this and all similar cases.

There are some things in which society is so profoundly interested that its interests take precedence of the interests of any group of men whatever. One of these things is the supply of the absolute necessaries of life. It would be intolerable if at any time any group of men by any process should be suffered to cut society off from the necessary supplies which sustain life. But those supplies are of no use unless they can be distributed, and in the matter of the distribution of goods, particularly of the goods that sustain life and industry, the interest of society is paramount to every other interest; and the difficulty about all situations like that which we have passed through is this—that the main partner is left out of the reckoning. These men were dealing with one another as if the only thing to settle was between themselves, whereas, the real thing to settle was what rights had the hundred million people of the United States. The business of government is to see that no other organization is as strong as itself; to see that no body or group of men, no matter what their private interest is, may come into competition with the authority of society, and the problem which Congress, because of the lateness of the session, has for a few months postponed, is this problem: By what means are we going to oblige persons who come to a controversy like this to admit the public into the partnership by which the thing is discussed and decided? That is not an easy problem. A great many different methods have been proposed, and one of the reasons why Congress thought it necessary to postpone the decision for a few months was that there were so many honest differences of opinion, not as to the object, but as to the method.

I want to suggest to you a method of testing your fellow-men, as to whether they know what they are talking about or not. It is not necessary for a man to come and argue with me an obvious moral principle, but I am very much interested when he comes and argues with me how he is going to make it work. And when men say, "We must not permit any organization to neglect the interests of society," I say "Amen!" but what I want to sit down and discuss with you is, how are we going to prevent it?

The only thing worth talking about in politics or any other sphere is the constructive idea. "How are you going to do it?" We all know, or, at any rate, we pretend to know, what we ought to do, but we do not all know how to do it, and the very difficult question which the American people is now face to face with, and which they are going to settle, is this: "How are we going to organize our participation as a partner in the settlement of disputes between capital and labor which interrupt the life of the nation?" Invite all subscribers to suggest a method!

The question is apt to be obscured in some quarters, as if we were saying that it was the right of the Government or of organized society, which is another term for the same thing, to say to a man: "You must work whether you want to or not." America is never going to say to any individual, "You must work whether you want to or not," but it is privileged to say to an organization of persons: "You must not interrupt the national life without consultings us." It is not a question of obliging individuals; it is a question of enforcing a partnership and seeing to it that no organization is stronger than that organization which we all belong to and support and call and love by the name of our own government.

So I laid a program before Congress by which, at any rate, a beginning might be made in that direction, and that program is going to be proceeded with. It is no fun in talking unless you can expect to do something. The only zest that ever comes into affairs for a man with red blood in his veins is the zest that comes when he is put to it to think out a difficult thing and do it; and I for my part congratulate the business men of America that some of their difficulties have been removed by legislation, that they have been fortified against certain forms of control which must have been intolerable to them, and that they have had their real commercial strength put at their service by such acts as the Federal Reserve act, for example, and that now, if they think they can conquer the world, it is up to them to do it; and that nobody is going to assist them, because it is a thing in which they cannot be assisted by anything but their own brain. We are now out in the open, competitors for the confidence of the world, and there is only one way to get it and that is to earn it.

I cannot imagine anything more inspiring than to be put on your mettle after legislation has taken the shackles off you and apprised you that you are no

man's servant. Reaction in this matter would shut
us up like a province. To turn back upon any portion of the road we have traveled would be craven.
To pretend that we are able to compete with the
world and then cringe at the opportunity would not
be worthy of any of the traditions of America, and
so for my part I am particularly proud to be sup-
ported by the business opinion of American men because I know myself to have a very great enthusiasm
for the triumphant development of American enterprise throughout the world.

THE MEXICAN PROBLEM AGAIN:
AN INTERVIEW

FROM THE "LADIES' HOME JOURNAL," OCTOBER, 1916.

LARGE questions are difficult to state in brief compass, but they can be intelligently comprehended only when fully stated, and must to all candid persons seem worthy of the pains. The Mexican question has never anywhere been fully stated, so far as I know, and yet it is one which is in need of all the light that can be thrown upon it, and can be intelligently discussed only by those who clearly see all that is involved.

In the first place, it is not a question which can be treated by itself as only a matter between Mexico and the United States. It is a part, a very intimate part, of the Pan-American question. The two Americas can be knitted together only by process of peace, friendship, helpfulness, and good will, and the nation which must of necessity take the initiative in proving the possibility of these processes is the United States.

A discussion of the Pan-American question must always begin with the Monroe Doctrine, and very little light will be thrown upon it unless we consider the Monroe Doctrine from the point of view of Latin-America rather than from the point of view of the United States.

In adopting the Monroe Doctrine the United States assumed the part of Big Brother to the rest of America. The primary purpose of the policy was to prevent the extension to the American Hemisphere of European influences, which seemed likely to involve South America and eventually ourselves as well in the net of European intrigue and reaction which was in that day being spread with so wide a sweep of purpose. But it was not adopted at the request of the American Republics. While it no doubt made them measurably free from the fear of European aggression or intervention in their affairs, it neither gave nor implied any guarantee on the part of the United States that we would use our power for their benefit and not for our own aggrandizement and advantage.

As the power of the United States has increased, the uneasiness of the Latin-American republics has increased with regard to the use we might make of that power in dealing with them.

Unfortunately we gave one very disquieting example of what we might do when we went to war with Mexico in Mr. Polk's time and got out of that war a great addition to our national territory.

The suspicion of our southern neighbors, their uneasiness as to our growing power, their jealousy that we should assume to play Big Brother to them without their invitation to do so, has constantly stood in the way of the amicable and happy relations we wished to establish with them. Only in very recent years have they extended their hands to us with anything like cordiality, and it is not likely that we shall ever have their entire confidence until we have succeeded in giving them satisfactory and conclusive proofs of our own friendly and unselfish purpose.

What is needed for the firm establishment of their faith in us is that we should give guaranties of some sort, in conduct as well as in promise, that we will as scrupulously respect their territorial integrity and their political sovereignty as we insist that European nations should respect them.

If we should intervene in Mexico, we should undoubtedly revive the gravest suspicions throughout all the states of America. By intervention I mean the use of the power of the United States to establish internal order there without the invitation of Mexico and determine the character and method of her political institutions. We have professed to believe that every nation, every people, has the right to order its own institutions as it will, and we must live up to that profession in our actions in absolute good faith.

Moreover, "order" has been purchased in Mexico at a terrible cost when it has been obtained by foreign assistance. The foreign assistance has generally come in the form of financial aid. The financial aid has almost invariably been conditioned upon "concessions" which have put the greater part of the resources of the country which have as yet been developed in the hands of foreign capitalists, and by the same token under the "protection" of foreign governments.

Those who have successfully maintained stable order in Mexico by such means have, like Diaz, found that they were the servants, not of Mexico, but of foreign *concessionaires*.

The economic development of Mexico has so far
been accomplished by such "concessions" and by the
exploitation of the fertile lands of the republic by
a very small number of owners who have accumulated under one title hundreds of thousands of acres,
swept within one ownership the greater part of the
states, and reduced the population of the country to
a sort of peonage.

Mexico is one of the treasure houses of the world.
It is exceedingly to be desired by those who wish to
amass fortunes. Its resources are indeed serviceable
to the whole world and are needed by the industries
of the whole world. No enterprising capitalist can
look upon her without coveting her. The foreign
diplomacy with which she has become bitterly familiar is the "dollar diplomacy," which has almost
invariably obliged her to give precedence to foreign
interests over her own. What she needs more than
anything else is financial support which will not
involve the sale of her liberties and the enslavement
of her people.

Property owned by foreigners, enterprises conducted by foreigners, will never be safe in Mexico
so long as their existence and the methods of their use
and conduct excite the suspicion and, upon occasion,
the hatred of the people of the country itself.

I would not be understood as saying that all or
even the majority of the foreigners who have owned
property in Mexico or who have developed her extraordinary resources have acted in a way to excite
the jealousy or deserve the dislike of the people of
the country. It is fortunately true that there have

been a great many who acted with the same honor
and public spirit there that characterized them at
home, and whose wish it has never been to exploit the
country to its own hurt and detriment.

I am speaking of a system and not uttering an indictment. The system by which Mexico has been
financially assisted has in the past generally bound
her hand and foot and left her in effect without a
free government. It has almost in every instance
deprived her people of the part they were entitled
to play in the determination of their own destiny and
development.

This is what every leader in Mexico has to fear,
and the history of Mexico's dealings with the United
States cannot be said to be reassuring.

It goes without saying that the United States must
do as she is doing—she must insist upon the safety
of her borders; she must, so fast as order is worked
out of chaos, use every instrumentality she can in
friendship employ to protect the lives and the property of her citizens in Mexico.

But she can establish permanent peace on her borders only by a resolute and consistent adoption in
action of the principles which underlie her own life.
She must respect the liberties and self-government of
Mexicans as she would respect her own. She has
professed to be the champion of the rights of small
and helpless states, and she must make the profession
good in what she does. She has professed to be the
friend of Mexico, and she must prove it by seeing
to it that every step she takes is a step of friendship
and helpfulness.

Our own principles and the peace of the world are conditioned upon the exemplification of those professions in action by ourselves and by all the nations of the world, and our dealings with Mexico afford us an opportunity to show the way.

Mexico must no doubt struggle through long processes of blood and terror before she finds herself and returns to the paths of peace and order; but other nations, older in political experience than she, have staggered and struggled through these dark ways for years together to find themselves at last, to come out into the light, to know the price of liberty, to realize the compulsion of peace, and the orderly processes of law.

It is painful to observe how few of the suggestions as to what the United States ought to do with regard to Mexico are based upon sympathy with the Mexican people or any effort even to understand what they need and desire. I can say with knowledge that most of the suggestions of action come from those who wish to possess her, who wish to use her, who regard her people with condescension and a touch of contempt, who believe that they are fit only to serve and not fit for liberty of any sort. Such men cannot and will not determine the policy of the United States. They are not of the true American breed or motive.

America will honor herself and prove the validity of her own principles by treating Mexico as she would wish Mexico to treat her.

ESSENTIAL TERMS OF PEACE IN EUROPE

ADDRESS TO THE UNITED STATES SENATE, JANUARY 22, 1917. FROM SENATE DOCUMENT 685, 64TH CONGRESS, 2D SESSION.

GENTLEMEN OF THE SENATE:

On the eighteenth of December last I addressed an identic note to the governments of the nations now at war requesting them to state, more definitely than they had yet been stated by either group of belligerents, the terms upon which they would deem it possible to make peace. I spoke on behalf of humanity and of the rights of all neutral nations like our own, many of whose most vital interests the war puts in constant jeopardy. The Central Powers united in a reply which stated merely that they were ready to meet their antagonists in conference to discuss terms of peace. The Entente Powers have replied much more definitely and have stated, in general terms, indeed, but with sufficient definiteness to imply details, the arrangements, guarantees, and acts of reparation which they deem to be the indispensable conditions of a satisfactory settlement. We are that much nearer a definite discussion of the peace which shall end the present war. We are that much nearer the discussion of the international concert which must thereafter hold the world at peace. In every discussion of the peace that must end this war it is taken for granted that

that peace must be followed by some definite concert of power which will make it virtually impossible that any such catastrophe should ever overwhelm us again. Every lover of mankind, every sane and thoughtful man must take that for granted.

I have sought this opportunity to address you because I thought that I owed it to you, as the counsel associated with me in the final determination of our international obligations, to disclose to you without reserve the thought and purpose that have been taking form in my mind in regard to the duty of our Government in the days to come when it will be necessary to lay afresh and upon a new plan the foundations of peace among the nations.

It is inconceivable that the people of the United States should play no part in that great enterprise. To take part in such a service will be the opportunity for which they have sought to prepare themselves by the very principles and purposes of their polity and the approved practices of their Government ever since the days when they set up a new nation in the high and honorable hope that it might in all that it was and did show mankind the way to liberty. They cannot in honor withhold the service to which they are now about to be challenged. They do not wish to withhold it. But they owe it to themselves and to the other nations of the world to state the conditions under which they will feel free to render it.

That service is nothing less than this, to add their authority and their power to the authority and force of other nations to guarantee peace and justice throughout the world. Such a settlement cannot now be long postponed. It is right that before it comes this Government should frankly formulate the conditions upon which it would feel justified in asking our people to approve its formal and solemn adherence to a League for Peace. I am here to attempt to state those conditions.

The present war must first be ended; but we owe it to candor and to a just regard for the opinion of mankind to say that, so far as our participation in guarantees of future peace is concerned, it makes a great deal of difference in what way and upon what terms it is ended. The treaties and agreements which bring it to an end must embody terms which will create a peace that is worth guaranteeing and preserving, a peace that will win the approval of mankind, not merely a peace that will serve the several interests and immediate aims of the nations engaged. We shall have no voice in determining what those terms shall be, but we shall, I feel sure, have a voice in determining whether they shall be made lasting or not by the guarantees of a universal covenant, and our judgment upon what is fundamental and essential as a condition precedent to permanency should be spoken now, not afterwards, when it may be too late.

No covenant of co-operative peace that does not include the peoples of the New World can suffice to keep the future safe against war; and yet there is only one sort of peace that the peoples of America could join in guaranteeing. The elements of that peace must be elements that engage the confidence and satisfy the principles of the American governments, elements consistent with their political faith and with the practical convictions which the peoples of America have once for all embraced and undertaken to defend.

I do not mean to say that any American government would throw any obstacle in the way of any terms of peace the governments now at war might agree upon, or seek to upset them when made, whatever they might be. I only take it for granted that mere terms of peace between the belligerents will not satisfy even the belligerents themselves. Mere agreements may not make peace secure. It will be absolutely necessary that a force be created as a guarantor of the permanency of the settlement so much greater than the force of any nation now engaged or any alliance hitherto formed or projected that no nation, no probable combination of nations could face or withstand it. If the peace presently to be made is to endure, it must be a peace made secure by the organized major force of mankind.

The terms of the immediate peace agreed upon will determine whether it is a peace for which such a guarantee can be secured. The question upon which the whole future peace and policy of the world depends is this: Is the present war a struggle for a just and secure peace, or only for a new balance of power? If it be only a struggle for a new balance of power, who will guarantee, who can guarantee the stable equilibrium of the new arrangement? Only a tranquil Europe can be a stable Europe. There must be, not a balance of power, but a community of power; not organized rivalries, but an organized common peace.

Fortunately we have received very explicit assurances on this point. The statesmen of both of the groups of nations now arrayed against one another have said, in terms that could not be misinterpreted, that it was no part of the purpose they had in mind to crush their antagonists. But the implications of these assurances may not be equally clear to all— may not be the same on both sides of the water. I think it will be serviceable if I attempt to set forth what we understand them to be.

They imply, first of all, that it must be a peace without victory. It is not pleasant to say this. I beg that I may be permitted to put my own interpretation upon it and that it may be understood that no other interpretation was in my thought. I am seeking only to face realities and to face them without soft concealments. Victory would mean peace forced upon the loser, a victor's terms imposed upon the vanquished. It would be accepted in humiliation, under duress, at an intolerable sacrifice, and would leave a sting, a resentment, a bitter memory upon which terms of peace would rest, not permanently, but only as upon quicksand. Only a peace between equals can last. Only a peace the very principle of which is equality and a common participation in a common benefit. The right state of mind, the right feeling between nations, is as necessary for a lasting peace as is the just settlement of vexed questions of territory or of racial and national allegiance.

The equality of nations upon which peace must be founded if it is to last must be an equality of rights;

the guarantees exchanged must neither recognize nor imply a difference between big nations and small, between those that are powerful and those that are weak. Right must be based upon the common strength, not upon the individual strength, of the nations upon whose concert peace will depend. Equality of territory or of resources there of course cannot be; nor any sort of equality not gained in the ordinary peaceful and legitimate development of the peoples themselves. But no one asks or expects anything more than an equality of rights. Mankind is looking now for freedom of life, not for equipoises of power.

And there is a deeper thing involved than even equality of right among organized nations. No peace can last, or ought to last, which does not recognize and accept the principle that governments derive all their just powers from the consent of the governed, and that no right anywhere exists to hand peoples about from sovereignty to sovereignty as if they were property. I take it for granted, for instance, if I may venture upon a single example, that statesmen everywhere are agreed that there should be a united, independent, and outonomous Poland, and that henceforth inviolable security of life, of worship, and of industrial and social development should be guaranteed to all peoples who have lived hitherto under the power of governments devoted to a faith and purpose hostile to their own.

I speak of this, not because of any desire to exalt an abstract political principle which has always been held very dear by those who have sought to build up liberty in America, but for the same reason that I have spoken of the other conditions of peace which seem to me clearly indispensable—because I wish frankly to uncover realities. Any peace which does not recognize and accept this principle will inevitably be upset. It will not rest upon the affections or the convictions of mankind. The ferment of spirit of whole populations will fight subtly and constantly against it, and all the world will sympathize. The world can be at peace only if its life is stable, and there can be no stability where the will is in rebellion, where there is not tranquillity of spirit and a sense of justice, of freedom, and of right.

So far as practicable, moreover, every great people now struggling towards a full development of its resources and of its powers should be assured a direct outlet to the great highways of the sea. Where this cannot be done by the cession of territory, it can no doubt be done by the neutralization of direct rights of way under the general guarantee which will assure the peace itself. With a right comity of arrangement no nation need be shut away from free access to the open paths of the world's commerce.

And the paths of the sea must alike in law and in fact be free. The freedom of the seas is the *sine qua non* of peace, equality, and co-operation. No doubt a somewhat radical reconsideration of many of the rules of international practice hitherto thought to be established may be necessary in order to make the seas indeed free and common in practically all circumstances for the use of mankind, but the motive for such changes is convincing and compelling.

There can be no trust or intimacy between the peoples of the world without them. The free, constant, unthreatened intercourse of nations is an essential part of the process of peace and of development. It need not be difficult either to define or to secure the freedom of the seas if the governments of the world sincerely desire to come to an agreement concerning it.

It is a problem closely connected with the limitation of naval armaments and the co-operation of the navies of the world in keeping the seas at once free and safe. And the question of limiting naval armaments opens the wider and perhaps more difficult question of the limitation of armies and of all programs of military preparation. Difficult and delicate as these questions are, they must be faced with the utmost candor and decided in a spirit of real accommodation if peace is to come with healing in its wings, and come to stay. Peace cannot be had without concession and sacrifice. There can be no sense of safety and equality among the nations if great preponderating armaments are henceforth to continue here and there to be built up and maintained. The statesmen of the world must plan for peace and nations must adjust and accommodate their policy to it as they have planned for war and made ready for pitiless contest and rivalry. The question of armaments, whether on land or sea, is the most immediately and intensely practical question connected with the future fortunes of nations and of mankind.

I have spoken upon these great matters without reserve and with the utmost explicitness because it has

seemed to me to be necessary if the world's yearning
desire for peace was anywhere to find free voice and
utterance. Perhaps I am the only person in high
authority amongst all the peoples of the world who
is at liberty to speak and hold nothing back. I am
speaking as an individual, and yet I am speaking
also, of course, as the responsible head of a great
government, and I feel confident that I have said
what the people of the United States would wish
me to say. May I not add that I hope and believe
that I am in effect speaking for liberals and friends
of humanity in every nation and of every program
of liberty? I would fain believe that I am speaking
for the silent mass of mankind everywhere who have
as yet had no place or opportunity to speak their
real hearts out concerning the death and ruin they
see to have come already upon the persons and the
homes they hold most dear.

And in holding out the expectation that the people
and Government of the United States will join the
other civilized nations of the world in guaranteeing
the permanence of peace upon such terms as I have
named I speak with the greater boldness and confidence because it is clear to every man who can think
that there is in this promise no breach in either our
traditions or our policy as a nation, but a fulfilment,
rather, of all that we have professed or striven for.

I am proposing, as it were, that the nations should
with one accord adopt the doctrine of President
Monroe as the doctrine of the world: that no nation
should seek to extend its polity over any other nation or people, but that every people should be left

free to determine its own polity, its own way of development, unhindered, unthreatened, unafraid, the little along with the great and powerful.

I am proposing that all nations henceforth avoid entangling alliances which would draw them into competitions of power; catch them in a net of intrigue and selfish rivalry, and disturb their own affairs with influences intruded from without. There is no entangling alliance in a concert of power. When all unite to act in the same sense and with the same purpose all act in the common interest and are free to live their own lives under a common protection.

I am proposing government by the consent of the governed; that freedom of the seas which in international conference after conference representatives of the United States have urged with the eloquence of those who are the convinced disciples of liberty; and that moderation of armaments which makes of armies and navies a power for order merely, not an instrument of aggression or of selfish violence.

These are American principles, American policies. We could stand for no others. And they are also the principles and policies of forward looking men and women everywhere, of every modern nation, of every enlightened community. They are the principles of mankind and must prevail.

SUBMARINE WARFARE AND THE BREAK WITH GERMANY

ADDRESS TO CONGRESS FEBRUARY 3, 1917. FROM THE "CONGRESSIONAL RECORD," 64TH CONGRESS, 2D SESSION, VOL. 54, PP. 2578-2579.

GENTLEMEN OF THE CONGRESS:

The Imperial German Government on the thirty-first of January announced to this Government and to the governments of other neutral nations that on and after the first day of February, the present month, it would adopt a policy with regard to the use of submarines against all shipping seeking to pass through certain designated areas of the high seas to which it is clearly my duty to call your attention.

Let me remind the Congress that on the eighteenth of April last, in view of the sinking on the twenty-fourth of March of the cross-channel passenger steamer *Sussex* by a German submarine, without summons or warning, and the consequent loss of the lives of several citizens of the United States who were passengers aboard her, this Government addressed a note to the Imperial German Government in which it made the following declaration:

If it is still the purpose of the Imperial Government to prosecute relentless and indiscriminate warfare against vessels of commerce by the use of submarines without regard to what the Government of the United States must consider the sacred and indisputable rules of international law and the universally recognized dictates of humanity, the Government of the United States is at last forced to the conclusion that there is but one course it can pursue. Unless the Imperial Government should now immediately declare and effect an abandonment of its present methods of submarine warfare against passenger and freight-carrying vessels, the Government of the United States can have no choice but to sever diplomatic relations with the German Empire altogether.

In reply to this declaration the Imperial German Government gave this Government the following assurance:

The German Government is prepared to do its utmost to confine the operations of war for the rest of its duration to the fighting forces of the belligerents, thereby also insuring the freedom of the seas, a principle upon which the German Government believes, now as before, to be in agreement with the Government of the United States.

The German Government, guided by this idea, notifies the Government of the United States that the German naval forces have received the following orders: In accordance with the general principles of visit and search and destruction of merchant vessels recognized by international law, such vessels, both within and without the area declared as naval war zone, shall not be sunk without warning and without saving human lives, unless these ships attempt to escape or offer resistance.

"But," it added, "neutrals can not expect that Germany, forced to fight for her existence, shall, for the sake of neutral interest, restrict the use of an effective weapon if her enemy is permitted to continue to apply at will methods of warfare violating the rules of international law. Such a demand would be incompatible with the character of neutrality, and the German Government is convinced that the Government of the United States does not think of making such a demand, knowing that the Government of the United States has repeatedly declared that it is determined to restore the principle of the freedom of the seas, from whatever quarter it has been violated.''

To this, the Government of the United States replied on the eighth of May, accepting, of course, the assurances given, but adding,

The Government of the United States feels it necessary to state that it takes it for granted that the Imperial German Government does not intend to imply that the maintenance of its newly announced policy is in any way contingent upon the course or result of diplomatic negotiations between the Government of the United States and any other belligerent Government, notwithstanding the fact that certain passages in the Imperial Government's note of the 4th instant might appear to be susceptible of that construction. In order, however, to avoid any possible misunderstanding, the Government of the United States notifies the Imperial Government that it cannot for a moment entertain, much less discuss, a suggestion that respect by German naval authorities for the rights of citizens of the United States upon the high seas should in any way or in the slightest degree be made contingent upon the conduct of any other Government affecting the rights of neutrals and noncombatants. Responsibility in such matters is single, not joint; absolute, not relative.

To this note of the eighth of May the Imperial German Government made no reply.

On the thirty-first of January, the Wednesday of the present week, the German Ambassador handed to the Secretary of State, along with a formal note, a memorandum which contains the following statement:

The Imperial Government, therefore, does not doubt that the Government of the United States will understand the situation thus forced upon Germany by the Entente-Allies' brutal methods of war and by their determination to destroy the Central Powers, and that the Government of the United States will further realize that the now openly disclosed intentions of the Entente-Allies give back to Germany the freedom of action which she reserved in her note addressed to the Government of the United States on May 4, 1916.

Under these circumstances Germany will meet the illegal measures of her enemies by forcibly preventing after February 1, 1917, in a zone around Great Britain, France, Italy, and in the Eastern Mediterranean all navigation, that of neutrals included, from and to England and from and to France, etc., etc. All ships met within the zone will be sunk.

I think that you will agree with me that, in view of this declaration, which suddenly and without prior intimation of any kind deliberately withdraws the solemn assurance given in the Imperial Government's note of the fourth of May, 1916, this Government has no alternative consistent with the dignity and honor of the United States but to take the course which, in its note of the eighteenth of April, 1916, it announced that it would take in the event that the German Government did not declare and effect an abandonment of the methods of submarine warfare which it was then employing and to which it now proposes again to resort.

I have, therefore, directed the Secretary of State to announce to His Excellency the German Ambassador that all diplomatic relations between the

United States and the German Empire are severed, and that the American Ambassador at Berlin will immediately be withdrawn; and, in accordance with this decision, to hand to His Excellency his passports.

Notwithstanding this unexpected· action of the German Government, this sudden and deeply deplorable renunciation of its assurances, given this Government at one of the most critical moments of tension in the relations of the two governments, I refuse to believe that it is the intention of the German authorities to do in fact what they have warned us they will feel at liberty to do. I cannot bring myself to believe that they will indeed pay no regard to the ancient friendship between their people and our own or to the solemn obligations which have been exchanged between them and destroy American ships and take the lives of American citizens in the wilful prosecution of the ruthless naval programme they have announced their intention to adopt. Only actual overt acts on their part can make me believe it even now.

If this inveterate confidence on my part in the sobriety and prudent foresight of their purpose should unhappily prove unfounded; if American ships and American lives should in fact be sacrificed by their naval commanders in heedless contravention of the just and reasonable understandings of international law and the obvious dictates of humanity, I shall take the liberty of coming again before the Congress, to ask that authority be given me to use any means that may be necessary for the protection of our seamen and our people in the prosecution of their peaceful and legitimate errands on the high seas. I can do nothing less. I take it for granted that all neutral governments will take the same course.

We do not desire any hostile conflict with the Imperial German Government. We are the sincere friends of the German people and earnestly desire to remain at peace with the Government which speaks for them. We shall not believe that they are hostile to us unless and until we are obliged to believe it; and we purpose nothing more than the reasonable defense of the undoubted rights of our people. We wish to serve no selfish ends. We seek merely to stand true alike in thought and in action to the immemorial principles of our people which I sought to express in my address to the Senate only two weeks ago,—seek merely to vindicate our right to liberty and justice and an unmolested life. These are the bases of peace, not war. God grant we may not be challenged to defend them by acts of wilful injustice on the part of the Government of Germany!

FOR DECLARATION OF WAR AGAINST
GERMANY

ADDRESS DELIVERED AT A JOINT SESSION OF THE TWO
HOUSES OF CONGRESS, APRIL 2, 1917. FORM THE 65TH
CONGRESS, 1ST SESSION, SENATE DOCUMENT NO. 5.

I HAVE called the Congress into extraordinary
session because there are serious, very serious,
choices of policy to be made, and made immediately,
which it was neither right nor constitutionally permissible that I should assume the responsibility of
making.

On the third of February last I officially laid before you the extraordinary announcement of the Imperial German Government that on and after the
first day of February it was its purpose to put aside
all restraints of law or of humanity and use its submarines to sink every vessel that sought to approach
either the ports of Great Britain and Ireland or the
western coasts of Europe or any of the ports controlled by the enemies of Germany within the Mediterranean. That had seemed to be the object of the
German submarine warfare earlier in the war, but
since April of last year the Imperial Government had
somewhat restrained the commanders of its undersea
craft in conformity with its promise then given to us
that passenger boats should not be sunk and that due
warning would be given to all other vessels which its

submarines might seek to destroy, when no resistance was offered or escape attempted, and care taken that their crews were given at least a fair chance to save their lives in their open boats. The precautions taken were meager and haphazard enough, as was proved in distressing instance after instance in the progress of the cruel and unmanly business, but a certain degree of restraint was observed. The new policy has swept every restriction aside. Vessels of every kind, whatever their flag, their character, their cargo, their destination, their errand, have been ruthlessly sent to the bottom without warning and without thought of help or mercy for those on board, the vessels of friendly neutrals along with those of belligerents. Even hospital ships and ships carrying relief to the sorely bereaved and stricken people of Belgium, though the latter were provided with safe conduct through the proscribed areas by the German Government itself and were distinguished by unmistakable marks of identity, have been sunk with the same reckless lack of compassion or of principle.

I was for a little while unable to believe that such things would in fact be done by any government that had hitherto subscribed to the humane practices of civilized nations. International law had its origin in the attempt to set up some law which would be respected and observed upon the seas, where no nation had right of dominion and where lay the free highways of the world. By painful stage after stage has that law been built up, with meager enough results, indeed, after all was accomplished that could be accomplished, but always with a clear view, at least, of what the heart and conscience of mankind demanded. This minimum of right the German Government has swept aside under the plea of retaliation and necessity and because it had no weapons which it could use at sea except these which it is impossible to employ as it is employing them without throwing to the winds all scruples of humanity or of respect for the understandings that were supposed to underlie the intercourse of the world. I am not now thinking of the loss of property involved, immense and serious as that is, but only of the wanton and wholesale destruction of the lives of non-combatants, men, women, and children, engaged in pursuits which have always, even in the darkest periods of modern history, been deemed innocent and legitimate. Property can be paid for; the lives of peaceful and innocent people cannot be. The present German submarine warfare against commerce is a warfare against mankind.

It is a war against all nations. American ships have been sunk, American lives taken, in ways which it has stirred us very deeply to learn of, but the ships and people of other neutral and friendly nations have been sunk and overwhelmed in the waters in the same way. There has been no discrimination. The challenge is to all mankind. Each nation must decide for itself how it will meet it. The choice we make for ourselves must be made with a moderation of counsel and a temperateness of judgment befitting our character and our motives as a nation. We must put excited feeling away. Our motive will not be revenge or the victorious assertion of the physical might of the nation, but only the vindication of right, of human right, of which we are only a single champion.

When I addressed the Congress on the twenty-sixth of February last I thought that it would suffice to assert our neutral rights with arms, our right to use the seas against unlawful interference, our right to keep our people safe against unlawful violence. But armed neutrality, it now appears, is impracticable. Because submarines are in effect outlaws when used as the German submarines have been used against merchant shipping, it is impossible to defend ships against their attacks as the law of nations has assumed that merchantmen would defend themselves against privateers or cruisers, visible craft giving chase upon the open sea. It is common prudence in such circumstances, grim necessity indeed, to endeavor to destroy them before they have shown their own intention. They must be dealt with upon sight, if dealt with at all. The German Government denies the right of neutrals to use arms at all within the areas of the sea which it has proscribed, even in the defense of rights which no modern publicist has ever before questioned their right to defend. The intimation is conveyed that the armed guards which we have placed on our merchant ships will be treated as beyond the pale of law and subject to be dealt with as pirates would be. Armed neutrality is ineffectual enough at best; in such circumstances and in the face of such pretensions it is worse than ineffectual: it is likely only to produce what it was meant to prevent; it is practically certain to draw us into the war without either the rights or the effectiveness of belligerents. There is one choice we cannot make,

we are incapable of making: we will not choose the
path of submission and suffer the most sacred rights
of our Nation and our people to be ignored or violated. The wrongs against which we now array ourselves are no common wrongs; they cut to the very
roots of human life.

With a profound sense of the solemn and even
tragical character of the step I am taking and of the
grave responsibilities which it involves, but in unhesitating obedience to what I deem my constitutional
duty, I advise that the Congress declare the recent
course of the Imperial German Government to be in
fact nothing less than war against the government
and people of the United States; that it formally
accept the status of belligerent which has thus been
thrust upon it; and that it take immediate steps not
only to put the country in a more thorough state
of defense but also to exert all its power and employ
all its resources to bring the Government of the German Empire to terms and end the war.

What this will involve is clear. It will involve the
utmost practicable coöperation in counsel and action
with the governments now at war with Germany, and,
as incident to that, the extension to those governments of the most liberal financial credits, in order
that our resources may so far as possible be added
to theirs. It will involve the organization and mobili-
zation of all the material resources of the country to
supply the materials of war and serve the incidental
needs of the Nation in the most abundant and yet the
most economical and efficient way possible. It will
involve the immediate full equipment of the navy in

all respects but particularly in supplying it with the best means of dealing with the enemy's submarines. It will involve the immediate addition to the armed forces of the United States already provided for by law in case of war at least five hundred thousand men, who should, in my opinion, be chosen upon the principle of universal liability to service, and also the authorization of subsequent additional increments of equal force so soon as they may be needed and can be handled in training. It will involve also, of course, the granting of adequate credits to the Government, sustained, I hope, so far as they can equitably be sustained by the present generation, by well conceived taxation.

I say sustained so far as may be equitable by taxation because it seems to me that it would be most unwise to base the credits which will now be necessary entirely on money borrowed. It is our duty, I most respectfully urge, to protect our people so far as we may against the very serious hardships and evils which would be likely to arise out of the inflation which would be produced by vast loans.

In carrying out the measures by which these things are to be accomplished we should keep constantly in mind the wisdom of interfering as little as possible in our own preparation and in the equipment of our own military forces with the duty,—for it will be a very practical duty,—of supplying the nations already at war with Germany with the materials which they can obtain only from us or by our assistance. They are in the field and we should help them in every way to be effective there.

I shall take the liberty of suggesting, through the several executive departments of the Government, for the consideration of your committees, measures for the accomplishment of the several objects I have mentioned. I hope that it will be your pleasure to deal with them as having been framed after very careful thought by the branch of the Government upon which the responsibility of conducting the war and safeguarding the Nation will most directly fall.

While we do these things, these deeply momentous things, let us be very clear, and make very clear to all the world what our motives and our objects are. My own thought has not been driven from its habitual and normal course by the unhappy events of the last two months, and I do not believe that the thought of the Nation has been altered or clouded by them. I have exactly the same things in mind now that I had in mind when I addressed the Senate on the twenty-second of January last; the same that I had in mind when I addressed the Congress on the third of February and on the twenty-sixth of February. Our object now, as then, is to vindicate the principles of peace and justice in the life of the world as against selfish and autocratic power and to set up amongst the really free and self-governed peoples of the world such a concert of purpose and of action as will henceforth insure the observance of those principles. Neutrality is no longer feasible or desirable where the peace of the world is involved and the freedom of its peoples, and the menace to that peace and freedom lies in the existence of autocratic governments backed by organized force which is controlled wholly by their will, not by the will of their people. We have seen the last of neutrality in such circumstances. We are at the beginning of an age in which it will be insisted that the same standards of conduct and of responsibility for wrong done shall be observed among nations and their governments that are observed among the individual citizens of civilized states.

We have no quarrel with the German people. We have no feeling towards them but one of sympathy and friendship. It was not upon their impulse that their government acted in entering this war. It was not with their previous knowledge or approval. It was a war determined upon as wars used to be determined upon in the old, unhappy days when peoples were nowhere consulted by their rulers and wars were provoked and waged in the interest of dynasties or of little groups of ambitious men who were accustomed to use their fellow men as pawns and tools. Self-governed nations do not fill their neighbor states with spies or set the course of intrigue to bring about some critical posture of affairs which will give them an opportunity to strike and make conquest. Such designs can be successfully worked out only under cover and where no one has the right to ask questions. Cunningly contrived plans of deception or aggression, carried, it may be, from generation to generation, can be worked out and kept from the light only within the privacy of courts or behind the carefully guarded confidences of a narrow and privileged class. They are happily impossible where public opinion commands and insists upon full information concerning all the nation's affairs.

A steadfast concert for peace can never be maintained except by a partnership of democratic nations. No autocratic government could be trusted to keep faith within it or observe its covenants. It must be a league of honor, a partnership of opinion. Intrigue would eat its vitals away; the plottings of inner circles who could plan what they would and render account to no one would be a corruption seated at its very heart. Only free peoples can hold their purpose and their honor steady to a common end and prefer the interests of mankind to any narrow interest of their own.

Does not every American feel that assurance has been added to our hope for the future peace of the world by the wonderful and heartening things that have been happening within the last few weeks in Russia? Russia was known by those who knew it best to have been always in fact democratic at heart, in all the vital habits of her thought, in all the intimate relationships of her people that spoke their natural instinct, their habitual attitude towards life. The autocracy that crowned the summit of her political structure, long as it had stood and terrible as was the reality of its power, was not in fact Russian in origin, character, or purpose; and now it has been shaken off and the great, generous Russian people have been added in all their naïve majesty and might to the forces that are fighting for freedom in the world, for justice, and for peace. Here is a fit partner for a League of Honor.

One of the things that has served to convince us that the Prussian autocracy was not and could never be our friend is that from the very outset of the present war it has filled our unsuspecting communities and even our offices of government with spies and set criminal intrigues everywhere afoot against our national unity of counsel, our peace within and without, our industries and our commerce. Indeed, it is now evident that its spies were here even before the war began; and it is unhappily not a matter of conjecture but a fact proved in our courts of justice that the intrigues which have more than once come perilously near to disturbing the peace and dislocating the industries of the country have been carried on at the instigation, with the support, and even under the personal direction of official agents of the Imperial Government accredited to the Government of the United States. Even in checking these things and trying to extirpate them we have sought to put the most generous interpretation possible upon them because we knew that their source lay not in any hostile feeling or purpose of the German people towards us (who were, no doubt as ignorant of them as we ourselves were), but only in the selfish designs of a Government that did what it pleased and told its people nothing. But they have played their part in serving to convince us at last that that Government entertains no real friendship for us and means to act against our peace and security at its convenience. That it means to stir up enemies against us at our very doors the intercepted note to the German Minister at Mexico City is eloquent evidence.

We are accepting this challenge of hostile purpose because we know that in such a Government, following such methods, we can never have a friend; and that in the presence of its organized power, always lying in wait to accomplish we know not what purpose, there can be no assured security for the democratic Governments of the world. We are now about to accept gauge of battle with this natural foe to liberty and shall, if necessary, spend the whole force of the nation to check and nullify its pretensions and its power. We are glad, now that we see the facts with no veil of false pretense about them, to fight thus for the ultimate peace of the world and for the liberation of its peoples, the German peoples included: for the rights of nations great and small and the privilege of men everywhere to choose their way of life and of obedience. The world must be made safe for democracy. Its peace must be planted upon the tested foundations of political liberty. We have no selfish ends to serve. We desire no conquest, no dominion. We seek no indemnities for ourselves, no material compensation for the sacrifices we shall freely make. We are but one of the champions of the rights of mankind. We shall be satisfied when those rights have been made as secure as the faith and the freedom of nations can make them.

Just because we fight without rancor and without selfish object, seeking nothing for ourselves but what we shall wish to share with all free peoples, we shall, I feel confident, conduct our operations as belligerents without passion and ourselves observe with proud punctilio the principles of right and of fair play we profess to be fighting for.

I have said nothing of the Governments allied with

the Imperial Government of Germany because they
have not made war upon us or challenged us to defend our right and our honor.   The Austro-Hungarian Government has, indeed, avowed its unqualified indorsement and acceptance of the reckless and
lawless submarine warfare adopted now without disguise by the Imperial German Government, and it
has therefore not been possible for this Government
to receive Count Tarnowski, the Ambassador recently
accredited to this Government by the Imperial and
Royal Government of Austria-Hungary; but that
Government has not actually engaged in warfare
against citizens of the United States on the seas, and
I take the liberty, for the present at least, of post-
poning a discussion of our relations with the authorities at Vienna.   We enter this war only where
we are clearly forced into it because there are no
other means of defending our rights.

It will be all the easier for us to conduct ourselves
as belligerents in a high spirit of right and fairness
because we act without animus, not in enmity towards
a people or with the desire to bring any injury or
disadvantage upon them, but only in armed opposi-
tion to an irresponsible government which has thrown
aside all considerations of humanity and of right
and is running amuck.   We are, let me say again, the
sincere friends of the German people, and shall desire nothing so much as the early reëstablishment of
intimate relations of mutual advantage between us,—
however hard it may be for them, for the time being,
to believe that this is spoken from our hearts.   We
have borne with their present Government through

all these bitter months because of that friendship,—
exercising a patience and forbearance which would
otherwise have been impossible. We shall, happily,
still have an opportunity to prove that friendship in
our daily attitude and actions towards the millions
of men and women of German birth and native sympathy who live amongst us and share our life, and
we shall be proud to prove it towards all who are
in fact loyal to their neighbors and to the Government in the hour of test. They are, most of them, as
true and loyal Americans as if they had never known
any other fealty or allegiance. They will be prompt
to stand with us in rebuking and restraining the few
who may be of a different mind and purpose. If
there should be disloyalty, it will be dealt with with
a firm hand of stern repression; but, if it lifts its
head at all, it will lift it only here and there and
without countenance except from a lawless and
malignant few.

It is a distressing and oppressive duty, Gentlemen
of the Congress, which I have performed in thus addressing you. There are, it may be, many months of
fiery trial and sacrifice ahead of us. It is a fearful
thing to lead this great peaceful people into war, into
the most terrible and disastrous of all wars, civilization itself seeming to be in the balance. But the right
is more precious than peace, and we shall fight for
the things which we have always carried nearest our
hearts,—for democracy, for the right of those who
submit to authority to have a voice in their own Governments, for the rights and liberties of small nations, for a universal dominion of right by such a

concert of free peoples as shall bring peace and safety to all nations and make the world itself at last free. To such a task we can dedicate our lives and our fortunes, everything that we are and everything that we have, with the pride of those who know that the day has come when America is privileged to spend her blood and her might for the principles that gave her birth and happiness and the peace which she has treasured. God helping her, she can do no other.

"AMERICA WAS BORN TO SERVE MANKIND"

MEMORIAL DAY ADDRESS AT ARLINGTON NATIONAL CEM-
ETERY, MAY 30, 1917. FROM "OFFICIAL BULLETIN,"
NO. 18.

THE program has conferred an unmerited dignity upon the remarks I am going to make by
calling them an address, because I am not here to
deliver an address. I am here merely to show in my
official capacity the sympathy of this great Government with the objects of this occasion, and also to
speak just a word of the sentiment that is in my own
heart.

Any Memorial Day of this sort is, of course, a day
touched with sorrowful memory, and yet I for one
do not see how we can have any thought of pity for
the men whose memory we honor to-day. I do not
pity them. I envy them, rather; because theirs is a
great work for liberty accomplished and we are in
the midst of a work unfinished, testing our strength
where their strength has already been tested.

There is a touch of sorrow, but there is a touch of
reassurance also in a day like this, because we know
how the men of America have responded to the call
of the cause of liberty and it fills our mind with a
perfect assurance that that response will come again
in equal measure, with equal majesty, and with a
result which will hold the attention of all mankind.

When you reflect upon it, these men who died to preserve the Union died to preserve the instrument which we are now using to serve the world—a free Nation espousing the cause of human liberty. In one sense the great struggle into which we have now entered is an American struggle, because it is in defense of American honor and American rights, but it is something even greater than that; it is a world struggle. It is a struggle of men who love liberty everywhere, and in this cause America will show herself greater than ever because she will rise to a greater thing.

We have said in the beginning that we planned this great Government that men who wished freedom might have a place of refuge and a place where their hope could be realized, and now, having established such a Government, having preserved such a Government, having vindicated the power of such a Government, we are saying to all mankind, "We did not set this Government up in order that we might have a selfish and separate liberty, for we are now ready to come to your assistance and fight out upon the field of the world the cause of human liberty."

In this thing America attains her full dignity and the full fruition of her great purpose.

No man can be glad that such things have happened as we have witnessed in these last fateful years, but perhaps it may be permitted to us to be glad that we have an opportunity to show the principles which we profess to be living principles which live in our hearts, and to have a chance by the pouring out of our blood and treasure to vindicate the thing which we have professed. For, my friends, the real fruition of life is to do the thing we have said we wished to do. There are times when words seem empty and only action seems great. Such a time has come, and in the providence of God America will once more have an opportunity to show to the world that she was born to serve mankind.

THE BIBLE

LETTER TO THE SOLDIERS AND SAILORS OF THE UNITED
STATES, AUGUST, 1917. FROM THE "CONGRESSIONAL
RECORD," VOL. 55, P. 6041.

THE Bible is the word of life. I beg that you
will read it and find this out for yourselves—
read, not little snatches here and there, but long
passages that will really be the road to the heart
of it. You will find it full of real men and women
not only, but also of things you have wondered about
and been troubled about all your life, as men have
been always; and the more you read the more it
will become plain to you what things are worth while
and what are not, what things make men happy—
loyalty, right dealings, speaking the truth, readiness
to give everything for what they think their duty,
and, most of all, the wish that they may have the
real approval of the Christ, who gave everything for
them—and the things that are guaranteed to make
men unhappy—selfishness, cowardice, greed, and
everything that is low and mean. When you have
read the Bible you will know that it is the Word of
God, because you will have found it the key to your
own heart, your own happiness, and your own duty.

WOODROW WILSON.

THE FOURTEEN POINTS SPEECH

ADDRESS DELIVERED AT A JOINT SESSION OF THE TWO HOUSES OF CONGRESS, JANUARY 8, 1918. FROM OFFICIAL GOVERNMENT PUBLICATION IN MR. WILSON'S FILES.

ONCE more, as repeatedly before, the spokesmen of the Central Empires have indicated their desire to discuss the objects of the war and the possible bases of a general peace. Parleys have been in progress at Brest-Litovsk between representatives of the Central Powers to which the attention of all the belligerents has been invited for the purpose of ascertaining whether it may be possible to extend these parleys into a general conference with regard to terms of peace and settlement. The Russian representatives presented not only a perfectly definite statement of the principles upon which they would be willing to conclude peace but also an equally definite program of the concrete application of those principles. The representatives of the Central Powers, on their part, presented an outline of settlement which, if much less definite, seemed susceptible of liberal interpretation until their specific program of practical terms was added. That program proposed no concessions at all either to the sovereignty of Russia or to the preferences of the populations with whose fortunes it dealt, but meant, in a word, that the Central Empires were to keep every foot of territory their armed forces had occupied,—every province, every city, every point of vantage,—as a permanent addition to their territories and their power. It is a reasonable conjecture that the general principles of settlement which they at first suggested originated with the more liberal statesmen of Germany and Austria, the men who have begun to feel the force of their own peoples' thought and purpose, while the concrete terms of actual settlement came from the military leaders who have no thought but to keep what they have got. The negotiations have been broken off. The Russian representatives were sincere and in earnest. They cannot entertain such proposals of conquest and domination.

The whole incident is full of significance. It is also full of perplexity. With whom are the Russian representatives dealing? For whom are the representatives of the Central Empires speaking? Are they speaking for the majorities of their respective parliaments or for the minority parties, that military and imperialistic minority which has so far dominated their whole policy and controlled the affairs of Turkey and the Balkan states which have felt obliged to become their associates in this war? The Russian representatives have insisted, very justly, very wisely, and in the true spirit of modern democracy, that the conferences they have been holding with the Teutonic and Turkish statesmen should be held within open, not closed, doors, and all the world has been audience, as was desired. To whom have we been listening, then? To those who speak the spirit and intention of the Resolutions of the German

Reichstag of the ninth of July last, the spirit and
intention of the liberal leaders and parties of Germany, or to those who resist and defy that spirit and
intention and insist upon conquest and subjugation?
Or are we listening, in fact, to both, unreconciled and
in open and hopeless contradiction? These are very
serious and pregnant questions. Upon the answer
to them depends the peace of the world.

But, whatever the results of the parleys at Brest-
Litovsk, whatever the confusions of counsel and of
purpose in the utterances of the spokesmen of the
Central Empires, they have again attempted to ac-
quaint the world with their objects in the war and
have again challenged their adversaries to say what
their objects are and what sort of settlement they
would deem just and satisfactory. There is no good
reason why that challege should not be responded
to, and responded to with the utmost candor. We
did not wait for it. Not once, but again and again,
we have laid our whole thought and purpose before
the world, not in general terms only, but each time
with sufficient definition to make it clear what sort of
definite terms of settlement must necessarily spring
out of them. Within the last week Mr. Lloyd George
has spoken with admirable candor and in admirable
spirit for the people and Government of Great
Britain. There is no confusion of counsel among the
adversaries of the Central Powers, no uncertainty of
principle, no vagueness of detail. The only secrecy
of counsel, the only lack of fearless frankness, the
only failure to make definite statement of the objects
of the war, lies with Germany and her Allies. The

issues of life and death hang upon these definitions.
No statesman who has the least conception of his
responsibility ought for a moment to permit himself
to continue this tragical and appalling outpouring of
blood and treasure unless he is sure beyond a perad-
venture that the objects of the vital sacrifice are part
and parcel of the very life of Society and that the
people for whom he speaks think them right and imperative as he does.

There is, moreover, a voice calling for these definitions of principle and of purpose which is, it seems
to me, more thrilling and more compelling than any
of the many moving voices with which the troubled
air of the world is filled. It is the voice of the Russian people. They are prostrate and all but helpless, it would seem, before the grim power of Germany, which has hitherto known no relenting and no
pity. Their power, apparently, is shattered. And
yet their soul is not subservient. They will not yield
either in principle or in action. Their conception of
what is right, of what it is humane and honorable
for them to accept, has been stated with a frankness,
a largeness of view, a generosity of spirit, and a universal human sympathy which must challenge the
admiration of every friend of mankind; and they
have refused to compound their ideals or desert
others that they themselves may be safe. They call
to us to say what it is that we desire, in what, if in
anything, our purpose and our spirit differ from
theirs; and I believe that the people of the United
States would wish me to respond, with utter simplicity and frankness. Whether their present lead-

ers believe it or not, it is our heartfelt desire and hope that some way may be opened whereby we may be privileged to assist the people of Russia to attain their utmost hope of liberty and ordered peace.

It will be our wish and purpose that the processes of peace, when they are begun, shall be absolutely open and that they shall involve and permit henceforth no secret understandings of any kind. The day of conquest and aggrandizement is gone by; so is also the day of secret covenants entered into in the interest of particular governments and likely at some unlooked-for moment to upset the peace of the world. It is this happy fact, now clear to the view of every public man whose thoughts do not still linger in an age that is dead and gone, which makes it possible for every nation whose purposes are consistent with justice and the peace of the world to avow now or at any other time the objects it has in view.

We entered this war because violations of right had occurred which touched us to the quick and made the life of our own people impossible unless they were corrected and the world secured once for all against their recurrence. What we demand in this war, therefore, is nothing peculiar to ourselves. It is that the world be made fit and safe to live in; and particularly that it be made safe for every peace-loving nation which, like our own, wishes to live its own life, determine its own institutions, be assured of justice and fair dealing by the other peoples of the world as against force and selfish aggression. All the peoples of the world are in effect partners in this interest, and for our own part we see very clearly that unless justice be done to others it will not be done to us. The program of the world's peace, therefore, is our program; and that program, the only possible program, as we see it, is this:

I. Open covenants of peace, openly arrived at, after which there shall be no private international understandings of any kind but diplomacy shall proceed always frankly and in the public view.

II. Absolute freedom of navigation upon the seas, outside territorial waters, alike in peace and in war, except as the seas may be closed in whole or in part by international action for the enforcement of international covenants.

III. The removal, so far as possible, of all economic barriers and the establishment of an equality of trade conditions among all the nations consenting to the peace and associating themselves for its maintenance.

IV. Adequate guarantees given and taken that national armaments will be reduced to the lowest point consistent with domestic safety.

V. A free, open-minded, and absolutely impartial adjustment of all colonial claims, based upon a strict observance of the principle that in determining all such questions of sovereignty the interests of the populations concerned must have equal weight with the equitable claims of the government whose title is to be determined.

VI. The evacuation of all Russian territory and such a settlement of all questions affecting Russia as will secure the best and freest coöperation of the other nations of the world in obtaining for her an unhampered and unembarrassed opportunity for the inde-

pendent determination of her own political development and national policy and assure her of a sincere
welcome into the society of free nations under institutions of her own choosing; and, more than a welcome, assistance also of every kind that she may need
nd may herself desire. The treatment accorded Russia
by her sister nations in the months to come will be the
acid test of their good will, of their comprehension of
her needs as distinguished from their own interests,
and of their intelligent and unselfish sympathy.

VII. Belgium, the whole world will agree, must
be evacuated and restored, without any attempt to
limit the sovereignty which she enjoys in common
with all other free nations. No other single act will
serve as this will serve to restore confidence among
the nations in the laws which they have themselves
set and determined for the government of their relations with one another. Without this healing act the
whole structure and validity of international law is
forever impaired.

VIII. All French territory should be freed and the
invaded portions restored, and the wrong done to
France by Prussia in 1871 in the matter of Alsace-
Lorraine, which has unsettled the peace of the world
for nearly fifty years, should be righted, in order
that peace may once more be made secure in the
interest of all.

IX. A readjustment of the frontiers of Italy should
be effected along clearly recognizable lines of nationality.

X. The peoples of Austria-Hungary, whose place
among the nations we wish to see safeguarded and as-

sured, should be accorded the freest opportunity of autonomous development.

XI. Rumania, Serbia, and Montenegro should be evacuated; occupied territories restored; Serbia accorded free and secure access to the sea; and the relations of the several Balkan states to one another determined by friendly counsel along historically established lines of allegiance and nationality; and international guarantees of the political and economic independence and territorial integrity of the several Balkan states should be entered into.

XII. The Turkish portions of the present Ottoman Empire should be assured a secure sovereignty, but the other nationalities which are now under Turkish rule should be assured an undoubted security of life and an absolutely unmolested opportunity of autonomous development, and the Dardanelles should be permanently opened as a free passage to the ships and commerce of all nations under international guarantees.

XIII. An independent Polish state should be erected which should include the territories inhabited by indisputably Polish populations, which should be assured a free and secure access to the sea, and whose political and economic independence and territorial integrity should be guaranteed by international covenant.

XIV. A general association of nations must be formed under specific covenants for the purpose of affording mutual guarantees of political independence and territorial integrity to great and small states alike.

In regard to these essential rectifications of wrong
and assertions of right we feel ourselves to be intimate partners of all the governments and peoples
associated together against the Imperialists.   We
cannot be separated in interest or divided in purpose.
We stand together until the end.

For such arrangements and covenants we are willing to fight and to continue to fight until they are
achieved; but only because we wish the right to prevail and desire a just and stable peace such as can
be secured only by removing the chief provocations
to war, which this program does not remove.   We
have no jealousy of German greatness, and there is
nothing in this program that impairs it.   We grudge
her no achievement or distinction of learning or of
pacific enterprise such as have made her record very
bright and very enviable.   We do not wish to injure
her or to block in any way her legitimate influence or
power.   We do not wish to fight her either with arms
or with hostile arrangements of trade if she is willing
to associate herself with us and the other peace-loving
nations of the world in covenants of justice and law
and fair dealing.   We wish her only to accept a place
of equality among the peoples of the world,—the new
world in which we now live,—instead of a place
of mastery.

Neither do we presume to suggest to her any alteration or modification of her institutions.   But it
is necessary, we must frankly say, and necessary as
a preliminary to any intelligent dealings with her on
our part, that we should know whom her spokesmen
speak for when they speak to us, whether for the

Reichstag majority or for the military party and the men whose creed is imperial domination.

We have spoken now, surely, in terms too concrete to admit of any further doubt or question. An evident principle runs through the whole program I have outlined. It is the principle of justice to all peoples and nationalities, and their right to live on equal terms of liberty and safety with one another, whether they be strong or weak. Unless this principle be made its foundation no part of the structure of international justice can stand. The people of the United States could act upon no other principle; and to the vindication of this principle they are ready to devote their lives, their honor, and everything that they possess. The moral climax of this the culminating and final war for human liberty has come, and they are ready to put their own strength, their own highest purpose, their own integrity and devotion to the test.

FOURTH LIBERTY LOAN

ADDRESS OPENING THE CAMPAIGN FOR THE FOURTH
LIBERTY LOAN DELIVERED IN NEW YORK CITY, SEP-
TEMBER 27, 1918. FROM OFFICIAL GOVERNMENT PUB-
LICATION IN MR. WILSON'S FILES.

I AM not here to promote the loan. That will be
done,—ably and enthusiastically done,—by the
hundreds of thousands of loyal and tireless men and
women who have undertaken to present it to you
and to our fellow citizens throughout the country;
and I have not the least doubt of their complete success; for I know their spirit and the spirit of the
country. My confidence is confirmed, too, by the
thoughtful and experienced coöperation of the bankers here and everywhere, who are lending their in-
valuable aid and guidance. I have come, rather, to
seek an opportunity to present to you some thoughts
which I trust will serve to give you, in perhaps
fuller measure than before, a vivid sense of the great
issues involved, in order that you may appreciate
and accept with added enthusiasm the grave significance of the duty of supporting the Government by
your men and your means to the utmost point of
sacrifice and self-denial. No man or woman who has
really taken in what this war means can hesitate to
give to the very limit of what he or she has; and it
is my mission here to-night to try to make it clear
once more what the war really means. You will

need no other stimulation or reminder of your duty.

At every turn of the war we gain a fresh consciousness of what we mean to accomplish by it. When
our hope and expectation are most excited we think
more definitely than before of the issues that hang
upon it and of the purposes which must be realized
by means of it. For it has positive and well-defined
purposes which we did not determine and which we
cannot alter. No statesman or assembly created
them; no statesman or assembly can alter them.
They have arisen out of the very nature and circumstances of the war. The most that statesmen or assemblies can do is to carry them out or be false to them.
They were perhaps not clear at the outset; but they
are clear now. The war has lasted more than four
years and the whole world has been drawn into it.
The common will of mankind has been substituted
for the particular purposes of individual states. Individual statesmen may have started the conflict, but
neither they nor their opponents can stop it as they
please. It has become a peoples' war, and peoples
of all sorts and races, of every degree of power and
variety of fortune, are involved in its sweeping
processes of change and settlement. We came into it
when its character had become fully defined and it
was plain that no nation could stand apart or be in-
different to its outcome. Its challenge drove to the
heart of everything we cared for and lived for. The
voice of the war had become clear and gripped our
hearts. Our brothers from many lands, as well as
our own murdered dead under the sea, were calling
to us, and we responded, fiercely and of course.

The air was clear about us. We saw things in their
full, convincing proportions as they were; and we
have seen them with steady eyes and unchanging
comprehension ever since. We accepted the issues
of the war as facts, not as any group of men either
here or elsewhere had defined them, and we can accept no outcome which does not squarely meet and
settle them. Those issues are these:

Shall the military power of any nation or group
of nations be suffered to determine the fortunes of
peoples over whom they have no right to rule except the right of force?

Shall strong nations be free to wrong weak nations and make them subject to their purpose and
interest?

Shall peoples be ruled and dominated, even in their
own internal affairs, by arbitrary and irresponsible
force or by their own will and choice?

Shall there be a common standard of right and
privilege for all peoples and nations or shall the
strong do as they will and the weak suffer without
redress?

Shall the assertion of right be haphazard and by
casual alliance or shall there be a common concert
to oblige the observance of common rights?

No man, no group of men, chose these to be the
issues of the struggle. They *are* the issues of it;
and they must be settled,—by no arrangement or
compromise or adjustment of interests, but definitely
and once for all and with a full and unequivocal acceptance of the principle that the interest of the
weakest is as sacred as the interest of the strongest.

This is what we mean when we speak of a permanent peace, if we speak sincerely, intelligently, and with a real knowledge and comprehension of the matter we deal with.

We are all agreed that there can be no peace obtained by any kind of bargain or compromise with the governments of the Central Empires, because we have dealt with the malready and have seen them deal with other governments that were parties to this struggle, at Brest-Litovsk and Bucharest. They have convinced us that they are without honor and do not intend justice. They observe no covenants, accept no principle but force and their own interest. We cannot "come to terms" with them. They have made it impossible. The German people must by this time be fully aware that we cannot accept the word of those who forced this war upon us. We do not think the same thoughts or speak the same language of agreement.

It is of capital importance that we should also be explicitly agreed that no peace shall be obtained by any kind of compromise or abatement of the principles we have avowed as the principles for which we are fighting. There should exist no doubt about that. I am, therefore, going to take the liberty of speaking with the utmost frankness about the practical implications that are involved in it.

If it be in deed and in truth the common object of the Governments associated against Germany and of the nations whom they govern, as I believe it to be, to achieve by the coming settlements a secure and lasting peace, it will be necessary that all who sit

down at the peace table shall come ready and willing
to pay the price, the only price, that will procure
it; and ready and willing, also, to create in some
virile fashion the only instrumentality by which it
can be made certain that the agreements of the peace
will be honored and fulfilled.

That price is impartial justice in every item of the
settlement, no matter whose interest is crossed; and
not only impartial justice, but also the satisfaction
of the several peoples whose fortunes are dealt with.
That indispensable instrumentality is a League of
Nations formed under covenants that will be efficacious. Without such an instrumentality, by which
the peace of the world can be guaranteed, peace will
rest in part upon the word of outlaws and only upon
that word. For Germany will have to redeem her
character, not by what happens at the peace table,
but by what follows.

And, as I see it, the constitution of that League
of Nations and the clear definition of its objects
must be a part, is in a sense the most essential part,
of the peace settlement itself. It cannot be formed
now. If formed now, it would be merely a new alliance confined to the nations associated against a
common enemy. It is not likely that it could be
formed after the settlement. It is necessary to guarantee the peace; and the peace cannot be guaranteed as an afterthought. The reason, to speak in
plain terms again, why it must be guaranteed is
that there will be parties to the peace whose promises have proved untrustworthy, and means must be
found in connection with the peace settlement itself

to remove that source of insecurity. It would be folly to leave the guarantee to the subsequent voluntary action of the Governments we have seen destroy Russia and deceive Rumania.

But these general terms do not disclose the whole matter. Some details are needed to make them sound less like a thesis and more like a practical program. These, then, are some of the particulars, and I state them with the greater confidence because I can state them authoritatively as representing this Government's interpretation of its own duty with regard to peace:

First, the impartial justice meted out must involve no discrimination between those to whom we wish to be just and those to whom we do not wish to be just. It must be a justice that plays no favorites and knows no standard but the equal rights of the several peoples concerned;

Second, no special or separate interest of any single nation or any group of nations can be made the basis of any part of the settlement which is not consistent with the common interest of all;

Third, there can be no leagues or alliances or special covenants and understandings within the general and common family of the League of Nations.

Fourth, and more specifically, there can be no special, selfish economic combinations within the League and no employment of any form of economic boycott or exclusion except as the power of economic penalty by exclusion from the markets of the world may be vested in the League of Nations itself as a means of discipline and control.

Fifth, all international agreements and treaties of every kind must be made known in their entirety to the rest of the world.

Special alliances and economic rivalries and hostilities have been the prolific source in the modern world of the plans and passions that produce war. It would be an insincere as well as insecure peace that did not exclude them in definite and binding terms.

The confidence with which I venture to speak for our people in these matters does not spring from our traditions merely and the well-known principles of international action which we have always professed and followed. In the same sentence in which I say that the United States will enter into no special arrangements or understandings with particular nations let me say also that the United States is prepared to assume its full share of responsibility for the maintenance of the common covenants and understandings upon which peace must henceforth rest. We still read Washington's immortal warning against "entangling alliances" with full comprehension and an answering purpose. But only special and limited alliances entangle; and we recognize and accept the duty of a new day in which we are permitted to hope for a general alliance which will avoid entanglements and clear the air of the world for common understandings and the maintenance of common rights.

I have made this analysis of the international situation which the war has created, not, of course, because I doubted whether the leaders of the great

nations and peoples with whom we are associated
were of the same mind and entertained a like purpose, but because the air every now and again gets
darkened by mist and groundless doubtings and
mischievous perversions of counsel and it is necessary once and again to sweep all the irresponsible
talk about peace intrigues and weakening morale
and doubtful purpose on the part of those in authority utterly, and if need be unceremoniously, aside
and say things in the plainest words that can be
found, even when it is only to say over again what
has been said before, quite as plainly if in less un-
varnished terms.

As I have said, neither I nor any other man in
governmental authority created or gave form to the
issues of this war. I have simply responded to them
with such vision as I could command. But I have
responded gladly and with a resolution that has
grown warmer and more confident as the issues have
grown clearer and clearer. It is now plain that they
are issues which no man can pervert unless it be
wilfully. I am bound to fight for them, and happy
to fight for them as time and circumstance have revealed them to me as to all the world. Our enthusiasm for them grows more and more irresistible as
they stand out in more and more vivid and unmistakable outline.

And the forces that fight for them draw into closer
and closer array, organize their millions into more and
more unconquerable might, as they become more and
more distinct to the thought and purpose of the
peoples engaged. It is the peculiarity of this great

war that while statesmen have seemed to cast about
for definitions of their purpose and have sometimes
seemed to shift their ground and their point of view,
the thought of the mass of men, whom statesmen are
supposed to instruct and lead, has grown more and
more unclouded, more and more certain of what it
is that they are fighting for. National purposes have
fallen more and more into the background and the
common purpose of enlightened mankind has taken
their place. The counsels of plain men have become
on all hands more simple and straightforward and
more unified than the counsels of sophisticated men
of affairs, who still retain the impression that they
are playing a game of power and playing for high
stakes. That is why I have said that this is a peoples'
war, not a statesmen's. Statesmen must follow the
clarified common thought or be broken.

I take that to be the significance of the fact that
assemblies and associations of many kinds made up
of plain workaday people have demanded, almost
every time they came together, and are still demanding, that the leaders of their Governments declare to
them plainly what it is, exactly what it is, that they
were seeking in this war, and what they think the
items of the final settlement should be. They are
not yet satisfied with what they have been told.
They still seem to fear that they are getting what
they ask for only in statesmen's terms,—only in the
terms of territorial arrangements and divisions of
power, and not in terms of broad-visioned justice and
mercy and peace and the satisfaction of those deep-
seated longings of oppressed and distracted men and

women and enslaved peoples that seem to them the
only things worth fighting a war for that engulfs
the world. Perhaps statesmen have not always recognized this changed aspect of the whole world of
policy and action. Perhaps they have not always
spoken in direct reply to the questions asked because
they did not know how searching those questions were
and what sort of answers they demanded.

But I, for one, am glad to attempt the answer
again and again, in the hope that I may make it
clearer and clearer that my one thought is to satisfy those who struggle in the ranks and are, perhaps
above all others, entitled to a reply whose meaning
no one can have any excuse for misunderstanding, if
he understands the language in which it is spoken
or can get some one to translate it correctly into
his own. And I believe that the leaders of the governments with which we are associated will speak,
as they have occasion, as plainly as I have tried to
speak. I hope that they will feel free to say whether
they think that I am in any degree mistaken in my
interpretation of the issues involved or in my purpose with regard to the means by which a satisfactory
settlement of those issues may be obtained. Unity
of purpose and of counsel are as imperatively necessary in this war as was unity of command in the
battlefield; and with perfect unity of purpose and
counsel will come assurance of complete victory. It
can be had in no other way. "Peace drives" can be
effectively neutralized and silenced only by showing that every victory of the nations associated
against Germany brings the nations nearer the sort

of peace which will bring security and reassurance
to all peoples and make the recurrence of another
such struggles of pitiless force and bloodshed forever
impossible, and that nothing else can. Germany is
constantly intimating the "terms" she will accept;
and always finds that the world does not want terms.
It wishes the final triumph of justice and fair dealing.

ARMISTICE TERMS

MESSAGE TO THE GERMAN GOVERNMENT THROUGH SEC-
RETARY LANSING AND MR. FREDERICK OEDERLIN,
CHARGE D'AFFAIRES OF SWITZERLAND, OCTOBER 23,
1918. FROM "OFFICIAL U. S. BULLETIN," NO. 445.

I HAVE the honor to acknowledge the receipt of
your note of the twenty-second transmitting a
communication under date of the twentieth from the
German Government and to advise you that the
President has instructed me to reply thereto as follows:

"Having received the solemn and explicit assurance of the German Government that it unreservedly
accepts the terms of peace laid down in his address
to the Congress of the United States on the eighth
of January, 1918, and the principles of settlement
enunciated in his subsequent addresses, particularly
the address of the twenty-seventh of September, and
that it desires to discuss the details of their application, and that this wish and purpose emanate, not
from those who have hitherto dictated German policy
and conducted the present war on Germany's behalf,
but from ministers who speak for the majority of
the Reichstag and for an overwhelming majority of
the German people; and having received also the
explicit promise of the present German Government
that the human rules of civilized warfare will be observed both on land and sea by the German armed

forces, the President of the United States feels that he cannot decline to take up with the Governments with which the Government of the United States is associated the question of an armistice.

"He deems it his duty to say again, however, that the only armistice he would feel justified in submitting for consideration would be one which should leave the United States and the powers associated with her in a position to enforce any arrangements that may be entered into and to make a renewal of hostilities on the part of Germany impossible. The President has, therefore, transmitted his correspondence with the present German authorities to the Governments with which the Government of the United States is associated as a belligerent, with the suggestion that, if those Governments are disposed to effect peace upon the terms and principles indicated, their military advisers and the military advisers of the United States be asked to submit to the Governments associated against Germany the necessary terms of such an armistice as will fully protect the interests of the peoples involved and insure to the associated Governments the unrestricted power to safeguard and enforce the details of the peace to which the German Government has agreed, provided they deem such an armistice possible from the military point of view. Should such terms of armistice be suggested, their acceptance by Germany will afford the best concrete evidence of her unequivocal acceptance of the terms and principles of peace from which the whole action proceeds.

"The President would deem himself lacking in

candor did he not point out in the frankest possible
terms the reason why extraordinary safeguards must
be demanded. Significant and important as the
constitutional changes seem to be which are spoken
of by the German Foreign Secretary in his note of
the twentieth of October, it does not appear that
the principle of a government responsible to the
German people has yet been fully worked out or that
any guarantees either exist or are in contemplation
that the alterations of principle and of practice now
partially agreed upon will be permanent. Moreover,
it does not appear that the heart of the present difficulty has been reached. It may be that future wars
have been brought under the control of the German
people, but the present war has not been; and it is
with the present war that we are dealing. It is
evident that the German people have no means of
commanding the acquiescence of the military authorities of the Empire in the popular will; that the
power of the King of Prussia to control the policy
of the Empire is unimpaired; that the determining
initiative still remains with those who have hitherto
been the masters of Germany.

"Feeling that the whole peace of the world depends now on plain speaking and straightforward
action, the President deems it his duty to say, without
any attempt to soften what may seem harsh words,
that the nations of the world do not and cannot trust
the word of those who have hitherto been the masters of German policy, and to point out once more
that in concluding peace and attempting to undo the
infinite injuries and injustices of this war the Gov-

ernment of the United States cannot deal with any but veritable representatives of the German people who have been assured of a genuine constitutional standing as the real rulers of Germany. If it must deal with the military masters and the monarchical autocrats of Germany now, or if it is likely to have to deal with them later in regard to the international obligations of the German Empire, it must demand, not peace negotiations, but surrender. Nothing can be gained by leaving this essential thing unsaid."

THANKSGIVING FOR VICTORY

THANKSGIVING PROCLAMATION, ISSUED NOVEMBER 16, 1918. FROM "UNITED STATES STATUTES AT LARGE," VOL. 40, PT. 2, PP. 1888-89.

IT has long been our custom to turn in the autumn of the year in praise and thanksgiving to Almighty God for His many blessings and mercies to us as a nation. This year we have special and moving cause to be grateful and to rejoice.

God has in His good pleasure given us peace. It has not come as a mere cessation of arms, a mere relief from the strain and tragedy of war. It has come as a great triumph of right. Complete victory has brought us, not peace alone, but the confident promise of a new day as well in which justice shall replace force and jealous intrigue among the nations. Our gallant armies have participated in a triumph which is not marred or stained by any purpose of selfish aggression. In a righteous cause they have won immortal glory and have nobly served their nation in serving mankind. God has indeed been gracious. We have cause for such rejoicing as revives and strengthens in us all the best traditions of our national history. A new day shines about us, in which our hearts take new courage and look forward with open hope to new and greater duties.

While we render thanks for these things, let us not forget to seek the Divine guidance in the performance of those duties, and Divine mercy and forgiveness for all errors of act or purpose, and pray that in all that we do we shall strengthen the ties of friendship and mutual respect upon which we must assist to built the new structure of peace and good will among the nations.

Wherefore, I, Woodrow Wilson, President of the United States of America, do hereby designate Thursday, the twenty-eighth day of November next as a day of thanksgiving and prayer and invite the people throughout the land to cease upon that day from their ordinary occupations and in their several homes and places of worship to render thanks to God, the ruler of nations.

ANNUAL MESSAGE

ADDRESS DELIVERED AT A JOINT SESSION OF THE TWO HOUSES OF CONGRESS, DECEMBER 2, 1918. FROM OFFICIAL GOVERNMENT PUBLICATION IN MR. WILSON'S FILES.

THE year that has elapsed since I last stood before you to fulfill my constitutional duty to give to the Congress from time to time information on the state of the Union has been so crowded with great events, great processes and great results that I cannot hope to give you an adequate picture of its transactions or of the far-reaching changes which have been wrought in the life of our nation and of the world. You have yourselves witnessed these things, as I have. It is too soon to assess them; and we who stand in the midst of them and are part of them are less qualified than men of another generation will be to say what they mean, or even what they have been. But some great outstanding facts are unmistakable and constitute, in a sense, part of the public business with which it is our duty to deal. To state them is to set the stage for the legislative and executive action which must grow out of them and which we have yet to shape and determine.

A year ago we had sent 145,819 men overseas. Since then we have sent 1,950,513, an average of 162,542 each month, the number in fact rising, in

May last to 245,951, in June to 278,760, in July to 307,182, and continuing to reach similar figures in August and September,—in August 289,570 and in September 257,438. No such movement of troops ever took place before, across three thousand miles of sea, followed by adequate equipment and supplies, and carried safely through extraordinary dangers of attack,—dangers which were alike strange and infinitely difficult to guard against. In all this movement only seven hundred and fifty-eight men were lost by enemy attack,—six hundred and thirty of whom were upon a single English Transport which was sunk near the Orkney Islands.

I need not tell you what lay back of this great movement of men and material. It is not invidious to say that back of it lay a supporting organization of the industries of the country and of all its productive activities more complete, more thorough in method and effective in result, more spirited and unanimous in purpose and effort than any other great belligerent had been able to effect. We profited greatly by the experience of the nations which had already been engaged for nearly three years in the exigent and exacting business, their every resource and every executive proficiency taxed to the utmost. We were their pupils. But we learned quickly and acted with a promptness and a readiness of coöperation that justify our great pride that we were able to serve the world with unparalleled energy and quick accomplishment.

But it is not the physical scale and executive efficiency of preparation, supply, equipment and dispatch that I would dwell upon, but the mettle and quality of the officers and men we sent over and of the sailors who kept the seas, and the spirit of the nation that stood behind them. No soldiers or sailors ever proved themselves more quickly ready for the test of battle or acquitted themselves with more splendid courage and achievement when put to the test. Those of us who played some part in directing the great processes by which the war was pushed irresistibly forward to the final triumph may now forget all that and delight our thoughts with the story of what our men did. Their officers understood the grim and exacting task they had undertaken and performed it with an audacity, efficiency and unhesitating courage that touch the story of convoy and battle with imperishable distinction at every turn, whether the enterprise were great or small,—from their great chiefs, Pershing and Sims, down to the youngest lieutenant; and their men were worthy of them,—such men as hardly need to be commanded, and go to their terrible adventure blithely and with the quick intelligence of those who know just what it is they would accomplish. I am proud to be the fellow countryman of men of such stuff and valor. Those of us who stayed at home did our duty; the war could not have been won or the gallant men who fought it given their opportunity to win it otherwise; but for many a long day we shall think ourselves "accurs'd we were not there, and hold our manhoods cheap while any speaks that fought" with these at St. Mihiel or Thierry. The memory of those days of triumphant battle will

go with these fortunate men to their graves; and
each will have his favorite memory. "Old men forget; yet all shall be forgot, but he'll remember with
advantages what feats he did that day!"

What we all thank God for with deepest gratitude is that our men went in force into the line of
battle just at the critical moment when the whole
fate of the world seemed to hang in the balance and
threw their fresh strength into the ranks of freedom in time to turn the whole tide and sweep of the
fateful struggle,—turn it once for all, so that henceforth it was back, back, back for their enemies, always back, never again forward! After that it was
only a scant four months before the commanders of
the Central Empires knew themselves beaten; and
now their very empires are in liquidation!

And throughout it all how fine the spirit of the
Nation was: what unity of purpose, what untiring
zeal! What elevation of purpose ran through all
its splendid display of strength, its untiring accomplishment. I have said that those of us who stayed
at home to do the work of organization and supply
will always wish that we had been with the men
whom we sustained by our labor; but we can never
be ashamed. It had been an inspiring thing to be
here in the midst of fine men who had turned aside
from every private interest of their own and devoted the whole of their trained capacity to the
tasks that supplied the sinews of the whole great undertaking! The patriotism, the unselfishness, the
thoroughgoing devotion and distinguished capacity
that marked their toilsome labors, day after day,

month after month, have made them fit mates and
comrades of the men in the trenches and on the sea.
And not the men here in Washington only. They
have but directed the vast achievement. Throughout innumerable factories, upon innumerable farms,
in the depths of coal mines and iron mines and copper mines, wherever the stuffs of industry were to
be obtained and prepared, in the shipyards, on the
railways, at the docks, on the sea, in every labor that
was needed to sustain the battle lines, men have vied
with each other to do their part and do it well. They
can look any man-at-arms in the face, and say, We
also strove to win and gave the best that was in us
to make our fleets and armies sure of their triumph!

And what shall we say of the women,—of their instant intelligence, quickening every task that they
touched; their capacity for organization and coöperation, which gave their action discipline and enhanced the effectiveness of everything they attempted; their aptitude at tasks to which they had
never before set their hands; their utter self-sacrifice alike in what they did and in what they gave?
Their contribution to the great result is beyond ap-
praisal. They have added a new luster to the annals of American womanhood.

The least tribute we can pay them is to make them
the equals of men in political rights as they have
proved themselves their equals in every field of practical work they have entered, whether for themselves or for their country. These great days of completed achievement would be sadly marred were we
to omit that act of justice. Besides the immense

practical services they have rendered, the women of
the country have been the moving spirits in the systematic economies by which our people have volun-
tarily assisted to supply the suffering peoples of
the world and the armies upon every front with food
and everything else that we had that might serve
the common cause. The details of such a story can
never be fully written, but we carry them at our
hearts and thank God that we can say that we are
the kinsmen of such.

And now we are sure of the great triumph for
which every sacrifice was made. It has come, come
in its completeness, and with the pride and inspiration of these days of achievement quick within us
we turn to the tasks of peace again,—a peace secure
against the violence of irresponsible monarchs and
ambitious military coteries and made ready for a new
order, for new foundations of justice and fair dealing.

We are about to give order and organization to
this peace not only for ourselves but for the other
peoples of the world as well, so far as they will suffer
us to serve them. It is international justice that we
seek, not domestic safety merely. Our thoughts have
dwelt of late upon Europe, upon Asia, upon the near
and the far East, very little upon the acts of peace
and accommodation that wait to be performed at our
own doors. While we are adjusting our relations
with the rest of the world is it not of capital importance that we should clear away all grounds of misunderstanding with our immediate neighbors and
give proof of the friendship we really feel? I hope

that the members of the Senate will permit me to speak once more of the unratified treaty of friendship and adjustment with the Republic of Colombia. I very earnestly urge upon them an early and favorable action upon that vital matter. I believe that they will feel, with me, that the stage of affairs is now set for such action as will be not only just but generous and in the spirit of the new age upon which we have so happily entered.

So far as our domestic affairs are concerned the problem of our return to peace is a problem of economic and industrial readjustment. That problem is less serious for us than it may turn out to be for the nations which have suffered the disarrangements and the losses of war longer than we. Our people, moreover, do not wait to be coached and led. They know their own business, are quick and resourceful at every readjustment, definite in purpose, and self-reliant in action. Any leading strings we might seek to put them in would speedily become hopelessly tangled because they would pay no attention to them and go their own way. All that we can do as their legislative and executive servants is to mediate the process of change here, there, and elsewhere as we may. I have heard much counsel as to the plans that should be formed and personally conducted to a happy consummation, but from no quarter have I seen any general scheme of "reconstruction" emerge which I thought it likely we could force our spirited business men and self-reliant laborers to accept with due pliancy and obedience.

While the war lasted we set up many agencies by

which to direct the industries of the country in the
services it was necessary for them to render, by which
to make sure of an abundant supply of the materials
needed, by which to check undertakings that could
for the time be dispensed with and stimulate those
that were most serviceable in war, by which to gain
for the purchasing departments of the Government a
certain control over the prices of essential articles
and materials, by which to restrain trade with alien
enemies, make the most of the available shipping, and
systematize financial transactions, both public and
private, so that there would be no unnecessary conflict or confusion,—by which, in short, to put every
material energy of the country in harness to draw the
common load and make of us one team in the accomplishment of a great task. But the moment we knew
the armistice to have been signed we took the harness off. Raw materials upon which the Government
had kept its hand for fear there should not be enough
for the industries that supplied the armies have been
released and put into the general market again.
Great industrial plants whose whole output and machinery have been taken over for the uses of the Government have been set free to return to the uses to
which they were put before the war. It has not been
possible to remove so readily or so quickly the control of foodstuffs and of shipping, because the world
has still to be fed from our granaries and the ships
are still needed to send supplies to our men oversea and to bring the men back as fast as the disturbed conditions on the other side of the water
permit; but even there restraints are being relaxed as

much as possible and more and more as the weeks
go by.

Never before have there been agencies in existence
in this country which knew so much of the field of
supply, of labor, and of industry as the War Industries Board, the War Trade Board, the Labor Department, the Food Administration, and the Fuel Administration have known since their labors became
thoroughly systematized; and they have not been
isolated agencies; they have been directed by men
which represented the permanent Departments of the
Government and so have been the centers of unified
and coöperative action. It has been the policy of the
Executive, therefore, since the armistice was assured
(which is in effect a complete submission of the
enemy) to put the knowledge of these bodies at the
disposal of the business men of the country and to
offer their intelligent mediation at every point and
in every matter where it was desired. It is surpris-
ing how fast the process of return to a peace footing
has moved in the three weeks since the fighting
stopped. It promises to outrun any inquiry that
may be instituted and any aid that may be offered.
It will not be easy to direct it any better than it will
direct itself. The American business man is of quick
initiative.

The ordinary and normal processes of private
initiative will not, however, provide immediate employment for all of the men of our returning armies.
Those who are of trained capacity, those who are
skilled workmen, those who have acquired familiarity
with established businesses, those who are ready and

willing to go to the farms, all those whose aptitudes
are known or will be sought out by employers will
find no difficulty, it is safe to say, in finding place
and employment. But there will be others who
will be at a loss where to gain a livelihood unless
pains are taken to guide them and put them in the
way of work. There will be a large floating residuum
of labor which should not be left wholly to shift
for itself. It seems to me important, therefore, that
the development of public works of every sort should
be promptly resumed, in order that opportunities
should be created for unskilled labor in particular,
and that plans should be made for such development
of our unused lands and our natural resources as we
have hitherto lacked stimulation to undertake.

I particularly direct your attention to the very
practical plans which the Secretary of the Interior
has developed in his annual report and before your
Committees for the declamation of arid, swamp, and
cut-over lands which might, if the States were willing and able to coöperate, redeem some three hundred
million acres of land for cultivation. There are said
to be fifteen or twenty million acres of land in the
West, at present arid, for whose reclamation water
is available, if properly conserved. There are about
two hundred and thirty million acres from which the
forests have been cut but which have never yet been
cleared for the plow and which lie waste and desolate.
These lie scattered all over the Union. And there
are nearly eighty million acres of land that lie under
swamps or subject to periodical overflow or too wet
for anything but grazing which it is perfectly feas-

ible to drain and protect and redeem. The Congress can at once direct thousands of the returning soldiers to the reclamation of the arid lands which it has already undertaken, if it will but enlarge the plans and appropriations which it has intrusted to the Department of the Interior. It is possible in dealing with our unused land to effect a great rural and agricultural development which will afford the best sort of opportunity to men who want to help themselves; and the Secretary of the Interior has thought the possible methods out in a way which is worthy of your most friendly attention.

I have spoken of the control which must yet for a while, perhaps for a long while, be exercised over shipping because of the priority of service to which our forces overseas are entitled and which should also be accorded the shipments which are to save recently liberated peoples from starvation and many devastated regions from permanent ruin. May I not say a special word about the needs of Belgium and northern France? No sums of money paid by way of indemnity will serve of themselves to save them from hopeless disadvantage for years to come. Something more must be done than merely find the money. If they had money and raw materials in abundance to-morrow they could not resume their place in the industry of the world to-morrow,—the very important place they held before the flame of war swept across them. Many of their factories are razed to the ground. Much of their machinery is destroyed or has been taken away. Their people are scattered and many of their best workmen are dead. Their

markets will be taken by others, if they are not in
some special way assisted to rebuild their factories
and replace their lost instruments of manufacture.
They should not be left to the vicissitudes of the
sharp competition for materials and for industrial
facilities which is now to set in. I hope, therefore,
that the Congress will not be unwilling, if it should
become necessary, to grant to some such agency as
the War Trade Board the right to establish priorities
of export and supply for the benefit of these people
whom we have been so happy to assist in saving from
the German terror and whom we must not now
thoughtlessly leave to shift for themselves in a pitiless competitive market.

For the steadying and facilitation of our own domestic business readjustments nothing is more important than the immediate determination of the taxes
that are to be levied for 1918, 1919 and 1920. As
much of the burden of taxation must be lifted from
business as sound methods of financing the Government will permit, and those who conduct the great
essential industries of the country must be told as
exactly as possible what obligations to the Government they will be expected to meet in the years immediately ahead of them. It will be of serious
consequence to the country to delay removing all uncertainties in this matter a single day longer than the
right processes of debate justify. It is idle to talk
of successful and confident business reconstruction
before those uncertainties are resolved.

If the war had continued it would have been necessary to raise at least eight billion dollars by taxa-

tion payable in the year 1919; but the war has ended
and I agree with the Secretary of the Treasury that
it will be safe to reduce the amount to six billions.
An immediate rapid decline in the expenses of the
Government is not to be looked for. Contracts made
for war supplies will, indeed, be rapidly canceled
and liquidated, but their immediate liquidation will
make heavy drains on the Treasury for the months
just ahead of us. The maintenance of our forces on
the other side of the sea is still necessary. A considerable proportion of those forces must remain in
Europe during the period of occupation, and those
which are brought home will be transported and de-
mobilized at heavy expense for months to come. The
interest on our war debt must of course be paid and
provision made for the retirement of the obligations
of the Government which represent it. But these
demands will of course fall much below what a continuation of military operations would have entailed
and six billions should suffice to supply a sound
foundation for the financial operations of the year.

I entirely concur with the Secretary of the Treasury in recommending that the two billions needed in
addition to the four billions provided by existing law
be obtained from the profits which have accrued and
shall accrue from war contracts and distinctively
war business, but that these taxes be confined to the
war profits accruing in 1918, or in 1919 from business originating in war contracts. I urge your acceptance of his recommendation that provision be
made now, not subsequently, that the taxes to be paid
in 1920 should be reduced from six to four billions.

And arrangements less definite than these would add elements of doubt and confusion to the critical period of industrial readjustment through which the country must now immediately pass, and which no true friend of the Nation's essential business interests can afford to be responsible for creating or prolonging. Clearly determined conditions, clearly and simply charted, are indispensable to the economic revival and rapid industrial development which may confidently be expected if we act now and sweep all interrogation points away.

I take it for granted that the Congress will carry out the naval program which was undertaken before we entered the war. The Secretary of the Navy has submitted to your Committees for authorization that part of the program which covers the building plans of the next three years. These plans have been prepared along the lines and in accordance with the policy which the Congress established, not under the exceptional conditions of the war, but with the intention of adhering to a definite method of development for the navy. I earnestly recommend the uninterrupted pursuit of that policy. It would clearly be unwise for us to attempt to adjust our programs to a future world policy as yet undetermined.

The question which causes me the greatest concern is the question of the policy to be adopted towards the railroads. I frankly turn to you for counsel upon it. I have no confident judgment of my own. I do not see how any thoughtful man can have who knows anything of the complexity of the problem. It is a problem which must be studied, studied immediately,

and studied without bias or prejudice. Nothing can
be gained by becoming partisans of any particular
plan of settlement.

It was necessary that the administration of the
railways should be taken over by the Government
so long as the war lasted. It would have been impossible otherwise to establish and carry through
under a single direction the necessary priorities of
shipment. It would have been impossible otherwise
to combine maximum production at the factories and
mines and farms with the maximum possible car supply to take the products to the ports and markets;
impossible to route troop shipments and freight shipments without regard to the advantage or disadvantage of the roads employed; impossible to subordinate,
when necessary, all questions of convenience to the
public necessity; impossible to give the necessary
financial support to the roads from the public treasury. But all these necessities have now been served,
and the question is, what is best for the railroads and
for the public in the future.

Exceptional circumstances and exceptional methods of administration were not needed to convince us
that the railroads were not equal to the immense
tasks of transportation imposed upon them by the
rapid and continuous development of the industries
of the country. We knew that already. And we
knew that they were unequal to it partly because their
full coöperation was rendered impossible by law and
their competition made obligatory, so that it has been
impossible to assign to them severally the traffic
which could best be carried by their respective lines

in the interest of expedition and national economy.

We may hope, I believe, for the formal conclusion of the war by treaty by the time spring has come. The twenty-one months to which the present control of the railways is limited after formal proclamation of peace shall have been made will run at the farthest, I take it for granted, only to the January of 1921. The full equipment of the railways which the federal administration had planned could not be completed within any such period. The present law does not permit the use of the revenues of the several roads for the execution of such plans except by formal contract with their directors, some of whom will consent while some will not, and therefore does not afford sufficient authority to undertake improvements upon the scale upon which it would be necessary to undertake them. Every approach to this difficult subject-matter of decision brings us face to face, therefore, with this unanswered question: What is it right that we should do with the railroads, in the interest of the public and in fairness to their owners?

Let me say at once that I have no answer ready. The only thing that is perfectly clear to me is that it is not fair either to the public or to the owners of the railroads to leave the question unanswered and that it will presently become my duty to relinquish control of the roads, even before the expiration of the statutory period, unless there should appear some clear prospect in the mean time of a legislative solution. Their release would at least produce one element of a solution, namely certainty and a quick stimulation of private initiative.

I believe that it will be serviceable for me to set forth as explicitly as possible the alternative courses that lie open to our choice. We can simply release the roads and go back to the old conditions of private management, unrestricted competition, and multiform regulation by both state and federal authorities; or we can go to the opposite extreme and establish complete Government control, accompanied, if necessary, by actual Government ownership; or we can adopt an intermediate course of modified private control, under a more unified and affirmative public regulation and under such alterations of the law as will permit wasteful competition to be avoided and a considerable degree of unification of administration to be effected, as, for example, by regional corporations under which the railways of definable areas would be in effect combined in single systems.

The one conclusion that I am ready to state with confidence is that it would be a disservice alike to the country and to the owners of the railroads to return to the old conditions unmodified. Those are conditions of restraint without development. There is nothing affirmative or helpful about them. What the country chiefly needs is that all its means of transportation should be developed, its railways, its waterways, its highways, and its countryside roads. Some new element of policy, therefore, is absolutely necessary,—necessary for the service of the public, necessary for the release of credit to those who are administering the railways, necessary for the protection of their security-holders. The old policy may be changed much or little, or surely it cannot wisely be

left as it was. I hope that the Congress will have
a complete and impartial study of the whole problem
instituted at once and prosecuted as rapidly as possible. I stand ready and anxious to release the roads
from the present control and I must do so at a very
early date if by waiting until the statutory limit of
time is reached I shall be merely prolonging the
period of doubt and uncertainty which is hurtful to
every interest concerned.

I welcome this occasion to announce to the Congress my purpose to join in Paris the representatives
of the governments with which we have been associated in the war against the Central Empires for the
purpose of discussing with them the main features of
the treaty of peace. I realize the great inconven-
iences that will attend my leaving the country, particularly at this time, but the conclusion that it was
my paramount duty to go has been forced upon me
by considerations which I hope will seem as conclusive to you as they have seemed to me.

The allied Governments have accepted the bases
of peace which I outlined to the Congress on the
eighth of January last, as the Central Empires also
have, and very reasonably desire my personal counsel in their interpretation and application, and it is
highly desirable that I should give it in order that
the sincere desire of our Government to contribute
without selfish purpose of any kind to settlements
that will be of common benefit to all the nations concerned may be made fully manifest. The peace settlements which are now to be agreed upon are of
transcendent importance both to us and to the rest

of the world, and I know of no business or interest
which should take precedence of them. The gallant
men of our armed forces on land and sea have consciously fought for the ideals which they knew to
be the ideals of their country; I have sought to express those ideals; they have accepted my statements
of them as the substance of their own thought and
purpose, as the associated Governments have accepted them; I owe it to them to see to it, so far as
in me lies, that no false or mistaken interpretation is
put upon them, and no possible effort omitted to
realize them. It is now my duty to play my full part
in making good what they offered their life's blood
to obtain. I can think of no call to service which
could transcend this.

I shall be in close touch with you and with affairs
on this side the water, and you will know all that I
do. At my request, the French and English Governments have absolutely removed the censorship of
cable news which until within a fortnight they had
maintained and there is now no censorship whatever
exercised at this end except upon attempted trade
communications with enemy countries. It has been
necessary to keep an open wire constantly available
between Paris and the Department of State and another between France and the Department of War.
In order that this might be done with the least possible interference with the other uses of the cables,
I have temporarily taken over the control of both
cables in order that they may be used as a single system. I did so at the advice of the most experienced
cable officials, and I hope that the results will justify

my hope that the news of the next few months may pass with the utmost freedom and with the least possible delay from each side of the sea to the other.

May I not hope, Gentlemen of the Congress, that in the delicate tasks I shall have to perform on the other side of the sea, in my efforts truly and faithfully to interpret the principles and purposes of the country we love, I may have the encouragement and the added strength of your united support? I realize the magnitude and difficulty of the duty I am undertaking; I am poignantly aware of its grave responsibilities. I am the servant of the Nation. I can have no private thought or purpose of my own in performing such an errand. I go to give the best that is in me to the common settlements which I must now assist in arriving at in conference with the other working heads of the associated Governments. I shall count upon your friendly countenance and encouragement. I shall not be inaccessible. The cables and the wireless will render me available for any counsel or service you may desire of me, and I shall be happy in the thought that I am constantly in touch with the weighty matters of domestic policy with which we shall have to deal. I shall make my absence as brief as possible and shall hope to return with the happy assurance that it has been possible to translate into action the great ideals for which America has striven.

CHRISTMAS GREETINGS TO THE SOLDIERS OF THE UNITED STATES

ADDRESS TO AMERICAN TROOPS AT HUMES, FRANCE, DECEMBER 25, 1918. FROM OFFICIAL GOVERNMENT PUBLICATION IN MR. WILSON'S FILES.

I WISH that I could give to each one of you the message that I know you are longing to receive from those at home who love you. I cannot do that, but I can tell you how everybody at home is proud of you; how everybody at home has followed every movement of this great Army with confidence and affection; and how the whole people of the United States are now waiting to welcome you home with an acclaim which probably has never greeted any other army. Because this is a war into which our country, like these countries we have been so proud to stand by, has put its whole heart, and the reason that we are proud of you is that you have put your heart into it; you have done your duty, and something more, you have done your duty and done it with a spirit which gave it distinction and glory.

And now we are to have the fruits of victory. You knew when you came over what you came over for, and you have done what it was appointed you to do. I know what you expect of me. Sometime ago a gentleman from one of the countries with which we are associated was discussing with me the moral aspects of this war, and I said that if we did not insist upon the high purposes for which this war was entered by the United States I could never look those gallant fellows across the seas in the face again. You knew what we expected of you and you did it. I know what you and the people at home expect of me; and I am happy to say, my fellow countrymen, that I do not find in the hearts of the great leaders with whom it is my privilege now to coöperate any difference of principle or of fundamental purpose. It happened that it was the privilege of America to present the chart for peace, and now the process of settlement has been rendered comparatively simple by the fact that all the nations concerned have accepted that chart and that the application of those principles laid down there will be their explication. The world will now know that the nations that fought this war, as well as the soldiers who represented them, are ready to make good—make good not merely in the assertion of their own interests, but make good in the establishment of peace upon the permanent foundations of right and of justice. Because this is not a war in which the soldiers of the free nations have obeyed masters. You have commanders, but you have no masters. Your very commanders represent you in representing the Nation of which you constitute so distinguished a part, and this being a people's war, everybody concerned in the settlement knows that it must be a people's peace, that nothing must be done in the settlement of the issues of the war which is not as handsome as the great achievements of the armies of the United States and the allies.

It is difficult, very difficult, men, in a formal speech like this to show you my real heart. You men probably do not realize with what anxious attention and care we have followed every step you have advanced, and how proud we are that every step was in advance and not in retreat; that every time you set your faces in any direction, you kept your faces in that direction. A thrill has gone through my heart, as it has gone through the heart of every American, with almost every gun that was fired and every stroke that was struck in the gallant fighting that you have done; and there has been only one regret in America, and that was the regret that every man there felt that he was not here in France, too. It has been a hard thing to perform civil tasks in the United States. It has been a hard thing to take part in directing what you did without coming over and helping you do it. It has taken a lot of moral courage to stay at home, but we are proud to back you up in every way that was possible to back you up, and now I am happy to find what splendid names you have made for yourselves among the civilian population of France as well as among your comrades in arms of the French Army. It is a fine testimony to you men that these people like you and love you and trust you, and the finest part of it all is that you deserve their trust.

I feel a comradeship with you to-day which is delightful as I look about upon these undisturbed fields and think of the terrible scenes through which you

have gone and realize now that the quiet peace, the
tranquillity of settled hope, has descended upon us
all; and while it is hard so far away from home
confidently to bid you a Merry Christmas, I can, I
think, confidently promise you a Happy New Year,
and I can from the bottom of my heart say, God bless
you.

AT THE GUILDHALL, LONDON

RESPONSE TO AN ADDRESS OF WELCOME BY THE LORD MAYOR AT THE GUILDHALL, LONDON, DECEMBER 28, 1918. FROM OFFICIAL GOVERNMENT PUBLICATION IN MR. WILSON'S FILES.

MR. LORD MAYOR:

We have come upon times when ceremonies like this have a new significance, and it is that significance which most impresses me as I stand here. The address which I have just heard is most generously and graciously conceived and the delightful accent of sincerity in it seems like a part of that voice of counsel which is now everywhere to be heard.

I feel that a distinguished honor has been conferred upon me by this reception, and I beg to assure you, sir, and your associates of my very profound appreciation, but I know that I am only part of what I may call a great body of circumstances. I do not believe that it was fancy on my part that I heard in the voice of welcome uttered in the streets of this great city and in the streets of Paris something more than a personal welcome. It seemed to me that I heard the voice of one people speaking to another people, and it was a voice in which one could distinguish a singular combination of emotions.

There was surely there the deep gratefulness that
the fighting was over. There was the pride that
the fighting had had such a culmination. There was
that sort of gratitude that the nations engaged had
produced such men as the soldiers of Great Britain
and of the United States and of France and of Italy
—men whose prowess and achievements they had witnessed with rising admiration as they moved from
culmination to culmination. But there was something more in it, the consciousness that the business
is not yet done, the consicousness that it now rests
upon others to see that those lives were not lost in
vain.

I have not yet been to the actual battlefields, but
I have been with many of the men who have fought
the battles, and the other day I had the pleasure of
being present at a session of the French Academy
when they admitted Marshal Joffre to their membership. The sturdy, serene soldier stood and uttered,
not the words of triumph, but the simple words of
affection for his soldiers, and the conviction which he
summed up, in a sentence which I will not try ac-
curately to quote but reproduce in its spirit, was that
France must always remember that the small and the
weak could never live free in the world unless the
strong and the great always put their power and
strength in the service of right. That is the afterthought—the thought that something must be done
now not only to make the just settlements, that of
course, but to see that the settlements remained and
were observed and that honor and justice prevailed
in the world. And as I have conversed with the sol-

diers, I have been more and more aware that they fought for something that not all of them had defined, but which all of them recognized the moment you stated it to them. They fought to do away with an old order and to establish a new one, and the center and characteristic of the old order was that unstable thing which we used to call the "balance of power"—a thing in which the balance was determined by the sword which was thrown in the one side or the other; a balance which was determined by the unstable equilibrium of competitive interests; a balance which was maintained by jealous watchfulness and an antagonism of interests which, though it was generally latent, was always deep-seated. The men who have fought in this war have been the men from free nations who were determined that that sort of thing should end now and forever.

It is very interesting to me to observe how from every quarter, from every sort of mind, from every concert of counsel, there comes the suggestion that there must now be, not a balance of power, not one powerful group of nations set off against another, but a single overwhelming, powerful group of nations who shall be the trustee of the peace of the world. It has been delightful in my conferences with the leaders of your Government to find how our minds moved along exactly the same line, and how our thought was always that the key to the peace was the guarantee of the peace, not the items of it; that the items would be worthless unless there stood back of them a permanent concert of power for their maintenance. That is the most reassuring thing that has

ever happened in the world. When this war began
the thought of a League of Nations was indulgently
considered as the interesting thought of closeted stu-
dents. It was thought of as one of those things that
it was right to characterize by a name which as a
university man I have always resented; it was said
to be academic, as if that in itself were a condemna-
tion, something that men could think about but never
get. Now we find the practical leading minds of the
world determined to get it. No such sudden and
potent union of purpose has ever been witnessed in
the world before. Do you wonder, therefore, gentlemen, that in common with those who represent you I
am eager to get at the business and write the sentences down; and that I am particularly happy that
the ground is cleared and the foundations laid—for
we have already accepted the same body of principles? Those principles are clearly and definitely
enough stated to make their application a matter
which should afford no fundamental difficulty. And
back of us is that imperative yearning of the world
to have all disturbing questions quieted, to have all
threats against peace silenced, to have just men everywhere come together for a common object. The
peoples of the world want peace and they want it
now, not merely by conquest of arms, but by agreement of mind.

It was this incomparably great object that brought
me overseas. It has never before been deemed ex-
cusable for a President of the United States to leave
the territory of the United States; but I know that
I have the support of the judgment of my colleagues

in the Government of the United States in saying that it was my paramount duty to turn away even from the imperative tasks at home to lend such counsel and aid as I could to this great, may I not say, final enterprise of humanity.

AT HIS GRANDFATHER'S CHURCH
AT CARLISLE

ADDRESS AT THE LOWTHER STREET CONGREGATIONAL CHURCH, CARLISLE, ENGLAND,[1] DECEMBER 29, 1918. FROM ORIGINAL COPY IN MR. WILSON'S FILES.

IT IS with unaffected reluctance that I project myself into this solemn service. I remember my grandfather very well, and, remembering him as I do, I am confident that he would not approve of it. I remember how much he required. I remember the stern lessons of duty he spoke to me. I remember also painfully the things which he expected me to know which I did not know. I know there has come a change of times when a layman like myself is permitted to speak in a congregation. But I was reluctant because the feelings that have been excited in me are too intimate and too deep to permit of public expression. The memories that have come to me to-day of the mother who was born here are very affecting, and her quiet character, her sense of duty and dislike of ostentation, have come back to me with increasing force as those years of duty have accumulated. Yet perhaps it is appropriate that in a place

[1] Woodrow Wilson's mother was born at Carlisle, England, December 20, 1826. His grandfather, Thomas Woodrow, was minister of the Lowther Street church. The President attended services and was unexpectedly called upon.

of worship I should acknowledge my indebtedness to her and to her remarkable father, because, after all, what the world is now seeking to do is to return to the paths of duty, to turn away from the savagery of interest to the dignity of the performance of right. And I believe that as this war has drawn the nations temporarily together in a combination of physical force we shall now be drawn together in a combination of moral force that will be irresistible.

It is moral force that is irresistible. It is moral force as much as physical that has defeated the effort to subdue the world. Words have cut as deep as the sword. The knowledge that wrong was being attempted has aroused the nations. They have gone out like men upon a crusade. No other cause could have drawn so many nations together. They knew that an outlaw was abroad who purposed unspeakable things. It is from quiet places like this all over the world that the forces accumulate which presently will overbear any attempt to accomplish evil on a large scale. Like the rivulets gathering into the river and the river into the seas, there come from communities like this streams that fertilize the consciences of men, and it is the conscience of the world that we are trying to place upon the throne which others would usurp.

IN FREE TRADE HALL, MANCHESTER

ADDRESS AT A LUNCHEON GIVEN DECEMBER 30, 1918. FROM OFFICIAL GOVERNMENT PUBLICATION IN MR. WILSON'S FILES.

MY LORD MAYOR, LADIES, AND GENTLE-MEN—PERHAPS I MAY BE PERMITTED TO ADD FELLOW CITIZENS:

You have made me feel in a way that is deeply delightful the generous welcome which you have accorded me. Back of it I know there lies the same sort of feeling for the great people whom I have the privilege of representing. There is a feeling of cordial fraternity and friendship between these two great nations, and as I have gone from place to place and been made everywhere to feel the pulse of sympathy that is now beating between us, I have been led to some very serious thoughts as to what the basis of it all is. For I think you will agree with me that friendship is not a mere sentiment. Patriotism is not a mere sentiment. It is based upon a principle—upon a principle that leads a man to give more than he demands. And, similarly, friendship is based not merely upon affection, but upon common service. A man is not your friend who is not willing to serve you, and you are not his friend unless you are willing to serve him, and out of that impulse of common interest and a desire of common service rises that

noble feeling which we have consecrated as friendship.

So it has seemed to me that the theme that we must
have in our minds now in this great day of settlement is the theme of common interest and the determination of what it is that is our common interest.
You know that heretofore the world has been governed, or at any rate an attempt has been made to
govern it, by partnerships of interest, and they have
broken down. Interest does not bind men together.
Interest separates men, for the moment there is the
slightest departure from the nice adjustment of interests jealousies begin to spring up. There is only
one thing that can bind people together and that is
a common devotion to right. Ever since the history of liberty began men have talked about their
rights, and it has taken several hundred years to
make them perceive that the principal part of right
is duty, and that unless a man performs his full duty
he is entitled to no right. This fine correlation of
the two things of duty and of right is the equipoise
and balance of society. So when we analyze the present situation and the future that we now have to
mold and control, it seems to me that there is no
other thought than that that can guide us.

You know that the United States has always felt
from the very beginning of her history that she must
keep herself separate from any kind of connection
with European politics, and I want to say very
frankly to you that she is not now interested in
European politics. But she is interested in the partnership of right between America and Europe. If

the future had nothing for us but a new attempt to keep the world at a right poise by a balance of power, the United States would take no interest, because she will join no combination of power which is not the combination of all of us. She is not interested merely in the peace of Europe, but in the peace of the world. Therefore it seems to me that in the settlement that is just ahead of us something more delicate and difficult than was ever attempted before is to be accomplished, a genuine concert of mind and of purpose. But while it is difficult there is an element present that makes it easy. Never before in the history of the world, I believe, has there been such a keen international consciousness as there is now. Men all over the world know that they have been embarrassed by national antagonisms and that the interest of each is the interest of all, and that men as men are the objects of government and international arrangements. There is a great voice of humanity abroad in the world just now which he who cannot hear is deaf. There is a great compulsion of the common conscience now in existence which if any statesman resist he has gained the most unenviable eminence in history. We are not obeying the mandates of parties or of politics. We are obeying the mandates of humanity. That is the reason why it seems to me that the things that are most often in our minds are the least significant. I am not hopeful that the individual items of the settlements which we are about to attempt will be altogether satisfactory. One has but to apply his mind to any one of the questions of boundary and of altered sovereignty and of

racial aspiration to do something more than conjecture that there is no man and no body of men
who know just how it ought to be settled. Yet if we
are to make unsatisfactory settlements, we must see
to it that they are rendered more and more satisfactory by the subsequent adjustments which are made
possible.

So that we must provide a machinery of readjustment in order that we may have a machinery of good
will and of friendship. Friendship must have a machinery. If I cannot correspond with you, if I cannot learn your mind, if I cannot coöperate with you,
I cannot be your friend, and if the world is to remain
a body of friends it must have the means of friendship, the means of constant friendly intercourse, the
means of constant watchfulness over the common interest—not making it necessary to make a great effort upon some great occasion and confer with one
another, but have an easy and constant method of
conference, so that troubles may be taken when they
are little and not allowed to grow until they are big.
I never thought that I had a big difference with a
man that I did not find when I came into conference
with him that, after all, it was rather a little difference and that if we were frank with one another, and
did not too much stand upon that great enemy of
mankind which is called pride, we could come together. It is the wish to come together that is more
than half of the process. This is a doctrine which
ought to be easy of comprehension in a great commercial center like this. You cannot trade with men
who suspect you. You cannot establish commercial

and industrial relations with those who do not trust
you. Good will is the forerunner of trade, and trade
is the great amicable instrument of the world on that
account.

I feel—I felt before I came here—at home in Manchester, because Manchester has so many of the char-
acteristics of our great American cities. I was
reminded of the anecdote of a humorous fellow countryman who was sitting at lunch in his club one day
and a man whom he did not like particularly came
by and slapped him on the shoulder. "Hello, Ollie,
old fellow, how are you?" he said. Ollie looked at
him coldly and said, "I don't know your face; I
don't know your name; but your manners are very
familiar." I don't know your names, but your manners are very familiar. They are very delightfully
familiar. So that I feel that in the community of interest and of understanding which is established in
great currents of trade, we are enabled to see international processes perhaps better than they can be
seen by others. I take it that I am not far from
right in supposing that that is the reason why Manchester has been a center of the great forward-
looking sentiments of men who had the instinct of
large planning, not merely for the city itself, but
for the Kingdom and the Empire and the world, and
with that outlook we can be sure that we can go
shoulder and shoulder together.

I wish that it were possible for us to do something like some of my very stern ancestors did, for
among my ancestors are those very determined persons who were known as the Covenanters. I wish

we could, not only for Great Britain and the United
States, but for France and Italy and the world, enter
into a great league and covenant, declaring ourselves,
first of all, friends of mankind and uniting ourselves together for the maintenance and the triumph
of right.

OPENING THE PEACE CONFERENCE

ADDRESS AT THE FIRST PLENARY SESSION, PARIS, JANU-
ARY 18, 1919. FROM OFFICIAL GOVERNMENT PUBLICA-
TION IN MR. WILSON'S FILES.

MR. CHAIRMAN:
It gives me great pleasure to propose as
permanent chairman of the conference M. Clemenceau, the president of the council. I would do this
as a matter of custom. I would do it as a tribute to
the French Republic. But I wish to do it as something more than that. I wish to do it as a tribute to
the man. France deserves the precedence not only
because we are meeting in her capital and because
she has undergone some of the most tragical sufferings of the war, but also because her capital, her
ancient and beautiful capital, has so often been the
center of conferences of this sort upon which the
fortunes of large parts of the world turned. It is a
very delightful thought that the history of the world,
which has so often centered here, will now be crowned
by the achievements of this conference. Because
there is a sense in which this is the supreme conference of the history of mankind. More nations are
represented here than were ever represented in such
a conference before. The fortunes of all peoples are
involved. A great war is ended which seemed about
to bring a universal cataclysm. The danger is passed.

A victory has been won for mankind, and it is delightful that we should be able to record these great results in this place.

But it is the more delightful to honor France because we can honor her in the person of so distinguished a servant. We have all felt in our participation in the struggles of this war the fine steadfastness which characterized the leadership of the French people in the hands of M. Clemenceau. We have learned to admire him, and those of us who have been associated with him have acquired a genuine affection for him. Moreover, those of us who have been in these recent days in constant consultation with him know how warmly his purpose is set toward the goal of achievement to which all our faces are turned. He feels as we feel, as I have no doubt everybody in this room feels, that we are trusted to do a great thing, to do it in the highest spirit of friendship and accommodation, and to do it as promptly as possible, in order that the hearts of men may have fear lifted from them and that they may return to those pursuits of life which will bring them happiness and content and prosperity. Knowing his brotherhood of heart in these great matters, it affords me a personal pleasure to propose not only that the president of the council of ministers, but M. Clemenceau, shall be the permanent chairman of this conference.

"MAKE THIS LEAGUE OF NATIONS A VITAL THING"

ADDRESS BEFORE THE SECOND PLENARY SESSION OF THE PEACE CONFERENCE; PARIS, JANUARY 25, 1919, FROM OFFICIAL GOVERNMENT PUBLICATION IN MR. WILSON'S FILES.

MR. CHAIRMAN:

I consider it a distinguished privilege to be permitted to open the discussion in this conference on the league of nations. We have assembled for two purposes, to make the present settlements which have been rendered necessary by this war, and also to secure the peace of the world, not only by the present settlements, but by the arrangements we shall make at this conference for its maintenance. The league of nations seems to me to be necessary for both these purposes. There are many complicated questions connected with the present settlements which perhaps cannot be successfully worked out to an ultimate issue by the decisions we shall arrive at here. I can easily conceive that many of these settlements will need subsequent reconsideration, but many of the decisions we make shall need subsequent alteration in some degree; for, if I may judge by my own study of some of these questions, they are not susceptible of confident judgments at present.

It is, therefore, necessary that we should set up

some machinery by which the work of this conference
should be rendered complete. We have assembled
here for the purpose of doing very much more than
making the present settlements. We are assembled
under very peculiar conditions of world opinion. I
may say without straining the point that we are not
representatives of Governments, but representatives
of peoples. It will not suffice to satisfy governmental
circles anywhere. It is necessary that we should
satisfy the opinion of mankind. The burdens of this
war have fallen in an unusual degree upon the whole
population of the countries involved. I do not need
to draw for you the picture of how the burden has
been thrown back from the front upon the older
men, upon the women, upon the children, upon the
homes of the civilized world, and how the real strain
of the war has come where the eye of government
could not reach, but where the heart of humanity
beats. We are bidden by these people to make a
peace which will make them secure. We are bidden
by these people to see to it that this strain does not
come upon them again, and I venture to say that it
has been possible for them to bear this strain because
they hoped that those who represented them could
get together after this war and make such another
sacrifice unnecessary.

It is a solemn obligation on our part, therefore, to
make permanent arrangements that justice shall be
rendered and peace maintained. This is the central
object of our meeting. Settlements may be temporary, but the action of the nations in the interest
of peace and justice must be permanent. We can set

up permanent processes. We may not be able to set
up permanent decisions. Therefore, it seems to me
that we must take, so far as we can, a picture of the
world into our minds. Is it not a startling circumstance, for one thing, that the great discoveries of
science, that the quiet studies of men in laboratories,
that the thoughtful developments which have taken
place in quiet lecture rooms, have now been turned
to the destruction of civilization? The powers of
destruction have not so much multiplied as gained
facility. The enemy whom we have just overcome
had at his seats of learning some of the principal
centers of scientific study and discovery, and he used
them in order to make destruction sudden and complete; and only the watchful, continuous coöperation
of men can see to it that science as well as armed
men is kept within the harness of civilization.

In a sense the United States is less interested in
this subject than the other nations here assembled.
With her great territory and her extensive sea borders, it is less likely that the United States should
suffer from the attack of enemies than that many of
the other nations here should suffer; and the ardor
of the United States—for it is a very deep and genuine ardor—for the society of nations is not an ardor
springing out of fear or apprehension, but an ardor
springing out of the ideals which have come to consciousness in this war. In coming into this war the
United States never for a moment thought that she
was intervening in the politics of Europe or the politics of Asia or the politics of any part of the world.
Her thought was that all the world had now become

conscious that there was a single cause which turned upon the issues of this war. That was the cause of justice and of liberty for men of every kind and place. Therefore, the United States should feel that its part in this war had been played in vain if there ensued upon it merely a body of European settlements. It would feel that it could not take part in guaranteeing those European settlements unless that guarantee involved the continuous superintendence of the peace of the world by the associated nations of the world.

Therefore, it seems to me that we must concert our best judgment in order to make this league of nations a vital thing—not merely a formal thing, not an occasional thing, not a thing sometimes called into life to meet an exigency, but always functioning in watchful attendance upon the interests of the nations—and that its continuity should be a vital continuity; that it should have functions that are continuing functions and that do not permit an intermission of its watchfulness and of its labor; that it should be the eye of the nations to keep watch upon the common interest, an eye that does not slumber, an eye that is everywhere watchful and attentive.

And if we do not make it vital, what shall we do? We shall disappoint the expectations of the peoples. This is what their thought centers upon. I have had the very delightful experience of visiting several nations since I came to this side of the water, and every time the voice of the body of the people reached me through any representative, at the front of its plea stood the hope for the league of nations. Gentlemen, the select classes of mankind are no longer the governors of mankind. The fortunes of mankind are now in the hands of the plain people of the whole world. Satisfy them, and you have justified their confidence not only, but established peace. Fail to satisfy them, and no arrangement that you can make will either set up or steady the peace of the world.

You can imagine, gentlemen, I dare say, the sentiments and the purpose with which representatives of the United States support this great project for a league of nations. We regard it as the keystone of the whole program which expressed our purposes and ideals in this war and which the associated nations have accepted as the basis of the settlement. If we returned to the United States without having made every effort in our power to realize this program, we should return to meet the merited scorn of our fellow citizens. For they are a body that constitutes a great democracy. They expect their leaders to speak their thoughts and no private purpose of their own. They expect their representatives to be their servants. We have no choice but to obey their mandate. But it is with the greatest enthusiasm and pleasure that we accept that mandate; and because this is the keystone of the whole fabric, we have pledged our every purpose to it, as we have to every item of the fabric. We would not dare abate a single part of the program which constitutes our instruction. We would not dare compromise upon any matter as the champion of this thing—this peace of the world, this attitude of justice, this principle that we are the masters of no people but are here to see that every people in the world shall choose its own masters and govern its own destinies, not as we wish, but as it wishes. We are here to see, in short, that the very foundations of this war are swept away. Those foundations were the private choice of small coteries of civil rulers and military staffs. Those foundations were the aggression of great powers upon the small. Those foundations were the holding together of empires of unwilling subject by the duress of arms. Those foundations were the power of small bodies of men to work their will upon mankind and use them as pawns in a game. And nothing less than the emancipation of the world from these things will accomplish peace. You can see that the representatives of the United States are, therefore, never put to the embarrassment of choosing a way of expediency, because they have never laid down for them the unalterable lines of principle. And, thank God, those lines have been accepted as the lines of settlement by all the high-minded men who have had to do with the beginnings of this great business.

I hope, Mr. Chairman, that when it is known, as I feel confident it will be known, that we have adopted the principle of the league of nations and mean to work out that principle in effective action, we shall by that single thing have lifted a great part of the load of anxiety from the hearts of men everywhere. We stand in a peculiar case. As I go about the streets here I see everywhere the American uniform. Those men came into the war after we had uttered our purposes. They came as crusaders, not merely to win a war, but to win a cause; and I am responsible

to them, for it fell to me to formulate the purposes
for which I asked them to fight, and I, like them,
must be a crusader for these things, whatever it costs
and whatever it may be necessary to do, in honor, to
accomplish the object for which they fought. I have
been glad to find from day to day that there is no
question of our standing alone in this matter, for
there are champions of this cause upon every hand.
I am merely avowing this in order that you may understand why, perhaps, it fell to us, who are disengaged from the politics of this great continent and of
the Orient, to suggest that this was the keystone of
the arch and why it occurred to the generous mind
of our president to call upon me to open this debate.
It is not because we alone represent this idea, but
because it is our privilege to associate ourselves with
you in representing it.

I have only tried in what I have said to give you
the fountains of the enthusiasm which is within us
for this thing, for those fountains spring, it seems
to me, from all the ancient wrongs and sympathies
of mankind, and the very pulse of the world seems
to beat to the surface in this enterprise.

BEFORE THE INTERNATIONAL LAW
SOCIETY

ADDRESS AT PARIS, MAY 9, 1919. FROM THE NEW YORK
"TIMES," MAY 11, 1919.

I ESTEEM it a very great pleasure to find myself in this distinguished company and in this companionship of letters. Sir Thomas [1] has been peculiarly generous, as have the gentlemen at the other end of the table, in what they have said of me, but they have given me too high a rôle to play up to. It is particularly difficult to believe oneself to be what has been described in so intimate a company as this. When a great body of people is present, one can assume a pose which is impossible when there is so small a number of critical eyes looking directly at you.

And yet there was one part of Sir Thomas's generous interpretation which was true. What I have tried to do, and what I have said in speaking for America, was to speak the mind of America, to speak the impulse and the principles of America. And the only proof I have of my success is that the spirit of America responded—responded without stint or limit —and proved that it was ready to do that thing which I was privileged to call upon it to do.

And we have illustrated in this spirit of America something which perhaps may serve as a partial

[1] Sir Thomas Barclay, President of the International Law Society.

guide for the future. May I say that one of the
things that has disturbed me in recent months is
the unqualified hope that men have entertained
everywhere of immediate emancipation from the
things that have hampered and oppressed them.
You cannot in human experience rush into the light.
You have to go through the twilight into the broaden-
ing day before the noon comes and the full sun is on
the landscape; and we must see to it that those who
hope are not disappointed, by showing them the
processes by which that hope must be realized—
processes of law, processes of slow disentanglement,
from the many things that have bound us in the past.

You cannot throw off the habits of society immediately any more than you can throw off the habits of
the individual immediately. They must be slowly got
rid of, or, rather, they must be slowly altered. They
must be slowly adapted, they must be slowly shapen
to the new ends for which we would use them. That is
the process of law, if law is intelligently conceived.

I thought it a privilege to come here to night, because your studies were devoted to one of the things
which will be of most consequence to men in the
future, the intelligent development of international
law. In one sense, this great, unprecedented war
was fought to give validity to international law, to
prove that it has a reality which no nation could afford to disregard; that, while it did not have the
ordinary sanctions, while there was no international
authority as yet to enforce it, it nevertheless had
something behind it which was greater than that,
the moral rectitude of mankind.

If we can now give to international law the kind of vitality which it can have only if it is a real expression of our moral judgment, we shall have completed in some sense the work which this war was intended to emphasize.

International law has perhaps sometimes been a little too much thought out in the closet. International law has—may I say it without offense?—been handled too exclusively by lawyers. Lawyers like definite lines. They like systematic arrangements. They are uneasy if they depart from what was done yesterday. They dread experiments. They like charted seas and, if they have no charts, hardly venture to undertake the voyage.

Now, we must venture upon uncharted seas, to some extent, in the future. In the new League of Nations we are starting out on uncharted seas, and therefore we must have, I will not say the audacity, but the steadiness of purpose which is necessary in such novel circumstances. And we must not be afraid of new things, at the same time that we must not be intolerant of old things. We must weave out of the old materials the new garments which it is necessary that men should wear.

It is a great privilege if we can do that kind of thinking for mankind—human thinking, thinking that is made up of comprehension of the needs of mankind. And when I think of mankind, I must say I do not always think of well-dressed persons. Most persons are not well dressed. The heart of the world is under very plain jackets, the heart of the world is at very simple firesides, the heart of the

world is in very humble circumstances; and, unless
you know the pressure of life of the humbler classes,
you know nothing of life whatever. Unless you
know where the pinch comes you do not know what
the pulse has to stand, you do not know what strain
the muscles have to bear, you do not know what
trial the nerves have to go through to hold on.

To hold on where there is no glee in life is the hard
thing. Those of us who can sit sometimes at leisure
and read pleasant books and think of the past, the
long past, that we have no part in, and project the
long future—we are not specimens of mankind. The
specimens of mankind have not time to do that, and
we must use our leisure when we have it to feel with
them and think for them, so that we can translate
their desire into a fact, so far as that is possible, and
see that that most complicated and elusive of all
things which we call justice is accomplished. An easy
word to say, and a noble word upon the tongue, but
one of the most difficult enterprises of the human
spirit!

It is hard to be just to those with whom you are
intimate; how much harder it is to conceive the problems of those with whom you are not intimate, and
be just to them. To live and let live, to work for
people and with people, is at the bottom of the kind
of experience which must underlie justice.

The sympathy that has the slightest touch of condescension in it has no touch of helpfulness about it.
If you are aware of stooping to help a man, you
cannot help him. You must realize that he stands on
the same earth with yourself and has a heart like

your own, and that you are helping him, standing on that common level and using that common impulse of humanity.

In a sense the old enterprise of national law is played out. I mean that the future of mankind depends more upon the relations of nations to one another, more upon the realization of the common brotherhood of mankind, than upon the separate and selfish development of national systems of law; so that the men who can, if I may express it so, think without language, think the common thoughts of humanity, are the men who will be most serviceable in the immediate future.

God grant that there may be many of them, that many men may see this hope and wish to advance it, and that the plain men everywhere may know that there is no language of society in which he has no brothers or colaborers, in order to reach the great ends of equity and of high justice.

"THAT QUICK COMRADESHIP OF LETTERS"

ADDRESS AT THE INSTITUTE OF FRANCE, PARIS, MAY 10, 1919. FROM ORIGINAL IN MR. WILSON'S FILES.

IT IS with the keenest sense of gratification and pleasure that I find myself in this company. You have not only said that I was at home here, but you have made me feel at home, sir, by the whole tone and tenor of your cordial welcome. I should in one sense in any case have felt at home, because I am more or less familiar with the works of the members of this Institute. I have worked in the same field. I have felt that quick comradeship of letters which is a very real comradeship, because it is a comradeship of thought and of principle. Therefore, I was prepared to feel at home in the company of men who have worked as I have in a common field.

Fortunately, sir, there is one thing which does not excite the jealousy of nations against one another. That is the distinction of thought, the distinction of literature, the achievement of the mind. Nations have always cheered one another in these accomplishments rather than envied one another. Their rivalry has been a generous rivalry, and never an antagonistic rivalry. They have coöperated in the fields of thought as they have not coöperated in other fields. Therefore, this is an old association of sentiment and of principle into which you have permitted me to enter. I would have liked very much sooner to take my actual seat in this company, except that I wanted to deserve your confidence by preferring my duty to my privilege. I wanted to be certain that I was not neglecting the things that you as well as my fellow countrymen would wish me to do in order to have the pleasure of being here in your presence and receiving a greeting, as well as giving to you my own very cordial greeting and adherence.

I have had in recent months one very deep sense of privilege. I have been keenly aware that there have been times when the peoples of Europe have not understood the people of the United States. We have been too often supposed to be a people devoted chiefly, if not entirely, to material enterprises. We have been supposed, in the common phrase, to worship the almighty dollar. We have accumulated wealth, sir, we have devoted ourselves to material enterprises, with extraordinary success, but there has underlain all of that all the time a common sense of humanity and a common sympathy with the high principles of justice, which have never grown dim in the field even of enterprise; and it has been my very great joy in these recent months to interpret the people of the United States to the people of the world. I have not done more, sir. I have not uttered in my public capacity my own private thoughts. I have uttered what I knew to be the thoughts of the great people whom I represent. I have uttered the things that have been stored up in their heart and purpose from the time of our birth as a nation. We came into the world consecrated to liberty, and whenever we see the cause of liberty imperilled we are ready to cast in our lot in common with the lot of those whose liberty is threatened. This is the spirit of the people of the United States, and they have been privileged to send two million men over here to tell you so. It has been their great privilege not merely to tell you so in words, but to tell you so in men and material,—the pouring out of their wealth and the offering of their blood.

So may I not take to myself the pleasant thought that in joining this company I am joining it in some sense as a representative of the people of the United States? Because my studies in the field of political science, sir, have been hardly more than my efforts as a public man. They have constituted an attempt to put into the words of learning the thoughts of a nation, the attitude of a people towards public affairs. A great many of my colleagues in American university life got their training even in political science, as so many men in the civil sciences did, in German universities. I have been obliged at various times to read a great deal of bad German, difficult German, awkward German, and I have been aware that the thought was as awkward as the phrase, that the thought was rooted in a fundamental misconception of the state and of the political life of people. And it has been a portion of my efforts to disengage the thought of American university teachers from this misguided instruction which they have received on this side of the sea. Their American spirit emancipated most of them as a matter of course, but the form of the thought sometimes misled them. They spoke too often of the State as a thing which could ignore the individual, as a thing which was privileged to dominate the fortune of men by a sort of inherent and sacred authority. Now, as an utter democrat I have never been able to accept that view of the State. My view of the State is that it must stoop and listen to what I have to say, no matter how humble I am, and that each man has the right to have his voice heard and his counsel heeded, in so far as it is worthy of heed.

I have always been among those who believed that the greatest freedom of speech was the greatest safety, because if a man is a fool, the best thing to do is to encourage him to advertise the fact by speaking. It cannot be so easily discovered if you allow him to remain silent and look wise, but if you let him speak, the secret is out and the world knows that he is a fool. So it is by the exposure of folly that it is defeated; not by the seclusion of folly, and in this free air of free speech men get into that sort of communication with one another which constitutes the basis of all common achievement. France through many vicissitudes and through many bitter experiences found the way to this sort of freedom, and now she stands at the front of the world as the representative of constitutional liberty.

SURESNES CEMETERY SPEECH

MEMORIAL DAY ADDRESS AT SURESNES CEMETERY, NEAR PARIS, MAY 30, 1919. FROM ORIGINAL IN MR. WILSON'S FILES.

NO ONE with a heart in his breast, no American, no lover of humanity, can stand in the presence of these graves without the most profound emotion. These men who lie here are men of a unique breed. Their like has not been seen since the far days of the Crusades. Never before have men crossed the seas to a foreign land to fight for a cause which they did not pretend was peculiarly their own, but knew was the cause of humanity and of mankind. And when they came, they found fit comrades for their courage and their devotion. They found armies of liberty already in the field—men who, though they had gone through three years of fiery trial, seemed only to be just discovering, not for a moment losing, the high temper of the great affair, men seasoned in the bloody service of liberty. Joining hands with these, the men of America gave that greatest of all gifts, the gift of life and the gift of spirit.

It will always be a treasured memory on the part of those who knew and loved those men that the testimony of everybody who saw them in the field of action was of their unflinching courage, their ardor to the point of audacity, their full consciousness of the high cause they had come to serve, and their constant vision of the issue. It is delightful to learn from those who saw these men fight and saw them waiting in the trenches for the summons to the fight that they had a touch of the high spirit of religion, that they knew they were exhibiting a spirit as well as a physical might, and those of us who know and love America know that they were discovering to the whole world the true spirit and devotion to their motherland. It was America who came in the person of these men and who will forever be grateful that she was so represented.

And it is the more delightful to entertain these thoughts because we know that these men, though buried in a foreign, are not buried in an alien soil. They are at home, sleeping with the spirits of those who thought the same thoughts and entertained the same aspirations. The noble women of Suresnes have given evidence of the loving sense with which they received these dead as their own, for they have cared for their graves, they have made it their interest, their loving interest, to see that there was no hour of neglect, and that constantly through all the months that have gone by, the mothers at home should know that there were mothers here who remembered and honored their dead.

You have just heard in the beautiful letter from Monsieur Clemenceau what I believe to be the real message of France to us on a day like this, a message of genuine comradeship, a message of genuine sympathy, and I have no doubt that if our British comrades were here, they would speak in the same spirit and in the same language. For the beauty of this war is that it has brought a new partnership and a new comradeship and a new understanding into the field of the effort of the nations.

But it would be no profit to us to eulogize these illustrious dead if we did not take to heart the lesson which they have taught us. They are dead; they have done their utmost to show their devotion to a great cause, and they have left us to see to it that that cause shall not be betrayed, whether in war or in peace. It is our privilege and our high duty to consecrate ourselves afresh on a day like this to the objects for which they fought. It is not necessary that I should rehearse to you what those objects were. These men did not come across the sea merely to defeat Germany and her associated powers in the war. They came to defeat forever the things for which the Central powers stood, the sort of power they meant to assert in the world, the arrogant, selfish dominance which they meant to establish; and they came, moreover, to see to it that there should never be a war like this again. It is for us, particularly for us who are civilians, to use our proper weapons of counsel and agreement to see to it that there never is such a war again. The nation that should now fling out of this common concord of counsel would betray the human race.

So it is our duty to take and maintain the safeguards which will see to it that the mothers of America and the mothers of France and England and Italy and Belgium and all the other suffering nations should never be called upon for this sacrifice again.

This can be done. It must be done. And it will be done. The thing that these men left us, though they did not in their counsels conceive it, is the great instrument which we have just erected in the League of Nations. The League of Nations is the covenant of governments that these men shall not have died in vain. I like to think that the dust of those sons of America who were privileged to be buried in their mother country will mingle with the dust of the men who fought for the preservation of the Union, and that as those men gave their lives in order that America might be united, these men have given their lives in order that the world might be united. Those men gave their lives in order to secure the freedom of a nation. These men have given theirs in order to secure the freedom of mankind; and I look forward to an age when it will be just as impossible to regret the results of their labor as it is now impossible to regret the result of the labor of those who fought for the Union of the States. I look for the time when every man who now puts his counsel against the united service of mankind under the League of Nations will be just as ashamed of it as if he now regretted the Union of the States.

You, are aware, as I am aware, that the airs of an older day are beginning to stir again, that the standards of an old order are trying to assert themselves again. There is here and there an attempt to insert into the counsel of statesmen the old reckonings of selfishness and bargaining and national advantage which were the roots of this war, and any man who counsels these things advocates the renewal of the

sacrifice which these men have made; for if this is
not the final battle for right, there will be another
that will be final. Let these gentlemen not suppose
that it is possible for them to accomplish this return
to an order of which we are ashamed and that we are
ready to forget. They cannot accomplish it. The
peoples of the world are awake and the peoples of the
world are in the saddle. Private counsels of statesmen cannot now and cannot hereafter determine the
destinies of nations. If we are not servants of
the opinion of mankind, we are of all men the littlest,
the most contemptible, the least gifted with vision.
If we do not know our age, we cannot accomplish our
purpose, and this age is an age which looks forward,
not backward; which rejects the standards of national
selfishness that once governed the counsel of nations
and demands that they shall give way to a new order
of things in which the only questions will be, ''Is it
right?'' ''Is it just?'' ''Is it in the interest of mankind?''

This is a challenge that no previous generation
ever dared to give ear to. So many things have happened, and they have happened so fast, in the last
four years, that I do not think many of us realize
what it is that has happened. Think how impossible
it would have been to get a body of responsible statesmen seriously to entertain the idea of the organization of a League of Nations four years ago! And
think of the change that has taken place! I was told
before I came to France that there would be confusion of counsel about this thing, and I found unity
of counsel. I was told that there would be opposi-

tion, and I found union of action. I found the statesmen with whom I was about to deal united in the
idea that we must have a League of Nations, that
we could not merely make a peace settlement and
then leave it to make itself effectual, but that we
must conceive some common organization by which
we should give our common faith that this peace
would be maintained and the conclusions at which
we had arrived should be made as secure as the
united counsels of all the great nations that fought
against Germany could make them. We have listened
to the challenge, and that is the proof that there shall
never be a war like this again.

Ladies and gentlemen, we all believe, I hope, that
spirits of these men are not buried with their bodies.
Their spirits live. I hope—I believe—that their
spirits are present with us at this hour. I hope that
I feel the compulsion of their presence. I hope that
I realize the significance of their presence. Think,
soldiers, of those comrades of yours who are gone.
If they were here, what would they say? They would
not remember what you are talking about to-day.
They would remember America which they left with
their high hope and purpose. They would remember
the terrible field of battle. They would remember
what they constantly recalled in times of danger,
what they had come for and how worth while it was
to give their lives for it. And they would say, "Forget all the little circumstances of the day. Be
ashamed of the jealousies that divide you. We command you in the name of those who, like ourselves,
have died to bring the counsels of men together, and

we remind you what America said she was born for. She was born, she said, to show mankind the way to liberty. She was born to make this great gift a common gift. She was born to show men the way of experience by which they might realize this gift and maintain it, and we adjure you in the name of all the great traditions of America to make yourselves soldiers now once for all in this common cause, where we need wear no uniform except the uniform of the heart, clothing ourselves with the principles of right and saying to men everywhere, 'You are our brothers and we invite you into the comradeship of liberty and of peace!' "

Let us go away hearing these unspoken mandates of our dead comrades.

If I may speak a personal word, I beg you to realize the compulsion that I myself feel that I am under. By the Constitution of our great country I was the commander-in-chief of these men. I advised the Congress to declare that a state of war existed. I sent these lads over here to die. Shall I—can I—ever speak a word of counsel which is inconsistent with the assurances I gave them when they came over? It is inconceivable. There is something better, if possible, that a man can give than his life, and that is his living spirit to a service that is not easy, to resist counsels that are hard to resist, to stand against purposes that are difficult to stand against, and to say, "Here stand I, consecrated in spirit to the men who were once my comrades and who are now gone, and who have left me under eternal bonds of fidelity."

EXPOSITION OF THE LEAGUE TO THE FOREIGN RELATIONS COMMITTEE

STATEMENT TO THE MEMBERS OF THE SENATE COMMIT-
TEE ON FOREIGN RELATIONS, AUGUST 19, 1919. FROM
66TH CONGRESS, 1ST SESSION. SENATE DOCUMENT
NO. 76.

MR. CHAIRMAN:

I have taken the liberty of writing out a little statement in the hope that it might facilitate discussion by speaking directly on some points that I know have been points of controversy and upon which I thought an expression of opinion would not be unwelcome. I am absolutely glad that the committee should have responded in this way to my intimation that I would like to be of service to it. I welcome the opportunity for a frank and full interchange of views.

I hope, too, that this conference will serve to expedite your consideration of the treaty of peace. I beg that you will pardon and indulge me if I again urge that practically the whole task of bringing the country back to normal conditions of life and industry waits upon the decision of the Senate with regard to the terms of the peace.

I venture thus again to urge my advice that the action of the Senate with regard to the treaty be taken at the earliest practicable moment because the problems with which we are face to face in the re-

adjustment of our national life are of the most pressing and critical character, will require for their
proper solution the most intimate and disinterested
coöperation of all parties and all interests, and cannot be postponed without manifest peril to our people
and to all the national advantages we hold most dear.
May I mention a few of the matters which cannot be
handled with intelligence until the country knows
the character of the peace it is to have? I do so only
by a very few samples.

The copper mines of Montana, Arizona and Alaska,
for example, are being kept open and in operation
only at a great cost and loss, in part upon borrowed
money; the zinc mines of Missouri, Tennessee and
Wisconsin are being operated at about one-half their
capacity; the lead of Idaho, Illinois and Missouri
reaches only a portion of its former market; there
is an immediate need for cotton belting, and also for
lubricating oil, which cannot be met—all because the
channels of trade are barred by war when there is
no war. The same is true of raw cotton, of which
the Central Empires alone formerly purchased nearly
4,000,000 bales. And these are only examples. There
is hardly a single raw material, a single important
foodstuff, a single class of manufactured goods which
is not in the same case. Our full, normal profitable
production waits on peace.

Our military plans of course wait upon it. We
cannot intelligently or wisely decide how large a
naval or military force we shall maintain or what our
policy with regard to military training is to be until
we have peace not only, but also until we know how

peace is to be sustained, whether by the arms of single nations or by the concert of all the great peoples. And there is more than that difficulty involved. The vast surplus properties of the army include not food and clothing merely, whose sale will affect normal production, but great manufacturing establishments also which should be restored to their former uses, great stores of machine tools, and all sorts of merchandise which must lie idle until peace and military policy are definitely determined. By the same token there can be no properly studied national budget until then.

The nations that ratify the treaty, such as Great Britain, Belgium and France, will be in a position to lay their plans for controlling the markets of Central Europe without competition from us if we do not presently act. We have no consular agents, no trade representatives there to look after our interests.

There are large areas of Europe whose future will lie uncertain and questionable until their people know the final settlements of peace and the forces which are to administer and sustain it. Without determinate markets our production cannot proceed with intelligence or confidence. There can be no stabilization of wages because there can be no settled conditions of employment. There can be no easy or normal industrial credits because there can be no confident or permanent revival of business.

But I will not weary you with obvious examples. I will only venture to repeat that every element of normal life amongst us depends upon and awaits the ratification of the treaty of peace; and also that we

cannot afford to lose a single summer's day by not
doing all that we can to mitigate the winter's suffering, which, unless we find means to prevent it, may
prove disastrous to a large portion of the world, and
may, at its worst, bring upon Europe conditions even
more terrible than those wrought by the war itself.

Nothing, I am led to believe, stands in the way of
ratification of the treaty except certain doubts with
regard to the meaning and implication of certain
articles of the Covenant of the League of Nations;
and I must frankly say that I am unable to understand why such doubts should be entertained. You
will recall that when I had the pleasure of a conference with your committee and with the committee
of the House of Representatives on Foreign Affairs
at the White House in March last the questions now
most frequently asked about the League of Nations
were all canvassed with a view to their immediate
clarification. The Covenant of the League was then
in its first draft and subject to revision. It was
pointed out that no express recognition was given
to the Monroe Doctrine; that it was not expressly
provided that the League should have no authority
to act or to express a judgment on matters of domestic
policy; that the right to withdraw from the League
was not expressly recognized; and that the constitutional right of the Congress to determine all questions
of peace and war was not sufficiently safeguarded.
On my return to Paris all these matters were taken
up again by the Commission on the League of Nations
and every suggestion of the United States was accepted.

The views of the United States with regard to the questions I have mentioned had, in fact, already been accepted by the commission and there was supposed to be nothing inconsistent with them in the draft of the Covenant first adopted—the draft which was the subject of our discussion in March—but no objection was made to saying explicitly in the text what all had supposed to be implicit in it. There was absolutely no doubt as to the meaning of any one of the resulting provisions of the Covenant in the minds of those who participated in drafting them, and I respectfully submit that there is nothing vague or doubtful in their wording.

The Monroe Doctrine is expressly mentioned as an understanding which is in no way to be impaired or interfered with by anything contained in the covenant and the expression "regional understandings like the Monroe Doctrine" was used, not because any one of the conferees thought there was any comparable agreement anywhere else in existence or in contemplation, but only because it was thought best to avoid the appearance of dealing in such a document with the policy of a single nation. Absolutely nothing is concealed in the phrase.

With regard to domestic questions Article 16 of the Covenant expressly provides that, if in case of any dispute arising between members of the League the matter involved is claimed by one of the parties "and is found by the council to arise out of a matter which by international law is solely within the domestic jurisdiction of that party, the council shall so report, and shall make no recommendation as to its settlement.'' The United States was by no means the only Government interested in the explicit adoption of this provision, and there is no doubt in the mind of any authoritative student of international law that such matters as immigration, tariffs, and naturalization are incontestably domestic questions with which no international body could deal without express authority to do so. No enumeration of domestic questions was undertaken because to undertake it, even by sample, would have involved the danger of seeming to exclude those not mentioned.

The right of any sovereign State to withdraw had been taken for granted, but no objection was made to making it explicit. Indeed, so soon as the views expressed at the White House conference were laid before the commission it was at once conceded that it was best not to leave the answer to so important a question to inference. No proposal was made to set up any tribunal to pass judgment upon the question whether a withdrawing nation had in fact fulfilled ''all its international obligations and all its obligations under the covenant.'' It was recognized that that question must be left to be resolved by the conscience of the Nation proposing to withdraw; and I must say that it did not seem to me worth while to propose that the article be made more explicit, because I knew that the United States would never itself propose to withdraw from the League if its conscience was not entirely clear as to the fulfillment of all its international obligations. It has never failed to fulfill them and never will.

Article 10 is in no respect of doubtful meaning

when read in the light of the covenant as a whole. The council of the League can only "advise upon" the means by which the obligations of that great article are to be given effect to. Unless the United States is a party to the policy or action in question, her own affirmative vote in the council is necessary before any advice can be given, for a unanimous vote of the council is required. If she is a party, the trouble is hers anyhow. And the unanimous vote of the council is only advice in any case. Each Government is free to reject it if it pleases. Nothing could have been made more clear to the conference than the right of our Congress under our Constitution to exercise its independent judgment in all matters of peace and war. No attempt was made to question or limit that right.

The United States will, indeed, undertake under Article 10 to "respect and preserve as against external aggression the territorial integrity and existing political independence of all members of the League," and that engagement constitutes a very grave and solemn moral obligation. But it is a moral, not a legal, obligation, and leaves our Congress absolutely free to put its own interpretation upon it in all cases that call for action. It is binding in conscience only, not in law.

Article 10 seems to me to constitute the very backbone of the whole covenant. Without it the League would be hardly more than an influential debating society.

It has several times been suggested, in public debate and in private conference, that interpretations of the sense in which the United States accepts the engagements of the covenant should be embodied in the instrument of ratification. There can be no reasonable objection to such interpretations accompanying the act of ratification provided they do not form a part of the formal ratification itself. Most of the interpretations which have been suggested to me embody what seems to me the plain meaning of the instrument itself. But if such interpretations should constitute a part of the formal resolution of ratification, long delays would be the inevitable consequence, inasmuch as all the many Governments concerned would have to accept, in effect, the language of the Senate as the language of the treaty before ratification would be complete. The assent of the German Assembly at Weimar would have to be obtained, among the rest, and I must frankly say that I could only with the greatest reluctance approach that Assembly for permission to read the treaty as we understand it and as those who framed it quite certainly understood it. If the United States were to qualify the document in any way, moreover, I am confident from what I know of the many conferences and debates which accompanied the formulation of the treaty that our example would immediately be followed in many quarters, in some instances with very serious reservations, and that the meaning and operative force of the treaty would presently be clouded from one end of its clauses to the other.

Pardon me, Mr. Chairman, if I have been entirely unreserved and plain-spoken in speaking of the great matters we all have so much at heart. If excuse is needed, I trust that the critical situation of affairs may serve as my justification. The issues that manifestly hang upon the conclusions of the Senate with regard to peace and upon the time of its action are so grave and so clearly insusceptible of being thrust on one side or postponed that I have felt it necessary in the public interest to make this urgent plea, and to make it as simply and as unreservedly as possible.

I thought that the simplest way, Mr. Chairman, to cover the points that I knew to be points of interest.

(Then follows the lengthy discussion between Mr. Wilson and the various members of the Senate Committee on Foreign Relations.)

ADDRESS

DELIVERED AT COLUMBUS, OHIO, SEPTEMBER 4, 1919.

MR. CHAIRMAN, GOVERNOR CAMPBELL, MY FELLOW CITIZENS:

It is with very profound pleasure that I find myself face to face with you. I have for a long time chafed at the confinement of Washington. I have for a long time wished to fulfill the purpose with which my heart was full when I returned to our beloved country, namely, to go out and report to my fellow countrymen concerning those affairs of the world which now need to be settled. The only people I owe any report to are you and the other citizens of the United States.

And it has become increasingly necessary, apparently, that I should report to you. After all the various angles at which you have heard the treaty held up, perhaps you would like to know what is in the treaty. I find it very difficult in reading some of the speeches that I have read to form any conception of that great document. It is a document unique in the history of the world for many reasons, and I think I cannot do you a better service, or the peace of the world a better service, than by pointing out to you just what this treaty contains and what it seeks to do.

In the first place, my fellow countrymen, it seeks to punish one of the greatest wrongs ever done in history, the wrong which Germany sought to do to the world and to civilization; and there ought to be no weak purpose with regard to the application of the punishment. She attempted an intolerable thing, and she must be made to pay for the attempt. The terms of the treaty are severe, but they are not unjust. I can testify that the men associated with me at the Peace Conference in Paris had it in their hearts to do justice and not wrong. But they knew, perhaps, with a more vivid sense of what had happened than we could possibly know on this side of the water, the many solemn covenants which Germany had disregarded, the long preparation she had made to overwhelm her neighbors, and the utter disregard which she had shown for human rights, for the rights of women, of children, of those who were helpless. They had seen their lands devasted by an enemy that devoted himself not only to the effort at victory, but to the effort at terror—seeking to terrify the people whom he fought. And I wish to testify that they exercised restraint in the terms of this treaty. They did not wish to overwhelm any great nation. They acknowledged that Germany was a great nation, and they had no purpose of overwhelming the German people, but they did think that it ought to be burned into the consciousness of men forever that no people ought to permit its government to do what the German Government did.

In the last analysis, my fellow countrymen, as we in America would be the first to claim, a people are

responsible for the acts of their Government. If
their Government purposes things that are wrong,
they ought to take measures to see to it that that purpose is not executed. Germany was self-governed;
her rulers had not concealed the purposes that they
had in mind, but they had deceived their people as
to the character of the methods they were going to
use, and I believe from what I can learn that there
is an awakened consciousness in Germany itself of
the deep iniquity of the thing that was attempted.
When the Austrian delegates came before the Peace
Conference, they in so many words spoke of the origination of the war as a crime and admitted in our
presence that it was a thing intolerable to contemplate. They knew in their hearts that it had done
them the deepest conceivable wrong, that it had put
their people and the people of Germany at the judgment seat of mankind, and throughout this treaty
every term that was applied to Germany was meant,
not to humiliate Germany, but to rectify the wrong
that she had done.

Look even into the severe terms of reparation—for
there was no indemnity. No indemnity of any sort
was claimed, merely reparation, merely paying for
the destruction done, merely making good the losses
so far as such losses could be made good which she
had unjustly inflicted, not upon the governments, for
the reparation is not to go to the governments, but
upon the people whose rights she had trodden upon
with absolute absence of everything that even resem-
bled pity. There was no indemnity in this treaty,
but there is reparation, and even in the terms of

reparation a method is devised by which the reparation shall be adjusted to Germany's ability to pay it.

I am astonished at some of the statements I hear made about this treaty. The truth is that they are made by persons who have not read the treaty or who, if they have read it, have not comprehended its meaning. There is a method of adjustment in that treaty by which the reparation shall not be pressed beyond the point which Germany can pay, but which will be pressed to the utmost point that Germany can pay—which is just, which is righteous. It would have been intolerable if there had been anything else. For, my fellow citizens, this treaty is not meant merely to end this single war. It is meant as a notice to every government which in the future will attempt this thing that mankind will unite to inflict the same punishment. There is no national triumph sought to be recorded in this treaty. There is no glory sought for any particular nation. The thought of the statesmen collected around that table was of their people, of the sufferings that they had gone through, of the losses they had incurred—that great throbbing heart which was so depressed, so forlorn, so sad in every memory that it had had of the five tragical years that have gone. Let us never forget those years, my fellow countrymen. Let us never forget the purpose—the high purpose, the disinterested purpose—with which America lent its strength not for its own glory but for the defense of mankind.

As I said, this treaty was not intended merely to end this war. It was intended to prevent any sim-

ilar war. I wonder if some of the opponents of the
League of Nations have forgotten the promises we
made our people before we went to that peace table.
We had taken by processes of law the flower of our
youth from every household, and we told those
mothers and fathers and sisters and wives and sweet-
hearts that we were taking those men to fight a war
which would end business of that sort; and if we do
not end it, if we do not do the best that human concert of action can do to end it, we are of all men
the most unfaithful, the most unfaithful to the
loving hearts who suffered in this war, the most unfaithful to those households bowed in grief and yet
lifted with the feeling that the lad laid down his life
for a great thing and, among other things, in order
that other lads might never have to do the same thing.
That is what the League of Nations is for, to end
this war justly, and then not merely to serve notice
on governments which would contemplate the same
things that Germany contemplated that they will do
it at their peril, but also concerning the combination
of power which will prove to them that they will do
it at their peril. It is idle to say the world *will*
.combine against you, because it may not, but it is
persuasive to say the world *is* combined against you,
and will remain combined against the things that
Germany attempted. The League of Nations is the
only thing that can prevent the recurrence of this
dreadful catastrophe and redeem our promises.

The character of the League is based upon the
experience of this very war. I did not meet a single
public man who did not admit these things, that

Germany would not have gone into this war if she
had thought Great Britain was going into it, and
that she most certainly would never have gone into
this war if she dreamed America was going into it.
And they all admitted that a notice beforehand that
the greatest powers of the world would combine to
prevent this sort of thing would prevent it absolutely. When gentlemen tell you, therefore, that
the League of Nations is intended for some other
purpose than this, merely reply this to them: If
we do not do this thing, we have neglected the central covenant that we made to our people, and there
will then be no statesman of any country who can
thereafter promise his people alleviation from the
perils of war. The passions of this world are not
dead. The rivalries of this world have not cooled.
They have been rendered hotter than ever. The harness that is to unite nations is more necessary now
than it ever was before, and unless there is this assurance of combined action before wrong is attempted, wrong will be attempted just as soon as the
most ambitious nations can recover from the financial
stress of this war.

Now, look what else is in the treaty. This treaty
is unique in the history of mankind, because the
center of it is the redemption of weak nations.
There never was a congress of nations before that
considered the rights of those who could not enforce
their rights. There never was a congress of nations
before that did not seek to effect some balance of
power brought about by means of serving the strength
and interest of the strongest powers concerned;

whereas this treaty builds up nations that never could have won their freedom in any other way; builds them up by gift, by largess, not by obligations; builds them up because of the conviction of the men who wrote the treaty that the rights of people transcend the rights of governments, because of the conviction of the men who wrote that treaty that the fertile source of war is wrong. The Austro-Hungarian Empire, for example, was held together by military force and consisted of peoples who did not want to live together, who did not have the spirit of nationality as towards each other, who were constantly chafing at the bands that held them. Hungary, though a willing partner of Austria, was willing to be a partner because she could share Austria's strength to accomplish her own ambitions, and her own ambitions were to hold under her the Jugo-Slavic peoples that lay to the south of her; Bohemia, an unhappy partner, a partner by duress, beating in all her veins the strongest national impulse that was to be found anywhere in Europe; and north of that, pitiful Poland, a great nation divided up among the great powers of Europe, torn asunder, kinship disregarded, natural ties treated with contempt, and an obligatory division among sovereigns imposed upon her—a part of her given to Russia, a part of her given to Austria, a part of her given to Germany—great bodies of Polish people never permitted to have the normal intercourse with their kinsmen for fear that that fine instinct of the heart should assert itself which binds families together. Poland could never have won her independ-

ence. Bohemia never could have broken away from
the Austro-Hungarian combination. The Slavic
peoples to the south, running down into the great
Balkan peninsula, had again and again tried to assert
their nationality and independence, and had as often
been crushed, not by the immediate power they were
fighting, but by the combined power of Europe. The
old alliances, the old balances of power, were meant
to see to it that no little nation asserted its right
to the disturbance of the peace of Europe, and every
time an assertion of rights was attempted they were
suppressed by combined influence and force.

This treaty tears away all that: says these people
have a right to live their own lives under the governments which they themselves choose to set up.
That is the American principle, and I was glad to
fight for it. When strategic claims were urged, it
was matter of common counsel that such considerations were not in our thought. We were not now
arranging for future wars. We were giving people
what belonged to them. My fellow citizens, I do not
think there is any man alive who has a more tender
sympathy for the great people of Italy than I have,
and a very stern duty was presented to us when we
had to consider some of the claims of Italy on the
Adriatic, because strategically, from the point of
view of future wars, Italy needed a military foothold
on the other side of the Adriatic, but her people did
not live there except in little spots. It was a Slavic
people, and I had to say to my Italian friends,
"Everywhere else in this treaty we have given territory to the people who lived on it, and I do not think

that it is for the advantage of Italy, and I am sure
it is not for the advantage of the world, to give Italy
territory where other people live.'' I felt the force
of the argument for what they wanted, and it was
the old argument that had always prevailed, namely,
that they needed it from a military point of view,
and I have no doubt that if there is no league of
nations, they will need it from a military point of
view; but if there is a league of nations, they will
not need it from a military point of view.

If there is no league of nations, the military point
of view will prevail in every instance, and peace
will be brought into contempt, but if there is a league
of nations, Italy need not fear the fact that the
shores on the other side of the Adriatic tower above
the lower and sandy shores on her side the sea, because there will be no threatening guns there, and
the nations of the world will have concerted, not
merely to see that the Slavic peoples have their rights,
but that the Italian people have their rights as well.
I had rather have everybody on my side than be
armed to the teeth. Every settlement that is right,
every settlement that is based on the principles I
have alluded to, is a safe settlement, because the
sympathy of mankind will be behind it.

Some gentlemen have feared with regard to the
League of Nations that we will be obliged to do
things we do not want to do. If the treaty were
wrong, that might be so, but if the treaty is right,
we will wish to preserve right. I think I know the
heart of this great people whom I, for the time being,
have the high honor to represent better than some

other men that I hear talk. I have been bred, and am proud to have been bred, in the old revolutionary school which set this Government up, when it was set up as the friend of mankind, and I know if they do not that America has never lost that vision or that purpose. But I have not the slightest fear that arms will be necessary if the purpose is there. If I know that my adversary is armed and I am not, I do not press the controversy, and if any nation entertains selfish purposes set against the principles established in this treaty and is told by the rest of the world that it must withdraw its claims, it will not press them.

The heart of this treaty then, my fellow citizens, is not even that it punishes Germany. That is a temporary thing. It is that it rectifies the age-long wrongs which characterized the history of Europe. There were some of us who wished that the scope of the treaty would reach some other age-long wrongs. It was a big job, and I do not say that we wished that it were bigger, but there were other wrongs elsewhere than in Europe and of the same kind which no doubt ought to be righted, and some day will be righted, but which we could not draw into the treaty because we could deal only with the countries whom the war had engulfed and affected. But so far as the scope of our authority went, we rectified the wrongs which have been the fertile source of war in Europe.

Have you ever reflected, my fellow countrymen, on the real source of revolution? Men do not start revolutions in a sudden passion. Do you remember what Thomas Carlyle said about the French Revolution? He was speaking of the so-called Hundred Days Terror which reigned not only in Paris, but throughout France, in the days of the French Revolution, and he reminded his readers that back of that hundred days lay several hundred years of agony and of wrong. The French people had been deeply and consistently wronged by their Government, robbed, their human rights disregarded, and the slow agony of those hundreds of years had after awhile gathered into a hot anger that could not be suppressed. Revolutions do not spring up over-night. Revolutions come from the long suppression of the human spirit. Revolutions come because men know that they have rights and that they are disregarded; and when we think of the future of the world in connection with this treaty we must remember that one of the chief efforts of those who made this treaty was to remove that anger from the heart of great peoples, great peoples who had always been suppressed, who had always been used, and who had always been the tools in the hands of governments, generally alien governments, not their own. The makers of the treaty knew that if these wrongs were not removed, there could be no peace in the world, because, after all, my fellow citizens, war comes from the seed of wrong and not from the seed of right. This treaty is an attempt to right the history of Europe, and, in my humble judgment, it is a measurable success. I say "measurable," my fellow citizens, because you will realize the difficulty of this:

Here are two neighboring peoples. The one people

have not stopped at a sharp line, and the settlements of the other people or their migrations have not begun at a sharp line. They have intermingled. There are regions where you cannot draw a national line and say there are Slavs on this side [illustrating] and Italians on that [illustrating]. It cannot be done. You have to approximate the line. You have to come as near to it as you can, and then trust to the processes of history to redistribute, it may be, the people that are on the wrong side of the line. There are many such lines drawn in this treaty and to be drawn in the Austrian treaty, where there are perhaps more lines of that sort than in the German treaty. When we came to draw the line between the Polish people and the German people—not the line between Germany and Poland; there was no Poland, strictly speaking, but the line between the German and the Polish people—we were confronted by such problems as the disposition of districts like the eastern part of Silesia, which is called Upper Silesia because it is mountainous and the other part is not. Upper Silesia is chiefly Polish, and when we came to draw the line of what should be Poland it was necessary to include Upper Silesia if we were really going to play fair and make Poland up of the Polish peoples wherever we found them in sufficiently close neighborhood to one another, but it was not perfectly clear that Upper Silesia wanted to be part of Poland. At any rate, there were Germans in Upper Silesia who said that it did not, and therefore we did there what we did in many other places. We said, "Very well, then, we will let the people that live there decide.

We will have a referendum. Within a certain length of time after the war, under the supervision of an international commission which will have a sufficient armed force behind it to preserve order and see that nobody interferes with the elections, we will have an absolutely free vote and Upper Silesia shall go either to Germany or to Poland, as the people in Upper Silesia prefer.'' That illustrates many other cases where we provided for a referendum, or a plebiscite, as they chose to call it. We are going to leave it to the people themselves, as we should have done, what Government they shall live under. It is none of my prerogative to allot peoples to this Government or the other. It is nobody's right to do that allotting except the people themselves, and I want to testify that this treaty is shot through with the American principle of the choice of the governed.

Of course, at times it went further than we could make a practical policy of, because various peoples were keen upon getting back portions of their population which were separated from them by many miles of territory, and we could not spot the map over with little pieces of separated States. I even reminded my Italian colleagues that if they were going to claim every place where there was a large Italian population, we would have to cede New York to them, because there are more Italians in New York than in any Italian city. But I hope, I believe, that the Italians in New York City are as glad to stay there as we are to have them. But I would not have you suppose that I am intimating that my Italian colleagues entered any claim for New York City.

We of all peoples in the world, my fellow citizens, ought to be able to understand the questions of this treaty without anybody explaining them to us, for we are made up out of all the peoples of the world. I dare say that in this audience there are representatives of practically all the people dealt with in this treaty. You do not have to have me explain national aspirations to you. You have been brought up on them. You have learned of them since you were children, and it is those national aspirations which we sought to release and give an outlet to in this great treaty.

But we did much more than that. This treaty contains among other things a Magna Charta of labor— a thing unheard of until this interesting year of grace. There is a whole section of the treaty devoted to arrangements by which the interests of those who labor with their hands all over the world, whether they be men or women or children, are sought to be safeguarded; and next month there is to meet the first assembly under this section of the league. Let me tell you, it will meet whether the treaty is ratified by that time or not. There is to meet an assembly which represents the interests of laboring men throughout the world. Not their political interests; there is nothing political about it. It is the interests of men concerning the conditions of their labor; concerning the character of labor which women shall engage in, the character of labor which children shall be permitted to engage in; the hours of labor; and, incidentally, of course, the remuneration of labor; that labor shall be remunerated in proportion, of course, to the maintenance of the standard of living, which is proper, for the man who is expected to give his whole brain and intelligence and energy to a particular task. I hear very little said about the Magna Charta of labor which is embodied in this treaty. It forecasts the day, which ought to have come long ago, when statesmen will realize that no nation is fortunate which is not happy and that no nation can be happy whose people are not contented; contented in their lives and fortunate in the circumstances of their lives.

If I were to state what seems to me the central idea of this treaty, it would be this: It is almost a discovery in international conventions that nations do not consist of their governments but consist of their people. That is a rudimentary idea. It seems to us in America to go without saying, but, my fellow citizens, it was never the leading idea in any other international congress that I ever heard of; that is to say, any international congress made up of the representatives of governments. They were always thinking of national policy, of national advantage, of the rivalries of trade, of the advantages of territorial conquest. There is nothing of that in this treaty. You will notice that even the territories which are taken away from Germany, like her colonies, are not given to anybody. There is not a single act of annexation in this treaty. Territories inhabited by people not yet to govern themselves, either because of economical or other circumstances, are put under the care of powers, who are to act as trustees—trustees responsible in the form of the world at the bar of the league of nations, and the terms upon which they are to exercise their trusteeship are outlined. They are not to use those people by way of draft to fight their wars for them. They are not to permit any form of slavery among them, or of enforced labor. They are to see to it that there are humane conditions of labor with regard not only to the women and children but to the men also. They are to establish no fortifications. They are to regulate the liquor and the opium traffic. They are to see to it, in other words, that the lives of the people whose care they assume—not sovereignty over whom they assume—are kept clean and safe and wholesome. There again the principle of the treaty comes out, that the object of the arrangement is the welfare of the people who live there, and not the advantage of the trustee.

It goes beyond that. It seeks to gather under the common supervision of the league of nations the various instrumentalities by which the world has been trying to check the evils that were in some places debasing men, like the opium traffic, like the traffic—for it was a traffic—in women and children, like the traffic in other dangerous drugs, like the traffic in arms among uncivilized people who could use arms only for their own detriment. It provides for sanitation, for the work of the Red Cross. Why, those clauses, my fellow citizens, draw the hearts of the world into league, draw the noble impulses of the world together and make a team of them.

I used to be told that this was an age in which mind was monarch, and my comment was that if that was true, the mind was one of those modern monarchs that reigns and does not govern; that, as a matter of fact, we were governed by a great representative assembly made up of the human passions, and that the best we could manage was that the high and fine passions should be in a majority so that they could control the baser passions, so that they could check the things that were wrong. This treaty seeks something like that. In drawing the humane endeavors of the world together it makes a league of the fine passions of the world, of its philanthropic passions, of its passion of pity, of its passion of human sympathy, of its passion of human friendliness and helpfulness, for there is such a passion. It is the passion which has lifted us along the slow road of civilization. It is the passion which has made ordered government possible. It is the passion which has made justice and established it in the world.

That is the treaty. Did you ever hear of it before? Did you ever know before what was in this treaty? Did anybody before ever tell you what the treaty was intended to do? I beg, my fellow citizens, that you and the rest of those Americans with whom we are happy to be associated all over this broad land will read the treaty yourselves, or, if you will not take the time to do that—for it is a technical document—that you will accept the interpretation of those who made it and know what the intentions were in the making of it. I hear a great deal, my fellow citizens, about the selfishness and the selfish ambitions of other governments, and I would not be doing justice to the gifted men with whom I was associated on

the other side of the water if I did not testify that
the purposes that I have outlined were their purposes. We differed as to the method very often. We
had discussions as to the details, but we never had
any serious discussion as to the principle. While we
all acknowledged that the principles might perhaps
in detail have been better realized, we are all back
of those principles. There is a concert of mind and
of purpose and of policy in the world that was never
in existence before. I am not saying that by way of
credit to myself or to those colleagues to whom I have
alluded, because what happened to us was that we
got messages from our people. We were under instructions, whether they were written down or not,
and we did not dare come home without fulfilling
those instructions. If I could not have brought back
the kind of treaty that I did bring back, I never
would have come back, because I would have been an
unfaithful servant, and you would have had the right
to condemn me in any way that you chose to use. So
that I testify that this is an American treaty not
only, but it is a treaty that expresses that heart of
the great peoples who were associated together in the
war against Germany.

I said at the opening of this informal address, my
fellow citizens, that I had come to make a report to
you. I want to add to that a little bit. I have not
come to debate the treaty. It speaks for itself, if
you will let it. The arguments directed against it
are directed against it with a radical misunderstanding of the instrument itself. Therefore, I am not
going anywhere to debate the treaty. I am going

to expound it, and I am going, as I do here, now, to-day, to urge you in every vocal method that you can use to assert the spirit of the American people in support of it. Do not let men pull it down. Do not let them misrepresent it. Do not let them lead this Nation away from the high purposes with which this war was inaugurated and fought. As I came through that line of youngsters in khaki a few minutes ago I felt that I could salute them because I had done the job in the way I promised them I would do it, and when this treaty is accepted, men in khaki will not have to cross the seas again. That is the reason I believe in it.

I say "when it is accepted," for it will be accepted. I have never entertained a moment's doubt of that, and the only thing I have been impatient of has been the delay. It is not dangerous delay, except for the temper of the peoples scattered throughout the world who are waiting. Do you realize, my fellow citizens, that the whole world is waiting on America? The only country in the world that is trusted at this moment is the United States, and the peoples of the world are waiting to see whether their trust is justified or not. That has been the ground of my impatience. I knew their trust was justified, but I begrudged the time that certain gentlemen wish to take in telling them so. We shall tell them so in a voice as authentic as any voice in history, and in the years to come men will be glad to remember that they had some part in the great struggle which brought this incomparable consummation of the hopes of mankind.

ADDRESS

MR. CHAIRMAN AND FELLOW COUNTRYMEN:

It is with a great deal of genuine pleasure that I find myself in Pueblo, and I feel it a compliment that I should be permitted to be the first speaker in this beautiful hall. One of the advantages of this hall, as I look about, is that you are not too far away from me, because there is nothing so reassuring to men who are trying to express the public sentiment as getting into real personal contact with their fellow citizens. I have gained a renewed impression as I have crossed the continent this time of the homogeneity of this great people to whom we belong. They come from many stocks, but they are all of one kind. They come from many origins, but they are all shot through with the same principles and desire the same righteous and honest things. I have received a more inspiring impression this time of the public opinion of the United States than it was ever my privilege to receive before.

The chief pleasure of my trip has been that it has nothing to do with my personal fortunes, that it has nothing to do with my personal reputation, that it has nothing to do with anything except great principles uttered by Americans of all sorts and of all parties which we are now trying to realize at this

crisis of the affairs of the world. But there have
been unpleasant impressions as well as pleasant impressions, my fellow citizens, as I have crossed the
continent. I have perceived more and more that men
have been busy creating an absolutely false impression of what the treaty of peace and the Covenant
of the League of Nations contain and mean. I find,
moreover, that there is an organized propaganda
against the League of Nations and against the treaty
proceeding from exactly the same sources that the
organized propaganda proceeded from which threatened this country here and there with disloyalty, and
I want to say—I cannot say too often—any man
who carries a hyphen about with him carries a dag-
ger that he is ready to plunge into the vitals of this
Republic whenever he gets ready. If I can catch
any man with a hyphen in this great contest I will
know that I have got an enemy of the Republic. My
fellow citizens, it is only certain bodies of foreign
sympathies, certain bodies of sympathy with foreign
nations that are organized against this great document which the American representatives have
brought back from Paris. Therefore, in order to
clear away the mists, in order to remove the impressions, in order to check the falsehoods that have clus-
tered around this great subject, I want to tell you a
few very simple things about the treaty and the
covenant.

Do not think of this treaty of peace as merely a
settlement with Germany. It is that. It is a very
severe settlement with Germany, but there is not anything in it that she did not earn. Indeed, she earned

more than she can ever be able to pay for, and the
punishment exacted of her is not a punishment
greater than she can bear, and it is absolutely necessary in order that no other nation may ever plot
such a thing against humanity and civilization. But
the treaty is so much more than that. It is not
merely a settlement with Germany; it is a readjustment of those great injustices which underlie the
whole structure of European and Asiatic society.
This is only the first of several treaties. They are
all constructed upon the same plan. The Austrian
treaty follows the same lines. The treaty with Hungary follows the same lines. The treaty with Bul-
garia follows the same lines. The treaty with
Turkey, when it is formulated, will follow the same
lines. What are those lines? They are based upon
the purpose to see that every government dealt with
in this great settlement is put in the hands of the
people and taken out of the hands of coteries and of
sovereigns who had no right to rule over the people.
It is a people's treaty, that accomplishes by a great
sweep of practical justice the liberation of men who
never could have liberated themselves, and the power
of the most powerful nations has been devoted not to
their aggrandizement but to the liberation of people
whom they could have put under their control if they
had chosen to do so. Not one foot of territory is demanded by the conquerors, not one single item of
submisison to their authority is demanded by them.
The men who sat around that table in Paris knew
that the time had come when the people were no
longer going to consent to live under masters, but

were going to live the lives that they chose themselves,
to live under such governments as they chose themselves to erect. That is the fundamental principle of
this great settlement.

And we did not stop with that. We added a great
international charter for the rights of labor. Reject this treaty, impair it, and this is the consequence
of the laboring men of the world, that there is no international tribunal which can bring the moral judgments of the world to bear upon the great labor
questions of the day. What we need to do with regard to the labor questions of the day, my fellow
countrymen, is to lift them into the light, is to lift
them out of the haze and distraction of passion, of
hostility, out into the calm spaces where men look at
things without passion. The more men you get into
a great discussion the more you exclude passion.
Just as soon as the calm judgment of the world is
directed upon the question of justice to labor, labor
is going to have a forum such as it never was supplied with before, and men everywhere are going to
see that the problem of labor is nothing more nor less
than the problem of the elevation of humanity. We
must see that all the questions which have disturbed
the world, all the questions which have eaten into the
confidence of men toward their governments, all the
questions which have disturbed the processes of industry, shall be brought out where men of all points
of view, men of all attitudes of mind, men of all kinds
of experience, may contribute their part of the settlement of the great questions which we must settle and
cannot ignore.

At the front of this great treaty is put the Covenant of the League of Nations. It will also be at the
front of the Austrian treaty and the Hungarian
treaty and the Bulgarian treaty and the treaty with
Turkey. Every one of them will contain the Covenant of the League of Nations, because you cannot
work any of them without the Covenant of the
League of Nations. Unless you get the united, concerted purpose and power of the great Governments
of the world behind this settlement, it will fall down
like a house of cards. There is only one power to
put behind the liberation of mankind, and that is the
power of mankind. It is the power of the united
moral forces of the world, and in the Covenant of
the League of Nations the moral forces of the world
are mobilized. For what purpose? Reflect, my fellow citizens, that the membership of this great
League is going to include all the great fighting nations of the world, as well as the weak ones. It is
not for the present going to include Germany, but
for the time being Germany is not a great fighting
country. All the nations that have power that can
be mobilized are going to be members of this League,
including the United States. And what do they
unite for? They enter into a solemn promise to one
another that they will never use their power against
one another for aggression; that they never will impair the territorial integrity of a neighbor; that they
never will interfere with the political independence
of a neighbor; that they will abide by the principle
that great populations are entitled to determine their
own destiny and that they will not interfere with

that destiny; and that no matter what differences
arise amongst them they will never resort to war
without first having done one or other of two things
—either submitted the matter of controversy to arbitration, in which case they agree to abide by the
result without question, or submitted it to the consideration of the council of the League of Nations,
laying before that council all the documents, all the
facts, agreeing that the council can publish the documents and the facts to the whole world, agreeing that
there shall be six months allowed for the mature consideration of those facts by the council, and agreeing
that at the expiration of the six months, even if they
are not then ready to accept the advice of the council
with regard to the settlement of the dispute, they will
still not go to war for another three months.   In
other words, they consent, no matter what happens,
to submit every matter of difference between them to
the judgment of mankind, and just so certainly as
they do that, my fellow citizens, war will be in the
far background, war will be pushed out of that foreground of terror in which it has kept the world for
generation after generation, and men will know that
there will be a calm time of deliberate counsel.   The
most dangerous thing for a bad cause is to expose
it to the opinion of the world.   The most certain
way that you can prove that a man is mistaken
is by letting all his neighbors know what he thinks,
by letting all his neighbors discuss what he thinks,
and if he is in the wrong you will notice that he will
stay at home, he will not walk on the street.   He will
be afraid of the eyes of his neighbors.   He will be

afraid of their judgment of his character. He will
know that his cause is lost unless he can sustain it by
the arguments of right and of justice. The same
law that applies to individuals applies to nations.

But, you say, "We have heard that we might be at
a disadvantage in the League of Nations." Well,
whoever told you that either was deliberately falsify-
ing or he had not read the Covenant of the League
of Nations. I leave him the choice. I want to give
you a very simple account of the organization of
the League of Nations and let you judge for yourselves. It is a very simple organization. The power
of the League, or rather the activities of the league,
lie in two bodies. There is the council, which consists of one representative from each of the principal
allied and associated powers—that is to say, the
United States, Great Britain, France, Italy, and
Japan, along with four other representatives of
smaller powers chosen out of the general body of the
membership of the League. The council is the source
of every active policy of the League, and no active
policy of the League can be adopted without a unanimous vote of the council. That is explicitly stated
in the Covenant itself. Does it not evidently follow
that the League of Nations can adopt no policy whatever without the consent of the United States? The
affirmative vote of the representative of the United
States is necessary in every case. Now, you have
heard of six votes belonging to the British Empire.
Those six votes are not in the council. They are in
the assembly, and the interesting thing is that the
assembly does not vote. I must qualify that state-

ment a little, but essentially it is absolutely true.
In every matter in which the assembly is given a
voice, and there are only four or five, its vote does
not count unless concurred in by the representatives
of all the nations represented on the council, so that
there is no validity to any vote of the assembly unless in that vote also the representative of the United
States concurs. That one vote of the United States
is as big as the six votes of the British Empire. I
am not jealous for advantage, my fellow citizens, but
I think that is a perfectly safe situation. There is
no validity in a vote, either by the council or the
assembly, in which we do not concur. So much for
the statements about the six votes of the British
Empire.

Look at it in another aspect. The assembly is the
talking body. The assembly was created in order
that anybody that purposed anything wrong should
be subjected to the awkward circumstance that everybody could talk about it. This is the great assembly
in which all the things that are likely to disturb the
peace of the world or the good understanding between nations are to be exposed to the general view,
and I want to ask you if you think it was unjust, unjust to the United States, that speaking parts should
be assigned to the several portions of the British Empire? Do you think it unjust that there should be
some spokesman in debate for that fine little stout
Republic down in the Pacific, New Zealand? Do you
think it was unjust that Australia should be allowed
to stand up and take part in the debate—Australia,
from which we have learned some of the most useful

progressive policies of modern time, a little nation
only five million in a great continent, but counting
for several times five in its activities and in its interest in liberal reform? Do you think it unjust that
that little Republic down in South Africa, whose gallant resistance to being subjected to any outside
authority at all we admired for so many months and
whose fortunes we followed with such interest,
should have a speaking part? Great Britain obliged
South Africa to submit to her sovereignty, but she
Immediately after that felt that it was convenient
and right to hand the whole self-government of that
colony over to the very men whom she had beaten.
The representatives of South Africa in Paris were
two of the most distinguished generals of the Boer
Army, two of the realest men I ever met, two men
that could talk sober counsel and wise advice, along
with the best statesmen in Europe. To exclude Gen.
Botha and Gen. Smuts from the right to stand up in
the parliament of the world and say something concerning the affairs of mankind would be absurd.
And what about Canada? Is not Canada a good
neighbor? I ask you, Is not Canada more likely to
agree with the United States than with Great Britain? Canada has a speaking part. And then, for
the first time in the history of the world, that great
voiceless multitude, that throng hundreds of millions
strong in India, has a voice, and I want to testify
that some of the wisest and most dignified figures
in the peace conference at Paris came from India,
men who seemed to carry in their minds an older wisdom than the rest of us had, whose traditions ran

back into so many of the unhappy fortunes of mankind that they seemed very useful counselors as to how some ray of hope and some prospect of happiness could be opened to its people. I for my part have no jealousy whatever of those five speaking parts in the assembly. Those speaking parts cannot translate themselves into five votes that can in any matter override the voice and purpose of the United States.

Let us sweep aside all this language of jealousy. Let us be big enough to know the facts and to welcome the facts, because the facts are based upon the principle that America has always fought for, namely, the equality of self-governing peoples, whether they were big or little—not counting men, but counting rights, not counting representation, but counting the purpose of that representation. When you hear an opinion quoted you do not count the number of persons who hold it; you ask, "Who said that?" You weigh opinions, you do not count them, and the beauty of all democracies is that every voice can be heard, every voice can have its effect, every voice can contribute to the general judgment that is finally arrived at. That is the object of democracy. Let us accept what America has always fought for, and accept it with pride that America showed the way and made the proposal. I do not mean that America made the proposal in this particular instance; I mean that the principle was an American principle, proposed by America.

When you come to the heart of the Covenant, my fellow citizens, you will find it in article ten, and I am very much interested to know that the other

things have been blown away like bubbles. There is
nothing in the other contentions with regard to the
league of nations, but there is something in article
ten that you ought to realize and ought to accept or
reject. Article ten is the heart of the whole matter.
What is article ten? I never am certain that I can
from memory give a literal repetition of its language,
but I am sure that I can give an exact interpretation
of its meaning. Article ten provides that every member of the league covenants to respect and preserve
the territorial integrity and existing political independence of every other member of the league as
against external aggression. Not against internal
disturbance. There was not a man at that table who
did not admit the sacredness of the right of self-
determination, the sacredness of the right of any
body of people to say that they would not continue
to live under the Government they were then living
under, and under article eleven of the Covenant they
are given a place to say whether they will live under
it or not. For following article ten is article eleven,
which makes it the right of any member of the League
at any time to call attention to anything, anywhere,
that is likely to disturb the peace of the world or the
good understanding between nations upon which the
peace of the world depends. I want to give you an
illustration of what that would mean.

You have heard a great deal—something that was
true and a great deal that was false—about that provision of the treaty which hands over to Japan the
rights which Germany enjoyed in the Province of
Shantung in China. In the first place, Germany did

not enjoy any rights there that other nations had not
already claimed. For my part, my judgment, my
moral judgment, is against the whole set of concessions. They were all of them unjust to China, they
ought never to have been exacted, they were all exacted by duress, from a great body of thoughtful and
ancient and helpless people. There never was any
right in any of them. Thank God, America never
asked for any, never dreamed of asking for any. But
when Germany got this concession in 1898, the Government of the United States made no protest whatever. That was not because the Government of the
United States was not in the hands of high-minded and
conscientious men. It was. William McKinley was
President and John Hay was Secretary of State—as
safe hands to leave the honor of the United States in as
any that you can cite. They made no protest because the state of international law at that time was
that it was none of their business unless they could
show that the interests of the United States were
affected, and the only thing that they could show
with regard to the interests of the United States was
that Germany might close the doors of Shantung
Province against the trade of the United States.
They, therefore, demanded and obtained promises
that we could continue to sell merchandise in Shantung. Immediately following that concession to
Germany there was a concession to Russia of the
same sort, of Port Arthur, and Port Arthur was
handed over subsequently to Japan on the very territory of the United States. Don't you remember
that when Russia and Japan got into war with one

another the war was brought to a conclusion by a
treaty written at Portsmouth, N. H., and in that
treaty without the slightest intimation from any
authoritative sources in America that the Government of the United States had any objection, Port
Arthur, Chinese territory, was turned over to Japan?
I want you distinctly to understand that there is no
no thought of criticism in my mind. I am expounding to you a state of international law. Now, read
articles ten and eleven. You will see that international law is revolutionized by putting morals into
it. Article ten says that no member of the League,
and that includes all these nations that have demanded these things unjustly of China, shall impair
the territorial integrity or the political independence
of any other member of the league. China is going
to be a member of the league. Article eleven says
that any member of the league can call attention to
anything that is likely to disturb the peace of the
world or the good understanding between nations,
and China is for the first time in the history of mankind afforded a standing before the jury of the world.
I, for my part, have a profound sympathy for China,
and I am proud to have taken part in an arrangement which promises the protection of the world to
the rights of China. The whole atmosphere of the
world is changed by a thing like that, my fellow citizens. The whole international practice of the world
is revolutionized.

But you will say, "What is the second sentence of
article ten? That is what gives very disturbing
thoughts." The second sentence is that the council

of the League shall advise what steps, if any, are
necessary to carry out the guaranty of the first sentence, namely, that the members will respect and preserve the territorial integrity and political independence of the other members. I do not know any other
meaning for the word "advise" except "advise."
The council advises, and it cannot advise without the
vote of the United States. Why gentlemen should
fear that the Congress of the United States would
be advised to do something that it did not want to
do I frankly cannot imagine, because they cannot
even be advised to do anything unless their own representative has participated in the advice. It may
be that that will impair somewhat the vigor of the
League, but, nevertheless, the fact is so, that we are
not obliged to take any advice except our own, which
to any man who wants to go his own course is a very
satisfactory state of affairs. Every man regards his
own advice as best, and I dare say every man mixes
his own advice with some thought of his own interest. Whether we use it wisely or unwisely, we can
use the vote of the United States to make impossible
drawing the United States into any enterprise that
she does not care to be drawn into.

Yet article ten strikes at the taproot of war. Article ten is a statement that the very things that have
always been sought in imperialistic wars are henceforth forgone by every ambitious nation in the world.
I would have felt very lonely, my fellow countrymen,
and I would have felt very much disturbed if, sitting
at the peace table in Paris, I had supposed that I
was expounding my own ideas. Whether you believe

it or not, I know the relative size of my own ideas;
I know how they stand related in bulk and proportion to the moral judgments of my fellow countrymen, and I proposed nothing whatever at the peace
table at Paris that I had not sufficiently certain
knowledge embodied the moral judgment of the citizens of the United States. I had gone over there
with, so to say, explicit instructions. Don't you remember that we laid down fourteen points which
should contain the principles of the settlement?
They were not my points. In every one of them I
was conscientiously trying to read the thought of
the people of the United States, and after I uttered
those points I had every assurance given me that
could be given me that they did speak the moral
judgment of the United States and not my single
judgment. Then when it came to that critical period
just a little less than a year ago, when it was evident
that the war was coming to its critical end, all the
nations engaged in the war accepted those fourteen
principles explicitly as the basis of the armistice and
the basis of the peace. In those circumstances I
crossed the ocean under bond to my own people and
to the other governments with which I was dealing.
The whole specification of the method of settlement
was written down and accepted beforehand, and we
were architects building on those specifications. It
reassures me and fortifies my position to find how before I went over men whose judgment the United
States has often trusted were of exactly the same
opinion that I went abroad to express. Here is something I want to read from Theodore Roosevelt:

"The one effective move for obtaining peace is by an agreement among all the great powers in which each should pledge itself not only to abide by the decisions of a common tribunal but to back its decisions by force. The great civilized nations should combine by solemn agreement in a great world league for the peace of righteousness; a court should be established. A changed and amplified Hague court would meet the requirements, composed of representatives from each nation, whose representatives are sworn to act as judges in each case and not in a representative capacity." Now there is article ten. He goes on and says this: "The nations should agree on certain rights that should not be questioned, such as territorial integrity, their right to deal with their domestic affairs, and with such matters as whom they should admit to citizenship. All such guarantee each of their number in possession of these rights."

Now, the other specification is in the Covenant. The Covenant in another portion guarantees to the members the independent control of their domestic questions. There is not a leg for these gentlemen to stand on when they say that the interests of the United States are not safeguarded in the very points where we are most sensitive. You do not need to be told again that the Covenant expressly says that nothing in this covenant shall be construed as affecting the validity of the Monroe doctrine, for example. You could not be more explicit than that. And every point of interest is covered, partly for one very interesting reason. This is not the first time that the Foreign Relations Committee of the Senate of the

United States has read and considered this covenant. I brought it to this country in March last in a tentative, provisional form, in practically the form that it now has, with the exception of certain additions which I shall mention immediately. I asked the Foreign Relations Committees of both Houses to come to the White House and we spent a long evening in the frankest discussion of every portion that they wished to discuss. They made certain specific suggestions as to what should be contained in this document when it was to be revised. I carried those suggestions to Paris, and every one of them was adopted. What more could I have done? What more could have been obtained? The very matters upon which these gentlemen were most concerned were, the right of withdrawal, which is now expressly stated; the safeguarding of the Monroe doctrine, which is now accomplished; the exclusion from action by the League of domestic questions, which is now accomplished. All along the line, every suggestion of the United States was adopted after the Covenant had been drawn up in its first form and had been published for the criticism of the world. There is a very true sense in which I can say this is a tested American document.

I am dwelling upon these points, my fellow citizens, in spite of the fact that I dare say to most of you they are perfectly well known, because in order to meet the present situation we have got to know what we are dealing with. We are not dealing with the kind of document which this is represented by some gentlemen to be; and inasmuch as we are deal-

ing with a document simon-pure in respect of the
very principles we have professed and lived up to,
we have got to do one or other of two things—we
have got to adopt it or reject it. There is no middle
course. You cannot go in on a special-privilege basis
of your own. I take it that you are too proud to ask
to be exempted from responsibilities which the other
members of the league will carry. We go in upon
equal terms or we do not go in at all; and if we do
not go in, my fellow citizens, think of the tragedy
of that result —the only sufficient guaranty to the
peace of the world withheld! Ourselves drawn apart
with that dangerous pride which means that we shall
be ready to take care of ourselves, and that means
that we shall maintain great standing armies and
an irresistible navy; that means we shall have the organization of a military nation; that means we shall
have a general staff, with the kind of power that
the general staff of Germany had; to mobilize this
great manhood of the Nation when it pleases, all the
energy of our young men drawn into the thought and
preparation for war. What of our pledges to the
men that lie dead in France? We said that they
went over there not to prove the prowess of America
or her readiness for another war but to see to it that
there never was such a war again. It always seems
to make it difficult for me to say anything, my fellow
citizens, when I think of my clients in this case. My
clients are the children; my clients are the next generation. They do not know what promises and bonds
I undertook when I ordered the armies of the United
States to the soil of France, but I know, and I in-

tend to redeem my pledges to the children; they shall not be sent upon a similar errand.

Again and again, my fellow citizens, mothers who lost their sons in France have come to me and, taking my hand, have shed tears upon it not only, but they have added, "God bless you, Mr. President!" Why, my fellow citizens, should they pray God to bless me? I advised the Congress of the United States to create the situation that led to the death of their sons. I ordered their sons oversea. I consented to their sons being put in the most difficult parts of the battle line, where death was certain, as in the impenetrable difficulties of the forest of Argonne. Why should they weep upon my hand and call down the blessings of God upon me? Because they believe that their boys died for something that vastly transcends any of the immediate and palpable objects of the war. They believe, and they rightly believe, that their sons saved the liberty of the world. They believe that wrapped up with the liberty of the world is the continuous protection of that liberty by the concerted powers of all civilized people. They believe that this sacrifice was made in order that other sons should not be called upon for a similar gift— the gift of life, the gift of all that died—and if we did not see this thing through, if we fulfilled the dearest present wish of Germany and now dissociated ourselves from those alongside whom we fought in the world, would not something of the halo go away from the gun over the mantelpiece, or the sword? Would not the old uniform lose something of its significance? These men were crusaders.

They were not going forth to prove the might of the
United States. They were going forth to prove the
might of justice and right, and all the world accepted them as crusaders, and their transcendent
achievement has made all the world believe in America as it believes in no other nation organized in the
modern world. There seem to me to stand between
us and the rejection or qualification of this treaty
the serried ranks of those boys in khaki, not only
these boys who came home, but those dear ghosts that
still deploy upon the fields of France.

My friends, on last Decoration Day I went to a
beautiful hillside near Paris, where was located the
cemetery of Suresnes, a cemetery given over to the
burial of the American dead. Behind me on the
slopes was rank upon rank of living American soldiers, and lying before me upon the levels of the
plain was rank upon rank of departed American
soldiers. Right by the side of the stand where I
spoke there was a little group of French women who
had adopted those graves, had made themselves
mothers of those dear ghosts by putting flowers every
day upon those graves, taking them as their own sons,
their own beloved, because they had died in the same
cause—France was free and the world was free because America had come! I wish some men in public
life who are now opposing the settlement for which
these men died could visit such a spot as that. I
wish that the thought that comes out of those graves
could penetrate their consciousness. I wish that they
could feel the moral obligation that rests upon us
not to go back on those boys, but to see the thing

through, to see it through to the end and make good
their redemption of the world. For nothing less depends upon this decision, nothing less than the liberation and salvation of the world.

You will say, ''Is the League an absolute guaranty
against war?'' No; I do not know any absolute guaranty against the errors of human judgment or the
violence of human passion, but I tell you this: With
a cooling space of nine months for human passion,
not much of it will keep hot. I had a couple of
friends who were in the habit of losing their tempers, and when they lost their tempers they were in
the habit of using very unparliamentary language.
Some of their friends induced them to make a promise that they never would swear inside the town
limits. When the impulse next came upon them, they
took a street car to go out of town to swear, and
by the time they got out of town they did not want
to swear. They came back convinced that they
were just what they were, a couple of unspeakable
fools, and the habit of getting angry and of swearing
suffered great inroads upon it by that experience.
Now, illustrating the great by the small, that is true
of the passions of nations. It is true of the passions
of men however you combine them. Give them space
to cool off. I ask you this: If it is not an absolute
insurance against war, do you want no insurance at
all? Do you want nothing? Do you want not only
no probability that war will not recur, but the probability that it will recur? The arrangements of justice do not stand of themselves, my fellow citizens.
The arrangements of this treaty are just, but they

need the support of the combined power of the great nations of the world. And they will have that support. Now that the mists of this great question have cleared away, I believe that men will see the truth, eye to eye and face to face. There is one thing that the American people always rise to and extend their hand to, and that is the truth of justice and of liberty and of peace. We have accepted that truth and we are going to be led by it, and it is going to lead us, and through us the world, out into pastures of quietness and peace such as the world never dreamed of before.

NATIONAL REFERENDUM ON THE LEAGUE OF NATIONS

AN APPEAL TO THE COUNTRY TO MAKE THE PRESIDEN-
TIAL ELECTION AN EXPRESSION OF THE NATION'S
OPINION ON THE LEAGUE OF NATIONS. OCTOBER 3,
1920. FROM THE NEW YORK "TIMES," OCTOBER 4,
1920.

THE issues of the present campaign are of such
tremendous importance, of such far-reaching
significance for the influence of the country and the
development of its future relations, and I have necessarily had so much to do with their development,
that I am sure you will think it natural and proper
that I should address to you a few words concerning
them.

Every one who sincerely believes in government by
the people must rejoice at the turn affairs have taken
in regard to this campaign. This election is to be a
genuine national referendum. The determination of
a great policy upon which the influence and authority of the United States in the world must depend is
not to be left to groups of politicians of either party,
but is to be referred to the people themselves for a
sovereign mandate to their representatives. They are
to instruct their own Government what they wish done.

The chief question that is put to you is, of course:
Do you want your country's honor vindicated and

the Treaty of Versailles ratified? Do you in particular approve of the League of Nations as organized and empowered in that treaty? And do you wish to see the United States play its responsible part in it?

You have been grossly misled with regard to the treaty, and particularly with regard to the proposed character of the League of Nations, by those who have assumed the serious responsibility of opposing it. They have gone so far that those who have spent their lives, as I have spent my life, in familiarizing themselves with the history and traditions and policies of the Nation, must stand amazed at the gross ignorance and impudent audacity which have led them to attempt to invent an "Americanism" of their own, which has no foundation whatever in any of the authentic traditions of the Government.

Americanism, as they conceive it, reverses the whole process of the last few tragical years. It would substitute America for Prussia in the policy of isolation and defiant segregation. Their conception of the dignity of the Nation and its interest is that we should stand apart and watch for opportunities to advance our own interests, involve ourselves in no responsibility for the maintenance of the right in the world or for the continued vindication of any of the things for which we entered the war to fight.

The conception of the great creators of the Government was absolutely opposite to this. They thought of America as the light of the world as created to lead the world in the assertion of the rights of peoples and the rights of free nations; as destined to set a responsible example to all the world of what free Government is and can do for the maintenance of right standards, both national and international.

This light the opponents of the League would quench. They would relegate the United States to a subordinate rôle in the affairs of the world.

Why should we be afraid of responsibilities which we are qualified to sustain and which the whole of our history has constituted a promise to the world we would sustain!

This is the most momentous issue that has ever been presented to the people of the United States, and I do not doubt that the hope of the whole world will be verified by an absolute assertion by the voters of the country of the determination of the United States to live up to all the great expectations which they created by entering the war and enabling the other great nations of the world to bring it to a victorious conclusion, to the confusion of Prussianism and everything that arises out of Prussianism. Surely we shall not fail to keep the promise sealed in the death and sacrifice of our incomparable soldiers, sailors and marines who await our verdict beneath the sod of France.

Those who do not care to tell you the truth about the League of Nations tell you that Article X of the Covenant of the League would make it possible for other nations to lead us into war, whether we will it by our own independent judgment or not. This is absolutely false. There is nothing in the Covenant which in the least interferes with or impairs the rights of Congress to declare war or not declare war, according to its own independent judgment, as our Constitution provides.

Those who drew the Covenant of the League were careful that it should contain nothing which interfered with or impaired the constitutional arrangements of any of the great nations which are to constitute its members. They would have been amazed and indignant at the things that are now being ignorantly said about this great and sincere document.

The whole world will wait for your verdict in November as it would wait for an intimation of what its future is to be.

"THE ROAD AWAY FROM REVOLUTION"

FROM THE "ATLANTIC MONTHLY," AUGUST, 1923.

IN THESE doubtful and anxious days, when all the world is at unrest and, look which way you will, the road ahead seems darkened by shadows which portend dangers of many kinds, it is only common prudence that we should look about us and attempt to assess the causes of distress and the most likely means of removing them.

There must be some real ground for the universal unrest and perturbation. It is not to be found in superficial politics or in mere economic blunders. It probably lies deep at the sources of the spiritual life of our time. It leads to revolution; and perhaps if we take the case of the Russian revolution, the outstanding event of its kind in our age, we may find a good deal of instruction for our judgment of present critical situations and circumstances.

What gave rise to the Russian revolution? The answer can only be that it was the product of a whole social system. It was not in fact a sudden thing. It had been gathering head for several generations. It was due to the systematic denial to the great body of Russians of the rights and privileges which all normal men desire and must have if they are to be contented and within rich of happiness. The lives of

the great mass of the Russian people contained no
opportunities, but were hemmed in by barriers
against which they were constantly flinging their
spirits, only to fall back bruised and dispirited. Only
the powerful were suffered to secure their rights or
even to gain access to the means of material success.

It is to be noted as a leading fact of our time that
it was against "capitalism" that the Russian leaders
directed their attack. It was capitalism that made
them see red; and it is against capitalism under one
name or another that the discontented classes everywhere draw their indictment.

There are thoughtful and well-informed men all
over the world who believe, with much apparently
sound reason, that the abstract thing, the system,
which we call capitalism, is indispensable to the industrial support and development of modern civilization. And yet everyone who has an intelligent
knowledge of social forces must know that great and
widespread reactions like that which is now unques-
tionably manifesting itself against capitalism do not
occur without cause or provocation; and before we
commit ourselves irreconcilably to an attitude of
hostility to this movement of the time, we ought
frankly to put to ourselves the question, Is the capitalistic system unimpeachable? which is another way
of asking, Have capitalists generally used their power
for the benefit of the countries in which their capital
is employed and for the benefit of their fellow men?

Is it not, on the contrary, too true that capitalists
have often seemed to regard the men whom they used
as mere instruments of profit, whose physical and

mental powers it was legitimate to exploit with as
slight cost to themselves as possible, either of money
or of sympathy? Have not many fine men who were
actuated by the highest principles in every other
relationship of life seemed to hold that generosity
and humane feeling were not among the imperative
mandates of conscience in the conduct of a banking
business, or in the development of an industrial or
commercial enterprise?

And, if these offenses against high morality and true
citizenship have been frequently observable, are we
to say that the blame for the present discontent and
turbulence is wholly on the side of those who are in
revolt against them? Ought we not, rather, to seek
a way to remove such offenses and make life itself
clean for those who will share honorably and cleanly
in it?

The world has been made safe for democracy.
There need now be no fear that any such mad design
as that entertained by the insolent and ignorant Ho-
henzollerns and their counselors may prevail against
it. But democracy has not yet made the world safe
against irrational revolution. That supreme task,
which is nothing less than the salvation of civilization, now faces democracy, insistent, imperative.
There is no escaping it, unless everything we have
built up is presently to fall in ruin about us; and the
United States, as the greatest of democracies, must
undertake it.

The road that leads away from revolution is clearly
marked, for it is defined by the nature of men and
of organized society. It therefore behooves us to

study very carefully and very candidly the exact nature of the task and the means of its accomplishment.

The nature of men and of organized society dictates the maintenance in every field of action of the highest and purest standards of justice and of right dealing; and it is essential to efficacious thinking in this critical matter that we should not entertain a narrow or technical conception of justice. By justice the lawyer generally means the prompt, fair, and open application of impartial rules; but we call ours a Christian civilization, and a Christian conception of justice must be much higher. It must include sympathy and helpfulness and a willingness to forego self-interest in order to promote the welfare, happiness, and contentment of others and of the community as a whole. This is what our age is blindly feeling after in its reaction against what it deems the too great selfishness of the capitalistic system.

The sum of the whole matter is this, that our civilization cannot survive materially unless it be redeemed spiritually. It can be saved only by becoming permeated with the spirit of Christ and being made free and happy by the practices which springs out of that spirit. Only thus can discontent be driven out and all the shadows lifted from the road ahead.

Here is the final challenge to our churches, to our political organizations, and to our capitalists—to everyone who fears God or loves his country. Shall we not all earnestly coöperate to bring in the new day?

"HIGH SIGNIFICANCE OF ARMISTICE DAY"

LAST PUBLIC ADDRESS, DELIVERED OVER THE RADIO,
NOVEMBER 10, 1923.

THE anniversary of Armistice Day should stir us to great exaltation of spirit because of the proud recollection that it was our day, a day above those early days of that never-to-be-forgotten November which lifted the world to the high levels of vision and achievement upon which the great war for democracy and right was fought and won, although the stimulating memories of that happy triumph are forever marred and embittered for us by the shameful fact that when the victory was won—won, be it remembered—chiefly by the indomitable spirit and ungrudging sacrifices of our own incomparable soldiers—we turned our backs upon our associates and refused to bear any responsible part in the administration of peace, or the firm and permanent establishment of the results of the war—won at so terrible a cost of life and treasure—and withdrew into a sullen and selfish isolation, which is deeply ignoble because manifestly cowardly and dishonorable.

This must always be a source of deep mortification to us and we shall inevitably be forced by the moral obligations of freedom and honor to retrieve that fatal error and assume once more the rôle of courage, self-respect, and helpfulness which every true Amer-

ican must wish to regard as our natural part in the
affairs of the world.

That we should have thus done a great wrong to
civilization at one of the most critical turning points
in the history of the world is the more to be deplored
because every anxious year that has followed has
made the exceeding need for such service as we might
have rendered more and more pressing as demoralizing circumstances which we might have controlled
have gone from bad to worse.

And now, as if to furnish a sort of sinister climax,
France and Italy between them have made waste
paper of the Treaty of Versailles, and the whole field
of international relationship is in perilous confusion.

The affairs of the world can be set straight only
by the firmest and most determined exhibition of
the will to lead and make right prevail.

Happily, the present situation in the world of affairs affords us the opportunity to retrieve the past
and to render to mankind the inestimable service of
proving that there is at least one great and powerful
nation which can turn away from programs of self-
interest and devote itself to practicing and establish-
ing the highest ideals of disinterested service and
the consistent standards of conscience and of right.

The only way in which we can worthily give proof
of our appreciation of the high significance of Armistice Day is by resolving to put self-interest away
and once more formulate and act upon the highest
ideals and purposes of international policy.

Thus, and only thus, can we return to the true
traditions of America.